DATE DUE

AUG 0 5 2009	
DEC 0 2 2010	
APR 2 1 2011	
FEB 1 0 2016	
DISCARD	

BRODART, CO.   Cat. No. 23-221-003

"Intimate" Violence against Women

"Intimate" Violence against Women

When Spouses, Partners, or Lovers Attack

Edited by Paula K. Lundberg-Love and Shelly L. Marmion

Women's Psychology
Michele A. Paludi, Series Editor

Westport, Connecticut
London

Library of Congress Cataloging-in-Publication Data

"Intimate" violence against women : when spouses, partners, or lovers attack / edited by Paula K. Lundberg-Love and Shelly L. Marmion.

p. cm. — (Women's psychology, ISSN 1931-0021)

Includes bibliographical references and index.

ISBN 0-275-98967-4 (alk. paper)

1. Women—Violence against—United States. 2. Abused women—United States. 3. Wife abuse—United States. 4. Psychological abuse—United States. 5. Dating violence—United States. 6. Sexual abuse victims—United States. I. Lundberg-Love, Paula K. II. Marmion, Shelly L., 1951-

HV6250.4.W65I574 2006

362.82′92—dc22   2006021002

British Library Cataloguing in Publication Data is available.

Library of Congress Catalog Card Number: 2006021002

ISBN: 0-275-98967-4

ISSN: 1931-0021

First published in 2006

Praeger Publishers, 88 Post Road West, Westport, CT 06881

An imprint of Greenwood Publishing Group, Inc.

www.praeger.com

Printed in the United States of America

The paper used in this book complies with the Permanent Paper Standard issued by the National Information Standards Organization (Z39.48-1984).

10 9 8 7 6 5 4 3 2

Contents

Preface

Both of us have been actively involved in providing therapeutic services to women who have been victims of intimate violence and/or in educating college graduate and undergraduate students of psychology about the issues of violence against women for over 20 years. As class sizes have increased and more and more of our graduates have chosen professions dedicated to helping victims of intimate violence, there are moments when we muse about the day when books like this will no longer need to be written. We try to imagine what it would be like for women to be able to walk down a street at night without worrying about the footsteps behind them. What would it be like to be alone with nature, with a beautiful full moon overhead, and feel serene? We contemplate what the world would be like if there were no longer a reason to tell women that they must stay vigilant to the possibility of abduction and assault. What would it be like to walk down the street of any city alone and be able to look men in the eye, smile, and be friendly without being misunderstood? How would it feel to wear the clothing one wanted and not feel self-conscious about the possible responses of men? We wonder how society would change if the prevalence of sexual assault, intimate partner violence, and other crimes against women radically decreased. What would it be like to be able to negotiate our way through the world and not have to worry about the possibility of being the victim of intrusive stares, harassment, "peeping Toms," exhibitionists, fondling, and unwanted physical and sexual battery? To what extent would the levels of depression, anxiety disorders, eating disorders, substance abuse disorders, sexual dysfunction, and numerous medical disorders decrease if the sexual abuse of children became nonexistent? For brief moments, we enjoy our vision of what it would be like to live in such a world. Then we come crashing back to reality.

Recently, the widely publicized cases of Kobe Bryant, Scott Peterson, and Mark Hacking have brought violence against women to the public eye. When the United States Congress passed the Violence Against Women Act (VAWA) in 1994, it was clear that domestic violence and sexual assault were no longer unsubstantiated "feminist" complaints. Although VAWA created a new climate that promoted victim safety, offender accountability, and a more responsive criminal justice system, millions of women continue to suffer at the hands of their abusers and lack the resources to begin their journeys toward safety, healing, and a better way of life.

Even though the high-profile cases of intimate violence against women receive societal attention, there remain hundreds of thousands of nameless, faceless women who are victimized about whom we hear and know nothing. For example, one of us recently conducted an initial client interview with a 17-year-old woman from a town near Tyler, Texas. She was formerly employed by a national pizza chain delivery/take-out restaurant. One day when she arrived at work, the store was short-handed because an employee had not shown up. The 40-something-year-old male manager was present as were two young male employees who were brothers. This young woman had worked with these individuals for awhile and trusted them. While they were working, there was verbal banter between the brothers and the young woman. Then, suddenly, one of the brothers started grabbing the girl's breasts. She protested, pushed him away, and resisted. His brother then came over and started to try to grab and fondle her breasts. The young woman continued to resist and attempted to get away. The young man who initiated the assault told his brother to grab her arms and hold them behind her back, which the brother did. The first young man then moved the young woman to the drive-through window and pulled up her shirt and bra, pressing her bare breasts against the window so that customers could see them. The manager sat there watching the assault and laughing. He did nothing to intervene or to help the young woman. She finally was able to break free of her attackers, and she fled the restaurant. She called a friend who came to get her and took her home. After an initial delay, she told her grandmother and the assault was reported to the police.

One morning, this young woman had awakened and her life was good. All she did was show up for work and her perceptions of the world and other people in it changed forever. She learned what too many women already know. Safety can never be taken for granted. There are many people in this world who will choose to victimize you because you are a woman. To live as a woman is to be always vigilant, never trusting too completely. Tragically, events like this happen daily, and society remains unaware of their frequency and oblivious to their long-lasting effects on women in this culture. As a nation, we are far too complacent. We are lacking the sense of outrage that should be our response when such actions are commonplace, when small acts of violence are laughed off, and when large acts of violence are met with curiosity followed by indifference.

There are events that occur on the international level that remind us that even as the world changes some attitudes and behaviors remain the same. For example, in mid-January 2006, the United States Secretary of State, Condoleezza Rice, criticized the Russian government for a gas conflict with the Ukraine. The news and analysis on-line publication *Pravda, RU* contained an article dated January 11, 2006, with an interview of Vladimir Zhirinovsky, the leader of the Liberal and Democratic Party of Russia, about Dr. Rice's comments. He said, "Condoleezza Rice released a coarse anti-Russian statement. This is because she is a single woman who has no children. She loses her reason because of her late single status." Later in the interview Zhirinovsky proclaims that:

> Ms. Rice's personal complexes affect the entire field of international politics. This is an irritating factor for everyone especially for the East and the Islamic world. When they look at her they go mad. Condoleezza Rice needs a company of soldiers. She needs to be taken to barracks where she would be satisfied. On the other hand, she can hardly be satisfied because of her age.... Condoleezza Rice is a very cruel, offended woman who lacks men's attention.[1]

Are his statements merely a reflection of an unenlightened male from a repressive regime? Unfortunately, he is not alone in his views. Men who have similar views are easily found in every culture. So, is there still a need for a book such as this? Absolutely.

"Intimate" Violence against Women will dispel the myths surrounding these crimes and replace them with the reality of this issue. This book will address the prevalence of intimate violence against women and describe its impact on their emotional and physical health and their views of the world. It will also describe the difficult legal issues involved in these crimes. Finally, the global and cultural issues regarding intimate violence against women will be addressed. This book will integrate the current research, theory, and advocacy on the topic of intimate violence against women so that you, the reader, will have the knowledge to help yourself or others who may become victims of such violence. Unfortunately, there is no way to know whether one's friend, intimate partner, or husband is a potential perpetrator. There is no magic checklist or

psychological test that can accurately predict who will commit intimate violence. So, while we will continue to imagine what it would be like to go to a place where there is no intimate violence, we will in the meantime arm ourselves and others with knowledge. We believe that these words of Elie Wiesel from his acceptance speech for the Nobel Peace Prize in 1986 must resonate with survivors of intimate violence and with those who work to eliminate that violence:

> There is so much to be done. There is so much that we can do. One person of integrity can make a difference, a difference of life and death. As long as one dissident is in prison, our freedom will not be true. As long as one child is hungry, our life will be filled with anguish and shame. What all victims need above all is to know that they are not alone; that we are not forgetting them, that when their voices are stifled we will lend them ours. . . .

All of the contributing authors of this book wrote their chapters to let survivors of violence know that they are not alone, and they are not forgotten. We hope that this book gives survivors and their experiences a loud, clear voice. We hope, as well, that the information provided, including the recommendations made to friends, families, therapists, and policy makers, will provide tools for every person to become part of the solution in fixing a pervasive problem that, in the end, affects us all.

Paula K. Lundberg-Love, Ph.D.
Shelly L. Marmion, Ph.D.

Acknowledgments

We would like to thank all of the contributors to this volume for their involvement and dedication. During its construction many individuals faced some major obstacles in their personal and professional lives, but they persevered, in spite of it all. We want them to know how much we value their commitment to this project.

We also want to thank Debbie Carvalko at the Greenwood Publishing Group for her support. She provided excellent guidance for and nurturance of the completion of this volume. When we needed some understanding and assistance, she rose to the occasion. Additionally, Lindsay Claire of Greenwood Publishing has kept us on course during the final stages of publication, and Laura Smith of Cadmus Professional Communications was instrumental in the final stages of the editing of this book. We thank both of them for their help.

Additionally, the contributors to this volume deserve our appreciation for all of the work that they do to aid in the healing of women who have been victims of intimate violence, and/or in educating college students and community members about the prevalence and consequences of such victimization. Indeed, Tyler, Texas is a proactive community for victims of intimate violence due to the efforts of many of these women.

I, (PLL), want to express my gratitude to Michele Paludi for the mentorship she has generously provided me throughout our graduate school years together, and our twenty-some years of friendship thereafter. When I made the transition from "rat research" to studying adult survivors of incest, Michele encouraged me. Also, she has afforded me invaluable opportunities to enhance my scholarship. Michele has been my touchstone. Thank you for believing in me. And to my daughter,

Jill Wright, thank you for being the best daughter any mother could have hoped for. You have enriched my life immeasurably.

We wish to dedicate this volume to our mothers, Alma Stern and Lois Gully. From our earliest recollections, they always told us we could achieve whatever we attempted. For some reason, we believed them. We also dedicate this volume to Alexis Wright and Jennifer Marmion and all the girls and young women who deserve to live in a world without intimate violence.

Writing this book was a more exhausting and exhilarating project than we initially anticipated. However, the contributors want the readers to know that this volume is not just a compendium of our collective knowledge. It is constructed from pieces of ourselves, rendered into a mosaic of hope and will.

Chapter 1

Violence against Women: The Extent of the Problem

Brittney Nichols

Violence against women is one of the most prevalent problems in America. The men who are committing these violent acts are not strangers to their victims. When women are attacked, it is most often by men they know. In 2004, men were as likely to be victimized by a stranger as by someone they knew, but women were most often victimized by someone they knew.[1]

The murder trial of Nicole Brown Simpson captivated the nation. The celebrity status of O.J. Simpson and race issues dominated public discussion, overshadowing the core issue of the case, which was domestic violence. The evidence presented at the trial included a history of domestic abuse, something O.J. didn't deny. During the investigation, it came to light that Nicole rented a safe-deposit box. The box contained a picture of Nicole with a black eye. It also held letters containing apologies from O.J. to Nicole for abusing her; in one letter, O.J. acknowledged the fact that he abused Nicole because she refused to have sex with him.[2] The prosecution tried to focus on domestic violence as being important to the case, but the brutal beatings that Nicole endured at the hands of O.J. were largely dismissed, even though it is common for domestic violence to escalate to homicide.[3] A former cop and friend of O.J. testified that, at Nicole's request, he had warned O.J. that he fit the pattern of an abuser.[4] Despite evidence to the contrary, one of defense lawyer Johnnie Cochran's arguments at trial was that not every man who beats his wife murders her.[5] Five days before

Nicole was brutally murdered, she phoned a shelter and was frightened that O.J. was going to kill her.[6] Domestic abuse advocates understand how domestic abuse and violence often escalate to murder, but this fact did not appear to be taken seriously at the trial. A juror called a 911 tape recording of Nicole begging for help as O.J. shouted at her "a waste of time."[7] O.J. Simpson was acquitted October 3, 1995.[8]

The disappearance of Laci Peterson caught the nation's attention in 2003. Laci was reported missing on December 24, 2002. Her body and that of her unborn son (already named Connor) washed up on the California shore in April 2003.[9] Although Laci's husband, Scott, was a suspect, Laci's family supported him in the early days of the investigation, describing him as a "loving husband" and "model son-in-law."[10] He was eventually convicted of killing his wife and dumping her body in the San Francisco Bay.[11] If Amber Frey, the woman with whom Scott was having an affair a month before Laci's disappearance, had not come forward, he might have gotten away with the murder. Amber helped the police catch Scott in several lies by cooperating with the investigation and taping his phone calls to her.[12]

Mark Hacking admitted to a Salt Lake City judge, "I intentionally shot Lori Hacking in the head with a .22 rifle on July 19, 2004."[13] After killing Lori, Mark had reported her missing, saying that she had not returned from a jog. Lori had recently discovered she was pregnant, and the couple had planned a move to North Carolina for Mark to attend medical school. They had found an apartment, arranged for a moving truck, and packed.[14] However, during the search for her body, it was discovered that Mark had been living a lie. Investigators learned that Mark had not been admitted to medical school (he never even applied); he also had not graduated from college.[15] Mark killed his wife after she discovered his secret.[16]

David Brame was a police chief. The city of Tacoma was shocked in April 2003, when he shot his wife before turning the gun on himself. What at first appeared to be a random act of violence was actually preceded by a history of domestic abuse. Crystal Brame had filed for divorce in February before the shooting. It was then that she spoke up about her husband's violence, revealing that he had choked her four times the year before, shoved her in a closet, and pointed a gun at her head. She also divulged to her psychologist that David was pressuring her to participate in group sex.[17] David kept Crystal in an intimidating environment not only through physical violence but also by playing mind games and making threats. David called her mentally unstable and threatened to take away her children (a son and a daughter), if she left.[18] Given David's position in the community, Crystal felt she had no one to turn to for help.

Although these cases appear to be isolated tragedies, they have consistent themes. One major theme is that of control. Many abusers feel a strong need to control the behavior of their partner. The threat of a breakup or divorce threatens that sense of control, while their need for it escalates. When abusers feel that they are losing control, they increase the violence and intimidation. Nicole and O.J. were divorced in 1992. In the time leading up to her murder, friends and family reported that Nicole was reducing her contact with O.J. and disengaging from her relationship with him. Instead of letting go, O.J. stalked Nicole by following her and peeking into her windows.

Crystal Brame described her husband's controlling behavior in court papers. His behavior included making her get permission to use their credit card and monitoring her trips to the grocery store by checking the car's odometer.[19] Leaving an abusive partner often triggers more controlling behavior, more abuse, and, all too often, murder.

Another common theme is manipulation. Like Scott Peterson and Mark Hacking, abusers often spin a web of lies to cover their tracks and even blame the victims for their behavior. Ironically, they are often well liked and popular, even charming—a trait that comes in handy when they need to hide the truth of what they are really like. A childhood friend of David Brame said that David never appeared to be a violent person. In fact, the friend described him as a "class act."[20] To continue his affair, Scott Peterson lied to Amber Frey about several things, including his marital status.[21] He also told Amber on the phone that he was celebrating New Year's Eve 2003 in Paris, when he was actually at a candlelight vigil for his missing wife in Modesto, California.[22] The lies told by these men gave them a temporary sense of control, but when the lies started to fall apart, their control quickly began to slip away. Like many abusers, these men were apparently so unable to deal with the loss of control they were willing to go to extreme lengths to regain control, even if it meant murder. Mark Hacking managed to convince everyone he knew that he was living a different life. He went to extremes to support the fantasy, such as picking out an apartment near the medical school he was never going to attend. When his wife discovered his secret, he panicked and killed her to protect the secrets of his false life. In general, the more the abusers feel the lack of control, the more they will act to regain it. Men often try to regain control with intimidation and violence, and all too often this has deadly consequences.

Some common triggers for an escalation of violence in a relationship are affairs, separation, and child custody battles. As in the cases of Lori Hacking and Laci Peterson, one important trigger was pregnancy and the changes it would bring. In fact, the number one cause of death in pregnant women is homicide. It outranks any health risk associated with pregnancy.[23] During pregnancy, the father may feel that he has little control over the situation. The wife or girlfriend begins turning more of her attention to taking care of herself and the child, while giving less attention to him and his needs. The baby to come may also be perceived as either competition or a burden, taking away from or even putting a strain on the father's social and financial freedom. The closer the due date gets, the more the father feels the strain and loss of control. In the Peterson trial, prosecutor Rick Distaso theorized that Scott's motive was not to continue the affair with Amber Frey but to gain "freedom from the burden of a wife and son, or if he divorced, freedom from paying child support."[24]

When Rae Carruth, former Carolina Panther, found out that his girlfriend, Cherica Adams, was pregnant, he pressured her to get an abortion. He did not want the financial burden, as he was already paying $3,000 a month in child support for another child he had fathered while still a teenager. When Cherica refused to get an abortion, he planned her murder. Rae and Cherica saw a movie together and then left in separate cars. Rae was driving in front of Cherica. Rae stopped his vehicle, blocking Cherica, while three men with whom Rae had conspired pulled alongside her vehicle and shot her. Cherica called 911 and lived long enough to tell how Rae had been blocking her car and that she thought he may have been involved. Cherica's son was saved via C-section before she died, but he suffered brain damage and is in the custody of his grandmother.[25]

On the surface, the men who commit these crimes do not appear to be cold-blooded killers or psychotic maniacs. Many are accomplished role models or the guy next door. They are our neighbors. They are seemingly upstanding citizens, from all walks of life. These cases, as shocking as they are, are not that unusual. We may want to believe that these crimes are committed under rare or unusual circumstances by people who are psychotic or monstrous, but it is not so. Perhaps the most horrendous thing about these crimes is that they and the people who commit them are not unique or unusual. Our society has not yet widely acknowledged how common these crimes are and what a challenge it is to address the circumstances that lead to such occurrences.

These stories are tragic. However, they help to bring attention to the rampant problem of violence against women in this country. This can provide a gateway for discussion, instill awareness, and help to spawn change. The diversity of the victims in these stories shows that abuse can happen to anyone. Victims of abuse should not feel stigmatized or alone in their experiences. It is hoped that these tragedies will encourage women suffering physical or emotional abuse to get help before their situation turns deadly. During the Simpson trial, as women realized that what had happened to Nicole could happen to them, domestic violence calls increased.

THREE MAJOR TYPES OF ABUSE: PHYSICAL, SEXUAL, AND EMOTIONAL

Physical abuse includes slapping, hitting, kicking, burning, punching, choking, shoving, beating, throwing things, locking a person out of the house, restraining, and other acts designed to injure, hurt, endanger, or cause physical pain.[26]

By the most conservative estimates, one million women in the United States suffer nonfatal violence by a spouse or partner each year.[27] In 2001, more than half a million American women (588,490) reported being victims of nonfatal violence committed by an intimate partner; undoubtedly, many other cases went unreported.[28] Physical abuse is such a common problem that it is very likely that someone you know has experienced it or is currently in an abusive relationship. Thirty percent of Americans say they know a woman who has been physically abused by her husband or boyfriend in the past year.[29] Although these statistics are staggering, they only give part of the picture. Many acts of violence go unreported and are hidden even from friends and family.

The following vignettes are examples of physical abuse:

Sarah is cooking dinner when her husband, Matt, comes home from work. He is angry that the meal isn't ready and begins to complain. He calls her incompetent and throws a pot of boiling water at her, causing serious burns.

Jennifer breaks up with her boyfriend Nick and begins dating another guy. Jealous, Nick follows her home one night and attacks her before she is safely inside. He kicks and punches her, calls her a slut, and leaves her with several bruises and a broken jaw.

Sharon's husband, Ted, is screaming at their five-year-old daughter for leaving a mess on the floor. Sharon suggests that he calm down. He then slaps Sharon, shouting that the house is his house and he can scream all he wants.

Sexual abuse includes sadism and forcing a person to have sex when he or she does not want to; forcing a person to engage in sexual acts that he or she does not like or finds unpleasant, frightening, or violent; forcing a person to have sex with others or while others watch; or forcing a person into acts that make him or her feel sexually demeaned or violated. Sexual abuse may also include forcing a woman into reproductive decisions that are contrary to her wishes or forcing her to have sex without protection against disease or pregnancy.[30]

When we think of rape in America, the typical scenario we imagine is a young woman being attacked in a dark alley by a stranger. Although rape is certainly perpetrated by strangers, this common stereotype of the crime does not convey the whole story or even the most common story. When women are sexually assaulted, it is most likely to be by a friend or acquaintance.[31] In their lifetime, one in four women are likely to experience sexual violence by an intimate partner.[32] In 2001, 41,470 women reported rape/sexual assault committed by an intimate partner.[33] However, these numbers only give us a fraction of the picture, because rape is the most underreported violent crime in the country. Victims often know their attacker. In a survey of victims who did not report either rape or attempted rape to the police, they stated the following reasons why no report was made: 43 percent thought nothing could be done, 27 percent felt it was a private matter, 12 percent were afraid of police response, and 12 percent felt it would not be seen as that important.[34]

All of the following vignettes are examples of sexual abuse:

Jeff secretly videotapes his girlfriend Shannon having sex with him. He then shows the tape to a group of his friends, knowing that Shannon would never have consented to such an act.

John forces his wife, Mary, to have sex when she doesn't want to do so. He laughs afterward, calling her a prude, and tells her that it is his right as her husband.

Bryan and Cindy have five children. Cindy is overwhelmed, and they have agreed not to have anymore children. To keep Cindy busy at home, Bryan tampers with her birth control and she becomes pregnant.

Emotional abuse includes consistently doing or saying things to shame, insult, ridicule, embarrass, demean, belittle, or mentally hurt another person. This may include calling a person names such as fat, lazy, stupid, bitch, silly, ugly, or failure, or telling someone he or she can't do anything right, is worthless, is undeserving, or is unwanted. Emotional abuse may also involve withholding money, affection, attention, or permission; destroying property; forcing a person to do things he or she does not want to do; manipulating; hurting or threatening children or pets; threatening to either abandon a person or take his or her children away. It may also include refusing to help someone who is sick or hurt; ridiculing a person's valued beliefs, religion, race, heritage, or class; or insulting a person's family or friends.[35]

Emotional abuse is less recognized as a significant social problem, but it is very harmful, quite common, and often occurs in conjunction with physical and sexual abuse. Due to the nature of emotional abuse, it is difficult to get accurate information on its prevalence. Some studies estimate that emotional abuse is 22 percent more prevalent than physical abuse.[36] Many people mistakenly believe that if there has been no physical damage, the behavior is not abusive and does not cause real harm. Ironically, emotional abuse is often described by victims as being worse than the physical abuse. The scars it leaves remain long after physical bruises have healed.

Here are examples of emotional abuse:

While Debbie fixes her hair in the morning, her live-in boyfriend, Tim, belittles her. He calls her names and tells her that she is wasting her time trying to look nice, because she will always be ugly.

Rob constantly comes home and complains that his wife, Sandra, is ruining his life. He tells her that he knows that he can find someone better and that someday he is going to take the children and leave.

Clearly, intimate violence against women has a profound impact on many facets of our society. It affects women of every age, race, or social status. Globally, one in three women has been beaten, coerced into sex, or otherwise abused in her lifetime.[37] According to the American Medical Association, family violence kills as many women every five years as the total number of Americans who died in the Vietnam War.[38] Financially speaking, the cost of domestic violence is tremendous. According to a study by the Centers for Disease Control and Prevention (CDC), the health-related costs of rape, physical assault, stalking, and homicide by intimate partners exceed $5.8 billion each year, including $4.1 billion in direct health care expenses, $900 million in lost productivity, and $900 million in lifetime earnings.[39] Businesses lose about $100 million annually in lost wages, sick leave, absenteeism, and nonproductivity as a direct result of domestic violence.[40]

Violence against women not only causes physical and emotional harm to women, it also affects the children. In a national survey of more than 6,000 American families, half of the men who frequently assaulted their wives also frequently assaulted their children.[41] Each year, an estimated 3.3 million children are exposed to violence by family members against their mothers or female caretakers.[42] Battered mothers are more likely than other mothers to abuse their children. Children whose mothers are abused are six times more likely to attempt suicide and 50 percent more likely to abuse drugs and alcohol. One study found that 63 percent of men between 15 and 20 years old who are incarcerated for homicide killed their mother's batterer. Domestic violence can also have detrimental effects on a woman's ability to support her family and herself. Victims are over-represented in the welfare population. Although studies show that these victims seek employment, they are often unable to maintain it because their abusers sabotage their efforts.[43] It is estimated that 50 percent of homeless women and children in the United States are fleeing domestic violence.[44]

These statistics show that despite the tendency in our country to dismiss violence between intimate partners as a private matter, the damage it causes reaches far beyond the closed doors it hides behind. The numbers clearly show that this is not an individual problem—this is society's problem. It is time to bring attention to this matter and ask ourselves why, in a country that glorifies rights and freedoms, we fail to deliver to women the right to live without fear of violence. Despite being the richest country in the world, the United States has some of the highest rates for rape, domestic violence, and spousal murder.[45] Rape, for instance, is 18 times higher in the United States than in Great Britain, and rape is one of the few categories of crime in the United States that has not seen a decrease in recent years.[46] Such numbers tell us that we are still too tolerant of violence directed at women. As a culture, we continue to believe that violence against women is a "normal" interaction between men and women. It is time that we find such behavior completely unacceptable.

Chapter 2

Dismantling the Myths about Intimate Violence against Women

Carol A. Grothues
Shelly L. Marmion

A number of myths or false beliefs exist about intimate partner abuse; some are more harmful than others. These myths are based on misinformation that is commonly held by both men and women, stemming from traditional values or attempts to understand the unbelievable—that a sane woman could actually be "stuck" in a bad relationship. People often try to make sense of these bad situations and end up maintaining harmful stereotypes.

Researchers studying domestic violence strive to publish studies that prove these myths to be untrue in order to stop their harmful effects. These beliefs are so common that they are often not questioned and are accepted by both men and women. All too often these myths are believed even by the victims themselves. Not only do they allow the violence and abuse to continue, but they keep victims stuck and lessen their opportunities to get the help they need. These myths must change if we will ever have any hope of stopping violence against women.

MYTH 1: DOMESTIC VIOLENCE IS USUALLY A ONE-TIME, ISOLATED OCCURRENCE

Battering is a pattern of power and control through use of force. It is not just one physical attack. Domestic violence includes the repeated use of a number of tactics, including intimidation, threats, economic deprivation (controlling all money in the relationship and only providing necessary living expenses when one chooses to do so, usually when the partner is submissive and acting "appropriate"), isolation (keeping all friends and family members away), and psychological and sexual abuse. This abuse typically involves demeaning, destructive comments that crush self-esteem and any sense of self-confidence. When someone tells you constantly that you are ugly and stupid and no one else could possibly love you, you begin to believe it.

This pattern of domestic violence tends to occur in cycles and usually involves three phases. The first is the *tension-building phase*, where anger and conflict start to grow. This is a very uncomfortable, tense time in the home, marked by negativity, emotional distance, and increased fear. When this tension builds high enough, violence erupts in the *acute battering phase*, often resulting in significant physical damage. Violence is usually followed by the *loving phase*, in which the batterer becomes sorrowful and repentant and promises never to do it again. Evidence is clear that the cycle continues and cycles more rapidly, with increasing levels of violence.[1] Moreover, even if the violence does not happen often, it remains a constant, hidden, terrorizing factor.

MYTH 2: MANY VICTIMS "ASK FOR" VIOLENT TREATMENT AND ABUSE

This belief is maintained by individuals who beat others, by persons who cannot understand why women just don't leave, and even by those who believe that women "deserve" to be beaten for overstepping the bounds of being a proper wife. Batterers "rationalize" that they had to hit or beat their wife because she needed to learn that what she had done was wrong or that it is better to let out the anger rather than hold it in. This is a blame factor that serves to take all responsibility from the person committing the violence. Even well-educated people sometimes conclude, for example, that if only dinner had been ready on time, then this would not have happened. Others get wrapped up in the mistaken logic that if the woman did not want it, she would just leave. Therefore, the situation is not so bad or perhaps she even likes it.

Victims do not ask for this abuse any more than do the victims of other types of crime. Victims of domestic violence have historically been characterized as masochistic women who enjoy being beaten. Evidence does not support this theory. Rather, victims of domestic violence desperately want the abuse to end, and they engage in various survival strategies, including calling the police or seeking help from family members, to protect themselves and their children.[2] Women may also use silence as a survival strategy, and they may endure a beating to keep the batterer from attacking the children. Clearly these strategies do not mean that women enjoy being beaten or abused, but these are ways that women have to lessen a dangerous situation. Some women will also admit to provoking the violence in order to get it over with in the hope of moving into the loving phase more quickly. This is certainly not evidence that this woman is "asking for" abuse. No one deserves to be hit. No one asks for it.

MYTH 3: IF A WOMAN IS ABUSED, SHE CAN EASILY LEAVE THE SITUATION

Many men and women believe this myth to be true, especially in America. In the land of democracy and free will, people believe that an individual can make absolutely any choice he or she wants to make, including leaving a violent spouse. "Just pack your bags and get out" is what battered women hear most often. The truth is that all women in battering relationships face barriers to leaving these relationships. First, they are at greater risk of being killed by the batterer than those who stay.[3] There is significant evidence that a women is at greater risk for being seriously injured or killed during the two years following departure than at any time she lived at home with the batterer.[4] In reality, victims make repeated attempts to leave violent relationships, but they are prevented from doing so by their partners, who tend to increase control and coercion through threats.

Economic issues are often a major reason for staying. Women who leave their spouse often have no good alternatives for housing or support for themselves or their children. Because of the nature of the abuse, which often involves increasing isolation from others, victims tend to have a very small support system. Shelters are not readily available in all communities, and even this option has limitations and has an impact on the children. It is not simply a case of not wanting to leave; most women do wish to do so. However, the costs of leaving are significant.

We also need to consider the complexities of these relationships that make leaving difficult. As stated before, the violent relationship is cyclical and almost always involves a loving phase that serves to maintain the loving feelings the woman has for her partner. She hopes he will change and wants desperately to believe it when he tells her that he will never harm her again. She does not want to give up on the dream she has for the happy family she once hoped to create.

MYTH 4: PERSONS WHO COMMIT SUCH VIOLENCE ARE SERIOUSLY PSYCHOLOGICALLY DERANGED OR PSYCHOTIC

Actually, male batterers often appear to be normal in every respect. Studies have found that batterers come from all walks of life and every

socioeconomic and ethnic group. There are no psychological characteristics that distinguish batterers from men who do not batter. Even
though some batterers do meet the criteria for antisocial personality
disorder or substance abuse, many do not.[5] Moreover, these characteristics are not immediately observable. Often people outside of the relationship have trouble believing that such a seemingly normal person
would be capable of such acts.

MYTH 5: VICTIMS SHOULD JUST GET OVER IT, BECAUSE THERE ARE NO LONG-LASTING EFFECTS AND A STRONG PERSON IS STRONGER WHEN THEY PUT IT IN THE PAST

In truth, there are significant long-lasting effects on a woman's physical and mental health. Although physical healing usually occurs fairly
rapidly, the emotional scars are long lasting and sometimes permanent.
Battered women tend to have low self-esteem as a result of constant or
chronic name-calling and criticism. They are made to feel powerless
and useless and begin to believe in these statements. Emotional abuse
is usually not a one-time incident that can be ignored or dismissed.
Most women report that the mental or emotional abuse is more destructive than the physical abuse.[6] Many women develop chronic low
self-esteem and even clinical depression.[7]

Although challenges often make us stronger, this is not usually the
case in domestic abuse situations due to the relatively long-term and
extremely personal nature of the relationship. We often hurt the ones
we love the most deeply, because we know all of their weaknesses and
insecurities. Batterers tend to be superb at finding these buttons and
pushing them often as they serve to enhance their control over others.

MYTH 6: SEXUAL ABUSE IS ABOUT SEX, AND IF A WOMAN WERE PROVIDING ADEQUATE SEX, HER HUSBAND WOULD NOT BE ABUSIVE (TO HER OR OTHERS)

The vast majority of sexual assault is about power, anger, and control, not about sexual gratification.[8] As in other forms of violence, the
perpetrator believes that he is entitled to force others to his will. It is
simply not true that men who rape or engage in sexual abuse of others
do so because their sexual needs are not being met by a partner. One
study found that rapists often have higher levels of consensual sexual
activity than other men.[9] The reality is that sexual abuse is not about
sex or sexual gratification at all. Although these perpetrators may
achieve sexual release through their actions, it is not their motivation
for engaging in such acts. When aggression is rewarded and associated
with increased power and even sexual gratification, the tendency

toward aggression will continue and even grow.[10] The motivation tends to be a desire for power and control, and the desire comes from a perceived powerlessness and the wish to gain power.

MYTH 7: MANY WOMEN ARE JUST AS VIOLENT AS MEN

The truth is that women who become violent or kill are far more likely to be responding to violence rather than starting it.[11] The idea that partners engage in "mutual combat" has been disproved. Although some women do engage in violent acts, they usually do it in self-defense.[12] Domestic violence is a serious issue for both men and women. According to the National Institute of Justice and the CDC, almost one-third of domestic violence is against men; however, men in general produce greater injury overall. The amount, frequency, severity, and consistency of violence against women are far greater than anything done by women to men.[13] The likelihood that women will become more violent in response to an escalating threat to their lives increases when they stay in an abusive relationship.

MYTH 8: VIOLENCE ONLY HAPPENS IN BAD OR POOR FAMILIES

Studies of domestic violence consistently have found that battering occurs among all types of families, regardless of income, profession, region, ethnicity, educational level, or race.[14] Although there are risk factors associated with higher rates of domestic violence, such as alcohol use, lower socioeconomic status, childhood exposure to abuse, early marriage or early parenthood, and stress, domestic violence occurs in all communities and among all types of people. Because many victims will not report family violence due to the stigma attached, we do not have a clear picture of differences across social classes or ethnicities. The fact that there are more calls received from poorer urban areas may not mean that the rate of domestic violence is higher among lower income groups.[15] It is important to remember that even men in respectable positions, like attorneys, physicians, or even psychologists, can be batterers.

MYTH 9: VIOLENCE AGAINST WOMEN IS WORSE IN OTHER COUNTRIES

This myth tries to dismiss gendered violence in this country as being less a problem compared to that in less modernized countries. The reality is that the United States has the highest levels of reported rape in the industrialized world. The rate is about 18 times higher than that in

England and 9 times higher than that in Canada.[16] Every six minutes a woman in this country is raped; every 18 seconds a woman is beaten, and every day four women are killed by their batterers. The rates of partner abuse tend to be high in other countries, but the rates in the United States are similar to many European countries.[17] About 25 percent of women in the United States will experience abuse during their lifetime, which means about three million women are abused each year.[18] Cultural differences may affect rates of reporting; therefore, actual rates in most countries can only be estimated.

Violence in the United States often occurs within the family, with the risk of injury for women and children being higher at home than on the most dangerous city streets.[19] Between one-third and one-half of women who are seen in U.S. hospitals are there due to injuries related to domestic violence.[20]

MYTH 10: IF I AM UNDERSTANDING AND PATIENT, THINGS WILL GET BETTER

Many women (as well as family and friends of battered couples) want to believe this myth and hope that things will get better. However, waiting and hoping a batterer will change is not a good plan. As stated earlier, abuse is typically a pattern that gets worse over time— growing in frequency and intensity—if active steps are not taken to change it.

There are things that women can do to prevent or escape abuse. In later chapters, many of the options and legal issues involved will be discussed. One of the first steps in preventing abuse is to understand the realities of the situation and dismantle the myths. Holding on to erroneous beliefs continues the cycle of violence and avoids putting blame on the batterer by blaming the victim instead. Studies have shown that more and more Americans believe that domestic violence is a serious crime, and all 50 states have passed laws to protect abused women. However, the continued belief of these myths keeps progress slow.

Chapter 3

Emotional Abuse of Women

Bobbie K. Burks

*The yelling I could take . . . the beating I could take . . . the pain and blood
I could take . . . but when he would tell me that he didn't love me and that
I was worthless, I felt myself dying inside.*

—*An emotional abuse survivor*

Emotion is defined as "the affective aspect of consciousness; a state of
feeling."[1] It is a concept, not a solid object; we can only witness the
expression of inner, personal emotional states, not the emotions themselves. How then does one define emotional violence? In her book *Emotional Abuse*, Marti Tamm Loring offers:

> Emotional abuse is an ongoing process in which one individual system-
> atically diminishes and destroys the inner self of another. The essential
> ideas, feelings, perceptions, and personality characteristics of the victim
> are constantly belittled. Eventually the victim begins to experience these
> aspects of the self as seriously eroded or belittled.[2]

Emotional abuse is often considered the worst kind of abuse.[3] It occurs
when those trusted to "provide you with care, love, and protection,
such as parents, other relatives, and teachers, say and do things that
make you feel bad about yourself."[4] Although it is widely considered
the most harmful form of relationship violence, emotional abuse is also
the most difficult to identify and prove and is almost impossible to use
as the basis for pressing relationship violence charges in the legal
system.

The mechanisms of emotional abuse—the specific weapons used to accomplish the goal of controlling and manipulating the behavior of another person—are numerous and varied. These mechanisms are often classified as *overt* (observable and identifiable) and *covert* (subtle, unobservable).[5] These mechanisms may take the following forms.

OVERT MECHANISMS OF ABUSE

1. Belittling: Telling a woman that she is less than she truly is;
2. Yelling: Raising vocal volume in an attempt to gain control of an interaction;
3. Name-calling: Labeling a woman in an effort to attack what she thinks about herself;
4. Criticizing: Finding fault with a woman or with what she does;
5. Ordering around: Exerting control over a woman to keep her at a power disadvantage;
6. Sulking: Withdrawing and/or pouting when the perpetrator does not get his or her way;
7. Withholding affection: Keeping physical, verbal, or psychological affirmation from a woman in an attempt to control her;
8. Ignoring: Completely dismissing a woman's presence to provoke or control her;
9. Isolating from family and friends: Keeping a woman from valuable support systems to maintain power and control over her;
10. Monitoring time and/or activities: Giving the impression to the woman being monitored that she is not in charge of her choices or actions;
11. Attempting to restrict resources (finances, telephone): Preventing a woman from calling for help or paying for escape;
12. Interfering with opportunities (job, medical care, education): Reinforcing a perception of helplessness and hopelessness in the victim;
13. Accusing the victim of engaging in repeated and/or purposively hurtful behaviors: Shifting the blame or creating fiction to further erode self-esteem;
14. Throwing objects, not necessarily at the victim: Showing power and giving a sense of danger to increase fearful obedience;
15. Slamming of objects or doors: Showing power to intimidate and manipulate;

16. Ridiculing the victim: Psychologically attacking the woman's self-esteem to produce a mind-set of learned helplessness and lack of hope;

17. Expressing disgust toward the victim: Trying to convince the woman that she is worthless and, therefore, that she needs the perpetrator;

18. Threatening to abandon (physically or emotionally): Generally occurring after the victim has been conditioned to believe that she cannot survive without the perpetrator;

19. Expressing excessive jealousy: Resulting from the perpetrator's fears that the victim may have a healthy relationship with some-one else and that she may realize the tactics being used against her;

20. Threatening life, pets, property, and/or family: Exercising emotional blackmail that makes the woman comply to protect her life and health or that of people and/or things that she cares about;

21. Exposing the victim to abuse of her children, pets, or parents: Inducing a state of posttraumatic stress in the woman, who will do anything to keep others safe;

22. Coercing the victim into illegal activity: Resulting from many items previously mentioned, this is an ultimate expression of the power the perpetrator has over his or her victim;

23. Provoking the victim into helpless flailing: Making the woman put up some sort of defense in a defenseless situation.

COVERT MECHANISMS OF ABUSE

1. Discounting: Minimizing an individual's accomplishments to prevent the building of self-esteem and a sense of having an ability to survive without the perpetrator;

2. Negation: Taking a victim's positive perception and restating it in a negative tone;

3. Projection/accusation: Blaming the victim for the perpetrator's feelings and actions in an effort to soothe those feelings;

4. Denial (of abuse by the abuser): Blaming the victim or telling the victim or others that the abuse never occurred. This reinforces helplessness in the victim and, at times, makes the victim doubt her memories of what happened;

5. Negative labeling: Telling the victim that she is defective in some way;

6. Subtle threats of physical and/or emotional abandonment or actual physical and/or emotional abandonment: Verbalizing threats to leave in an attempt to control a situation.[6]

The scars of emotional attacks on the core of the self are long lasting and often impossible to erase. The fruits of these attacks, as described later in this chapter, are lives that may never reach their full potential for health and happiness due to destruction of the victim's belief in her ability to adequately meet the challenges of the world. The victim may also experience a skewed sense of identity and have difficulty finding her place in productive society.

RATIONALES CITED BY EMOTIONAL ABUSERS

As with other subtypes of abuse, the ultimate goal is power and control over the victim. "Power . . . is defined as the capability of carrying out one's own will and assuming control over others, with or without legitimacy, based on having a larger share of physical, psychological, and/or material resources."[7] One emotional abuse perpetrator explained her rationale this way:

> He didn't have the drive I thought it would take to get us to where we wanted to be. We lived in a crappy house with a crappy car and crappy friends who had about as much get-up-and-go as he did. I found out that if I nagged him about how worthless he was as a husband, he would shape up for a while and give us what we wanted. But it didn't last long, and I had to keep nagging and nagging until he started staying at work all the time. The money was good, but one day he just didn't come home.

Most abusers attack their victims emotionally to feel better about themselves and their situations. There is a perceived inequality of power in the relationship, and abusers fill their need for a sense of personal power and control over their circumstances by stealing the power of others. Of the many analogies and metaphors for abusers' behavioral choices, the term *emotional vampire* seems to best describe what they do when they enter a room: They seem to suck the very emotional "lifeblood" out of their victims, each time their own power/control "tank" is nearing empty. The victims often avoid the presence of the abusers, seeking refuge away from home when in a position to do so or in other areas of the house shared with the abuser. Countless victims have told the story of hearing the abuser's car pull into the driveway and watching their families scatter from sight. They tell tales of their initial interactions with the abuser, who may come through the door of the house with angry words and frightening behaviors.

I had worked all day just trying to make a living for my family. My boss jumped all over me for something that wasn't my fault and I got a written reprimand in my personnel file. I get home and the house is a mess, the kids are filthy, and the wife is just looking at me like a deer in the headlights. No dinner on the table, no hugs when I came in . . . what would YOU do if you came home to something like that? A man has a right to expect to be king in his own castle."[8]

Emotional abuse is a tool abusers use to help them fill their need for a sense of power and control. By belittling the efforts of an exhausted, frustrated wife to perform to his exacting standards of perfection, a controlling husband convinces her that she is not worthy of his affection or anyone else's approval. The abusers' standards are generally unrealistically high and virtually impossible to attain. By setting the bar too high, the emotional abuse perpetrators assure that they will have many opportunities to siphon off the self-esteem of others.

Emotional abuse is not limited to male-female or other romantic relationships. Parents may use shame as the tool of choice to keep their children toeing the family line, keeping family secrets, or fulfilling their parents' need for living out their dreams through the accomplishments of their children. They may purge themselves of uncomfortable feelings by heaping them on their children—those who are more vulnerable and who have fewer coping skills to deflect them. Shame—a major result of emotional abuse—is the most powerful tool of the abuser. "Shame is the intensely painful feeling or experience of believing we are flawed and therefore unworthy of acceptance and belonging."[9] Shame transcends guilt. Guilt is the recognition of having done something bad, whereas shame is the perception of being bad because of something one has done. Appropriate guilt is ended by making amends. Shame, on the other hand, can be used by the abuser who often finds a shame-prone individual to mold into a victim. The cycle of shame is passed from generation to generation, and behavioral traits that perpetuate this cycle are reinforced through social learning and negative behavioral modification methods. A lowered sense of self-worth is often learned through membership in a family system built on secrets and silence. "Unhealthy shame is the faulty conviction that one is somehow innately defective, as compared to the norm."[10]

Specific tools used by the perpetrator to induce shame and powerlessness include[11] neglect or deprivation, abandonment, isolation, role reversals, severe criticism, manipulation, extreme control, witnessing the abuse of others, harsh punishments, inconsistent discipline, cruel comments, and inappropriate lecturing and/or yelling.

SYMPTOMS OF EMOTIONAL ABUSE

When individuals come into counseling with any or all of the following symptoms, they should be carefully questioned to discover whether their history of emotional abuse begins in their family of origin or in relationships they formed after they left the family fold.

- Low self-esteem/self-worth/self-efficacy (feeling capable of self-care);
- Difficulty taking risks of any magnitude (fear of failure or harm, as well as perceptions that they will not be able to do the task);
- Difficulties in relationships (sustaining relationships, choosing healthy partners, etc.);
- Withdrawal mechanisms for emotional safety (excessive shyness, social phobias, etc.);
- Difficulty engaging with others in conversations or at events (fear of being inadequate or being found unintelligent);
- Developmental issues due to socialization challenges and lack of family encouragement and support (feelings of greater comfort with those who are significantly older or younger);
- Feelings of incompetence (resulting from being told that they were not capable);
- Suicidal ideation or fantasy (desire to be released from the pressure and/or pain);
- Expressions of being unworthy of love and affection (from being told so by the abuser);
- Inaccurate body image due to messages from others (feeling as if the abuser is the only one who would ever be able to love them because of internalized messages of ugliness or deformity);
- Fear of self-expression or assertive behavior (feelings of inadequacy);
- Detachment from other people and feelings of being alone, and unable to trust anyone (the ability to attach is disrupted by early caregiver abuse or occurrences in later formative relationships);
- Sexual dysfunction and/or sexual desire issues based on old messages;
- Self-mutilation or self-injury (creating physical pain to block emotional pain);
- Substance abuse/addiction (self-medicating to escape negative thoughts or perceptions);
- Behavioral addiction (behaviors that the victims learn will ease distress);

- Intense perfectionism (in an attempt to make up for abuser-communicated shortcomings);
- Eating disorders (anorexia, bulimia, binge eating to control at least one part of their lives);
- Physical complaints with no medical evidence (stress-induced ailments provide medical explanations when psychological explanations seem inadequate); and
- Promiscuous/risky sexual behavior (an attempt to control or prove self-worth).

There are many more symptoms that are sometimes seen in the treatment of emotional abuse survivors. The foundation for most of these symptoms is that sense of shame. Victims create a reality for themselves that perpetuates the lies that they have come to believe are truths.

> It started in my family. I didn't look like they did . . . my father always used to joke—and everyone joined in with him—that I must have been the outcome of my mother banging the milkman or something. They laughed, and I can hear their laughter to this day. The old man is dead, and I still hear him laughing sometimes in the night.
>
> —*Male survivor*

> My parents divorced, and I was the child who got dragged along to every new guy's home that my mom went to live in. I was a throw-away child. All of my "uncles" would make fun of me because my mom was so pretty and I wasn't . . . at least they said I wasn't. A few of them used me and I let them, because at least when they were doing it, they said nice things to me. I kept on letting men do whatever they wanted because at least then they weren't cutting me down. I had something they wanted, and they were willing to trade compliments for what I had to offer.
>
> —*Female survivor*

EFFECTS OF EMOTIONAL ABUSE ACROSS THE LIFESPAN

Childhood

Even in the youngest children, emotional abuse leaves deep wounds. If one considers Erik Erikson's developmental model,[12] when persons who are charged with providing basic care to the infant fail to do so, the child may grow up with a sense of mistrust about the world and those in his or her immediate circle of influence. In the toddler, if the challenge of autonomy development is not met, then early shame is left in its wake. Initiative is unable to take root, and this lack colors the individual's life with guilt and feelings of incompetence. The child's belief in his or her ability to survive in the world is removed, and feelings of inferiority and a lack of belief in his or her ability to move through life with any success fills the emotional void.

Attachment issues[13] are also a major concern during this stage of development. Altered attachment to others is the result of neglect and the outcomes described above. A possible result is that the child will form an insecure or anxious attachment to caregivers, showing great distress when separated from them. This may forever slow the individual's progress toward developing meaningful relationships on many levels.

As toddlers begin to explore the world, a constant assault on their emotions in the form of parental criticism may result in their failure to thrive in social environments. Acting-out behaviors may become the rule of the day. When children take their cues from emotionally abusive parents, they seek to control their world through intimidation and manipulation.

Social learning theory[14] provides an explanation for the repetition of emotional abuse patterns across generations. Children who observe or experience a parent having his or her needs met through emotional manipulation and abuse may come to believe that this is an appropriate way for them to operate in their environment. In some cases, emotionally abusive parents may even reward the abusive behaviors of their children as part of an "it was good enough for me, it's good enough for them" rationalization.

When emotionally abused children begin to attend school, the rules of their environments change. Abusive behaviors and outbursts may not be tolerated in the classroom, and these children become confused about the rules for behavior. Their acting out may increase due to the conflict between their home existence in a world without healthy boundaries and a school system that tries to enforce healthy socialization. This confusion may be exhibited in:

- Behavioral disturbances;
- Emotional outbursts;
- Learning and attention issues (that may be misdiagnosed as attention deficit hyperactivity disorder [ADHD], childhood bipolar disorder, or learning disabilities);
- Enuresis (inability to control urination), encopresis (inability to control passing feces), and other regressive behaviors;
- Selective mutism (choosing not to talk because it may be safer to be quiet);
- Excessive clinging to healthy authority figures (bonding quickly and deeply to a teacher who is a healthy role model);
- Lying or cheating on class work (to appear worthy or better than they believe they are);

- Violence in the classroom or playground resulting in the victimization of others; and
- Self-mutilation or self-injury (for attention or to reduce emotional pain).

Preadolescence

Children entering junior high or middle schools face enormous developmental challenges, even without the presence or history of emotional abuse in their lives. When abuse is part of the picture, the emotional growth of these individuals may become even more difficult. Society and the media have a combined influence in creating unrealistic expectations of physical attributes, intellectual achievement, and social status for young people. Puberty, known to most parents as "hormone hell," is the spark that threatens to set off an explosion of insecurity, inadequacy, low self-esteem, low self-worth, and general misery for preteens living in situations where emotional abuse is typical. Young people who already believe they are worthless have no difficulty accepting the same messages from peers who are playing the power-and-control game they may have been taught in their own homes.

The rising number of reported incidents of school violence in this age group is alarming. Many children are labeled as troublemakers, because they are either perpetrators or victims of bullying and/or emotional assault and manipulation. They do not believe in themselves, yet they are thrust into an environment that is designed to force them into believing in something much bigger than the individual. One local middle school divides their students into teams to help them gain a sense of pride and accomplishment. This effort is a double-edged sword; competition is so intense at times that the students set out to sabotage the efforts of other teams and humiliate opposing team members. Authority issues come to the forefront during these years and create either fear or loathing of rules and boundaries in children who have experienced emotionally abusive environments.

Adolescence/High School

Our culture is witnessing an erosion of individuals' belief in their ability to achieve beyond the level of their parents. Teens who have experienced emotional abuse are more prone to develop a defeatist attitude about their abilities. They are less likely to attach to healthy school organizations and will, instead, seek out disenfranchised neofamilies (e.g., gangs) that offer protection and acceptance to those who have felt the sting of abandonment and rejection either at home or in other relationships. The teen's self-image comes from their identification with the peer group, and their loyalty to the "family" may bring with it a dedication to doing whatever it takes to preserve its safety and sanctity. If students are not members of a group, and they refuse to consider joining, they may be treated with disdain and, in some cases, violence. Colors, clothing styles, and other personal grooming choices give visual identity to the "family" unit.

Self-medication can become more of an issue for emotional abuse victims and survivors during this time of life. Experimentation with substances is sometimes seen as a rite of passage, but teens who feel overwhelmingly intense emotional pain will abuse alcohol and drugs of all kinds to temporarily dull or eliminate this pain. The effects of self-medication are seen in poor scholastic performance, excessive truancy, defiance of authority, vandalism, lack of motivation to achieve or succeed, and higher drop-out rates. Efforts to self-medicate cross from the chemical to the behavioral, with abuse survivors indulging in eating disorders, self-injury, promiscuity, criminal activity, and other actions that bring an adrenaline "rush" and temporary relief from the constant thoughts of inadequacy and worthlessness.

Adulthood

If we follow the effects of emotional abuse from infancy to adulthood, the results for the survivor seem hopeless. Many survivors are not able to successfully resolve the developmental challenges that make for healthy adulthood. If the emotional abuse was confined to the family of origin, then at the age of majority the survivor is freed from the confines and control of the family home environment only to emerge ill-equipped to handle the everyday pressures of self-support and connection with others for social and personal fulfillment. These adults may be unable to sustain meaningful relationships, with a growing withdrawal syndrome as the hallmark of their future. They may seek out partners who perpetuate the abuse they experienced earlier in life; they move toward the familiar, because they know the rules of that environment and can exist there with the coping skills they have learned. Educational underachievement may limit the goals of these adult survivors, as they face underemployment, job dissatisfaction, and a sense of not having turned their dreams into reality.

The concept of the "generational curse" of emotional abuse may become more evident when these individuals take on a parenting role. Parenting skills learned in the family of origin may have been limited to the effectiveness of shame as a corrective tool. Individuals who reported that they had vowed never to use the same tactics on their children have said they found themselves reverting to their parents' strategies in moments of disciplinary stress. Thus, the curse is perpetuated and a new generation of individuals is shaped with the distinct potential for doing even more damage to more individuals in the future.

> I didn't know why I yelled at my little girl like that . . . the things that came out of my mouth even shocked me! The look on her face—a face that looks so much like mine—was like looking into a time-traveling mirror where I could see myself as my mother yelled at me. I was channeling my mom, and it felt sickening. I apologized to my daughter—I even cried while I was doing it, just like my mom—but I know the damage has been done. And I will spend the rest of my life trying to make it up to her.
>
> —*Survivor mother*

EMOTIONAL ABUSE BY INSTITUTIONS

To this point, discussion has centered on person-to-person emotional violence. The sad fact is that emotional abuse is also a tool of various societal and cultural institutions, resulting in just as much damage as that experienced in families. Correction through shame is a powerful tool in the workplace and educational environment, with individuals utilizing it and rationalizing it as being necessary to productivity. Intense competition is encouraged in schools with unrealistic criteria for perfection (e.g., ideal body types for students in sports and performing arts), which can lower self-esteem and lead to eating disorders, steroid use, and exercise addiction. Media institutions perpetuate myths of desirability in ads for everything from body lotions to lingerie to automobiles.

Law enforcement agencies may also be unwitting contributors to the under-reporting of all types of abusive behaviors, as noted by one survivor who speaks for many:

> He wouldn't stop yelling. He got right against my ear and yelled as loud as he could until the pain forced me to run and call the police. When they got there, they asked me if he had hit me . . . if I had any bruises or blood anywhere they could see. When I told them what he had done and what he said, one officer just rolled his eyes and told me that without physical proof of injury, he couldn't do anything for me. I cried and tried to explain how much the yelling hurt and the profanity and horrible names had affected me and my kids. He pulled me to the side and said, "If I were you, the next time he throws something or tries to hit you, step in the way and let it do some damage. Then we can take him to jail." I took him at his word and didn't call the police again until he almost killed me.[15]

To their credit, some police and sheriff's departments often enforce time-outs or cooling off periods for couples who make domestic violence calls, even without proof of physical injury. This policy may give individuals time to clear their thoughts and decide what to do in response to the violent incident. Courts are granting family protective orders in many communities, which are short-term separations that allow the parties to seek intervention for their respective needs and to prepare for reconciliation or permanent separation in the future.

One institution that has been in the abuse spotlight in recent years is the church. Various denominations and religions have used shame effectively to control and correct their congregants/parishioners through certain rituals and codes of silence. Carefully chosen pieces of scriptural text have been used by all faiths to perpetuate the expectation of the "long-suffering" nature of the woman in marriage, and the concept of submission in marriage has often been perverted by perpetrators to justify violence. Male clergy who are uncomfortable counseling a female church member who reports inequities and abuse of any type in her marriage may minimize the situation and encourage her to give her husband just one more chance. Many of these women leave the church due to a sense of betrayal by not only the spiritual leader or counselor but also by the God that they represent. It may take them a lifetime to reattach with a church body and continue spiritual development. There is also a history of the church discounting emotionally abused victims who come to the church for support, because the church leaders have not been trained to recognize the symptoms of this abuse. The good news is that most seminaries and schools now train clergy in how to respond to relationship violence, and messages to stop all kinds of abuse are preached from the pulpit. Many larger churches have installed counseling ministries with clinically trained professionals to serve the needs of their membership, and in-house support groups have been initiated to address emotional abuse (as well as all forms of relationship violence) and its outcomes.

VICTORY OVER EMOTIONAL ABUSE

Recovery from an emotionally abusive past occurs most successfully within a community that aims to make all forms of abuse unacceptable. Victims need a supportive environment that validates their existence and value to the world to begin challenging and changing the lessons learned during the time of emotional assault. Many survivors must first come to the realization that they have been victims of abuse in order to assign responsibility for their memories to the perpetrator. Twelve-Step recovery groups (such as Codependents Anonymous, Al-Anon, and

Celebrate Recovery) call this "coming out of denial." It is a time of moving from a mind-set of low self-worth to a sense of hope and value through healthy group interaction. Taking responsibility for one's healing is another important component of recovery. Connections to support groups, a trained counselor, and other avenues of education concerning coping skills and self-forgiveness help the victim move to survivor status. One survivor relates her recovery experience:

> I never really knew what codependency meant until I went to Celebrate Recovery at a local church. A friend told me about their codependency group for women who had been through situations like mine, and I had come to the point that I figured it couldn't hurt to see what it was all about. When they talked about denial, I cried so hard! I realized I had taken responsibility for what my husband had done to me and the kids, and thought of myself as weak and stupid because he told me so for many years. By sharing in the women's codependency group without being afraid someone might think I was crazy, I found my voice. Now I can talk freely about my past. I have given responsibility to my ex-husband for what he did and forgiven myself, and I now have hope for the future . . . a future free from being put down and made to feel like I didn't deserve to be loved.[16]

Cognitive restructuring is a major component of recovery from emotional abuse. In cognitive restructuring, negative messages are replaced by self-talk that affirms the individual's worth and promise. Behavior modification techniques are also included in the recovery plan. The individual must intentionally and purposefully rehearse new, assertive behaviors and thereby gain positive reinforcement for the right for honest self-expression without feeding off the reactions of others as a way of determining self-worth. Life coaching in the areas of employment, self-image, educational advancement, and pursuit of pleasurable activities also may assist the survivor to thrive in new environments and situations.

Emotional abuse recovery progresses through a predictable continuum: realize what is going on, assign responsibility for behaviors and attitudes, and then reach out to connect with individuals and organizations that have the potential to add to the healing mix. Recovery is a lifelong process. There is no "cure" for an abuse-filled past; there is only a daily determination to overcome its effects and to learn positive lessons from experiences.

PREVENTING EMOTIONAL ABUSE: THE WRITER'S OPINION

If one holds to the hypothesis that emotional abuse is a by-product of the perpetrators' feelings of powerlessness and lack of control, it would be best to address that problem at the very start of socialization rather than to wait until it is made evident through the perpetrators' choice of violent acts. Organizations such as Parents Anonymous offer parenting skills classes for all age groups, from expectant individuals to those who are court mandated to receive training in parenting skills. Many courts require divorcing parents to attend educational programs that encourage putting the emotional safety needs of the children first, above any efforts to control or gain power over an ex-spouse through manipulation and intimidation of the children. Child protective service agencies may refer a caregiver to mandatory individual and/or group counseling to resolve issues that may interfere with effective parenting outcomes. Many abuse behaviors stem from the perpetrators' history of abuse by an authority figure in their past, and their challenges may come from learning not to repeat abusive behaviors they were taught. It seems as if prevention is a more effective approach than remediation, but prevention requires a far-reaching plan of action that must be embraced by all segments of society.

Media campaigns targeting relationship violence have attempted to eradicate the mind-set that this type of behavior is acceptable. One of the biggest obstacles to this goal is the portrayal and promotion of violence in the media. Many of the highest grossing movies feature heroes or anti-heroes for whom violence is a way of life. On television, the viewing public's appetite for violence is whetted by more and more programs that have power, control, or violence as a central theme. Millions of dollars in production budgets are being spent on special effects to make the physical effects of violence look more painful and lifelike. Just a few generations ago, the viewing public seemed content with westerns in which a person was shot and fell to the ground without copious blood and body parts displayed on screen. Now, we are treated to slow-motion multi-angle views of graphic violence. The popularity just a few years ago of the *Faces of Death* video series (in which actual deaths of persons or animals were shown in detail) among young men, in particular, was a forewarning of things to come. Video games now feature scantily clad females in full combat with males, in gruesome fight-to-the-death competitions, leaving the players thirsty for more violently aggressive game playing. The video game industry has responded to criticism with a ratings system to warn parents of violence, but the majority of games are purchased by children with allowances or birthday money far from the eyes of parents who might censor their choices. The games come home and are played frequently and repeatedly in rooms with closed doors, until the game is mastered and a new game comes out with even more sensational violence.

The music industry is not without its culpability. Music videos that show women as objects of ridicule or physical pleasure abound, and there are videos with explicit violence against women—some made by women themselves—that are shown in tight rotation on the video channels. Some rap music is littered with references to keeping women in line with violence, and some artists have included lyrics about hating parents that etch themselves into the memories of those who listen to the songs over and over again.

Television talk shows have encouraged verbal, emotional, and physical abuse for the pleasure of the viewing audience. There are many other areas in our society in which the promotion of pro-violent messages needs to be addressed. The individual who has been a victim of emotional abuse must acknowledge the maltreatment for recovery to begin. It is now being proposed that this same revelation moment must be reached by society. We must agree to address the problem as a whole for each of us to begin our own healing from a culture that condones and even rewards aggression in all its forms.

Parents must begin to screen the materials viewed and heard by their children. Our country enjoys freedom of speech to protect an artist's right to express their views, but parents must exercise the right to raise their children to respect life rather than demean it. The media, schools, churches, and law enforcement agencies must band together to send out a central message of the unacceptability of violence in any form and then work together to end it. We must provide healing environments and support to empower survivors to fulfill their potential. Abusers must be given the message that there are consequences for their choices and that abusive behaviors will not be tolerated at any level of severity. Only when abuse or violence becomes socially unacceptable, when perpetrators are treated with the disgust and swift condemnation they deserve, will we begin to see a brighter tomorrow for the victims of today and the victims who will otherwise inevitably follow.

The answer begins with each of us. We must take responsibility for our interaction styles and become aware of our tendencies to seek power in situations through manipulation or intimidation. Only when we see our role in this system of abuse will we begin the journey out of denial and toward a world that empowers individuals and does not attempt to control through shame and intimidation.

Chapter 4

Battered Women

Paula K. Lundberg-Love
D. Karen Wilkerson

We were married for five years before my husband shoved me during an argument. It took me by surprise as he had never done anything like that. He seemed truly upset by what had happened. He apologized profusely. He cried and begged for my forgiveness and swore it would never happen again. He gave me flowers. We went to dinner. Nothing else happened for another year. Then it happened again, except this time it was a shove and a slap. Soon the violence escalated and slaps became punches. The beatings occurred more frequently. Dan began to drink more, which only resulted in more vicious outbursts. Then one night I thought he was going to kill me. I locked myself in the bedroom. But he knocked the door down and knocked me unconscious. When I regained consciousness, there was an incredible pain in the back of my neck. I realized I was bleeding. I screamed and asked what he had done. He responded that he had cut me. I begged for him to call 911 as I was dying. He said he was calling. I could hear him on the phone, but nothing happened. No one came. I told him to call again. Once again I heard him reporting an emergency. I crawled down the hall. While he was on the phone acting as if he were talking to 911, the phone was unplugged. I begged him to plug in the phone and save my life. He did nothing until I said the magic words, "I promise I will not press charges. Just let me live." He finally called 911, and I barely survived.[1]

It is hard to imagine that anyone living in modern society does not know what battering is. Popular books, movies, and television programs have depicted violent relationships between intimates for many years. Rarely, in fact, does one open a newspaper or watch the local news without hearing of a tragic incident in which a spouse or lover has injured, or even killed, the one-time object of their affection. For the record, the term *battering* includes: *physical abuse*, defined as any use of size, strength, or presence to hurt or control someone else; *emotional abuse*, which includes any use of words, voice, action, or lack of action meant to control, hurt, or demean another person; and *sexual abuse*, the use of sexual behavior meant to control, manipulate, humiliate, or demean another person.

The range of behaviors that qualify for battering in all its ugly forms therefore may encompass a broad variety of actions, from those that seem harmless (such as a shove or push, the display of a clenched fist, chasing a partner, making a sarcastic comment, name-calling, or criticism) to levels of violence that most people readily recognize as well beyond the bounds of "normal" behavior. The extreme degrees of the latter category include punching holes in walls or doors, destroying or sabotaging automobiles and property, abandoning a partner in a dangerous place, making threats with objects or weapons, making threats against friends or family members (including children and pets), engaging in physical assaults or public humiliation, stalking, threatening suicide, and committing murder.[2]

There is, unfortunately, no end to the tortures people commit upon those they claim to have loved. Even worse, only the most vicious levels of these acts are considered criminal. Hence, many of the behavioral indicators leading up to a tragic outcome are often ignored or minimized by friends, family, law enforcement, and the judicial system until it is too late.

CHARACTERISTICS OF BATTERERS

How, then, does one identify a batterer? Wilson identifies 17 warning signs found in people who abuse their intimate partners[3]:

1. Jealousy: Batterers are possessive. They question who their partner talks to and "drop by" work or call often to check up on their partner. They may even review the mileage on the car or phone records.

2. Controlling behavior: Batterers claim concern for their partner's welfare, but they may refuse their partner's independence in personal decisions, such as freedom to come and go, spend money, join a church or club, or determine personal appearance.

3. Quick involvement: Batterers knew their partner less than six months before becoming engaged or living together, claiming love at first sight. Batterers often pressure their partners for early commitment.

4. Unrealistic expectations: Batterers are emotionally dependent on their partners, idealizing the partner and expecting him or her to take care of everything.

5. Isolation: Batterers destroy their partner's support system of friends of either sex, family, and co-workers. Often they move the partner to a rural or remote area where he or she does not have access to a telephone or automobile.

6. Blames others for own problems: For almost anything that goes wrong in the batterers' lives (mistakes, loss of job, financial difficulties, sexual problems), they perceive their partner to be the person at fault. Occasionally they blame others, but the batterers always remain free from responsibility.

7. Blames others for own feelings: Batterers tell their partners, "You made me do it," "It's your fault I'm angry," or "You're trying to hurt me by not doing what I ask," to manipulate them and to avoid discussions of decisions.

8. Hypersensitivity: Batterers are easily "set off" by slight setbacks or rebuffs. Batterers claim hurt feelings and rage about the unfairness of life as if things that happen are directly targeted toward them.

9. Cruelty to animals or children: Batterers brutally punish or are insensitive to pain and suffering of animals. They have unrealistic expectations for children and punish them when they fail. They may tease children until they cry or spank infants for soiling diapers.

10. "Playful" use of force in sex: Batterers may hold their partner down or want to act out sexual fantasies in which the partner is helpless. They may also sulk or use anger to manipulate their partner into having sex and initiate or demand sex with a partner who is sleeping, ill, or tired.

11. Verbal abuse: Batterers degrade or curse their partner and demean their partner's accomplishments or ability to function without the batterer. They may also awaken the partner to verbally abuse him or her or not permit him or her to sleep while verbal abuse occurs.

12. Rigid sex roles: For male batterers, the partner is expected to serve and obey. The partner is viewed as inferior and as an incomplete person without the relationship to the batterer.

13. Jekyll-and-Hyde personality: Batterers may have explosive mood swings, particularly when related to hypersensitivity and other characteristics. Their attitudes and behaviors may also be completely different around friends and family than when the couple is alone.

14. Past battering: Batterers may admit to having hit partners in the past, but they say the victim made them do it and minimize what occurred. Former partners or family members may warn of a violent history. Battering behavior does not just go away.

15. Threats of violence: Batterers threaten physical force to control their partners, although they tell their partners that everybody talks like that.

16. Breaking or striking objects: Batterers break things, throw objects, and beat on tables or walls to terrorize their partners into submission.

17. Use of any force during arguments: Batterers often hold their partners down, keep their partners from leaving the room, and push and shove their partners, particularly while arguing.

PATTERNS IN A VIOLENT RELATIONSHIP

Lenore Walker, author of *The Battered Woman*, identified a cycle of escalating violence that is apparent in approximately two-thirds of battering relationships. Even though these relationships are not violent at all times, the degree and frequency of violence tends to escalate over time. Further, there is a predictable three-stage cycle of each violent event, even though the victim may be unaware of the pattern.

In the *tension-building* stage, which begins some time after a loving courtship and eventual commitment, the woman senses that something is wrong in the relationship. As the tension escalates, there may be minor incidents, but she begins to believe that her efforts to appease her partner will keep him from becoming angry. The second stage, or *acute-battering incident*, begins with a violent attack on the woman, which temporarily discharges the tension. This abusive event lasts only a few minutes or hours, usually as long as the batterer wishes to continue the attack. The woman experiences physical and emotional injury, shock, and disbelief as she begins to realize she has no control over the batterer during this phase. Then the remorse begins—a period of *loving contrition* and *absence of tension*. The batterer apologizes profusely and offers gifts and solemn assurances that he will never repeat the attack. It is during this period that batterers may also make rationalized explanations and excuses for their behavior, indirectly pushing blame and guilt onto the woman. Unfortunately, the "kiss and make-up" portion of the cycle reminds women of the early courtship period prior to commencement of violence in the relationship, strengthening their desire to stay in the relationship and their false hope in the belief that he will change.[4]

Usually, however, within a few days, weeks, or months, the tension begins to build as the cycle starts again. And the beat goes on. Until or unless the battered partner escapes, or the battering partner comes to a clear realization of the need for significant and permanent behavioral change, this horrible pattern of torment can continue for a lifetime. One comedienne remarked, "Our wedding vows said 'until death do us part.' I guess that means I'm going to have to kill him." Sadly, that way of ending a marriage occurs more often than any of us wants to realize.

ESTIMATES OF THE INCIDENCE AND PREVALENCE OF BATTERING

In chapter 5, the problems concerning studies that attempt to determine the incidence (number of cases over a specific time period) and prevalence (numbers of people who have ever experienced a particular event) of violence against women are discussed. As in the case of sexual assault, the true numbers of battered women are unknown and the estimates we have are probably underestimates of the magnitude of the problem. Available data come primarily from two sources—crime statistics and research projects involving nationally representative self-report surveys. Crime-related statistics are compiled by the CDC and the National Institute of Justice (NIJ). In turn, the CDC and Bureau of Justice Statistics (BJS) data are derived from the Uniform Crime Reports (UCR), the reports of intentional injuries from the National Electronic Injury Surveillance System (NEISS), the government reports of homicide, the Federal Bureau of Investigation (FBI) Supplemental Homicide Reports (SHR), and the results of the National Crime Victimization Survey (NCVS).[5] Some of the most important research projects conducted to determine the incidence and/or prevalence of battered women include the National Family Violence Surveys (NFVS),[6,7] National Violence Against Women Survey (NVAWS),[8] and the National Survey of Families and Households (NSFH).[9]

According to the NVAWS, approximately 1.3 million women are beaten by a past or current intimate partner every year. The results of the NFVS suggest that the prevalence of physical assaults among married and divorced women is 12.3 percent for nonsevere violence and 4.4 percent for severe violence. Data from the NCVS of all crimes committed against intimates in 1998 indicate that women experience five times as many incidents of nonfatal violence as men.[10] Also in the NCVS study, when one looks at the percentage of women who are victimized by physical assaults in terms of their relationship to the offender, we find that only 38.4 percent of the perpetrators are strangers, 61.6 percent are people known to the victims, 20.7 percent are current or ex-spouses or boyfriends, and 34.3 percent are friends or acquaintances.

In another study that examined NIJ and CDC data, it was found that 22.1 percent of women and only 7.4 percent of men were physically assaulted by their spouses, ex-spouses, cohabitors, or dates. NCVS data indicate that among the nearly one million crimes committed by current or former partners, women were the victims in nearly 85 percent of the cases (15 percent for men), and the rate of victimization for women separated from their partners was three times the rate for divorced women and 25 times the rate for married women.[11] Another recent study has shown that men perpetrate far more domestic violence than women.[12]

Furthermore, a woman does not have to be married to be battered. The prevalence of domestic violence among couples living together (22 percent) was higher than that for dating partners (10.6 percent) or married couples (10.5 percent).[13] Battering also is not limited to heterosexual partners. In a survey of gay, lesbian, bisexual, and transgendered individuals, the lifetime percentage of physical abuse was 32 percent.[14]

Clearly, the data indicate that the battering of women is a significant problem in the United States. But is that true for our neighboring country of Canada? In a study of over 7,000 Canadian women, only 3.7 percent of Canadian-born women, 2.4 percent of immigrant women from developed countries, and 5.5 percent of immigrant women from developing countries were victims of domestic violence.[15] Based upon these data, it appears that greater numbers of women are battered in the United States than in Canada. The question that comes to mind is *why*. So far, there is no simple answer to this question. Indeed, the answer to why there is such a difference in the prevalence of domestic violence in two countries of similar origin could probably be the topic of an entire book. However, it is a critical question for which our society needs to seek an answer.

CONSEQUENCES OF BATTERING

I watched my mother endure 20 years of marriage to a batterer. I watched her gradually "morph" from an energetic, confident, assertive woman to a defeated, depressed victim of subjugation. As I grew older, sometimes I would ask her why we had to live like this. Why couldn't we leave my father? She would always offer reasons, most of which were economic. She couldn't afford to support three children on her own . . . we would not be able to live in a decent neighborhood with decent schools on her salary . . . my father's salary was so modest that child support payments would not ease her financial burden. So she stayed. One night when I was 20, my father was slapping my mother around in the kitchen with more force than usual. Of course he had been drinking more than usual. As things escalated, I seriously thought that this time he might kill her. As I picked up the kitchen phone, I screamed at him, "I am not going to let you kill my mother. I am calling the police!" Then he picked up a cast iron frying pan and came after me. I looked him right in the eyes and told him, "Go ahead and kill me. I would rather be dead than live like this." That stopped the violence that night. But she still stayed. Then nearly a month later he came after my eighty-some-year-old grandmother. That night we fled. It was very difficult for the first six months but at least we were no longer chronically terrified. I left college and got a job. Together my mother and I created a good, violence-free life for my siblings and my grandmother. I eventually finished college by attending evening and Saturday classes.[16]

One of the least understood issues regarding battered women is why they remain with their batterers for as long as they do. Whether they are students, clients, or people in general, we routinely hear, "Well, if that ever happened to me, I would leave immediately. He wouldn't do that to me again!" But battered women do not stay in battering homes because they are unconcerned about their safety. They stay because there are a number of obstacles that must be overcome in order for them to be able to leave and to survive. Also there are many psychological consequences of battering that compromise women's ability to leave. Some of the obstacles that can prevent women from leaving a violent home include fear of retaliation, lack of economic resources, children, and societal influences. Psychological consequences of battering range from low self-esteem, coping and problem-solving deficits, learned helplessness, depression, substance abuse, posttraumatic stress disorder (PTSD), and the hostage syndrome. The following section will discuss the obstacles battered women face when they attempt to leave, as well as the psychological effects of being battered.

OBSTACLES BATTERED WOMEN FACE WHEN THEY ATTEMPT TO LEAVE

In order for a battered woman to leave her batterer she must come to change some of her beliefs. Researchers have found that a woman needs to (1) acknowledge that the relationship is unhealthy; (2) realize that the relationship will not get better; (3) experience some catalyst event, for example, abuse of another family member; (4) give up the dream of an idealized relationship; and (5) accept that to some extent the relationship will never be over if there are children and child custody/visitation issues.[17] Even when victims are ready to leave, they need to be able to find safe places to go, and they need to know what community agencies are available to help them. Sometimes local shelters are filled, and the battered woman will need assistance from her local crisis center to find the closest shelter where there is space available. Nevertheless, the following issues often prevent women from leaving. For any woman reading this volume who needs resource information to assist her in leaving her batterer, see Appendix 1: Safety Recommendations for Victims of Intimate Partner Violence.

Fear

It is not surprising that fear permeates the life of a battered woman. She often fears the unknown, fears what will happen to her and her children if they leave, and she fears that her partner will retaliate in some way if she does leave. In a historical story of 10 women living in a shelter, Hyden identified several successive stages of fear through which battered women progress: general fearfulness that had no specific target, specific fear of the male partner, and a chronic, generalized background fear. These fears are illustrated in the following quote:

> When I first came here, what I was mostly thinking about, was that I was so frightened. It didn't matter how many locked doors there were. I couldn't even feel protected here, so I was really afraid . . . . It's like I just sat on a chair, and I remember I was thinking "somebody's got to come and help me now," because I am completely paralyzed . . . completely unable to change my life . . . alone.[18]

Battered women have a legitimate reason to be fearful, because the most dangerous time for her is when she leaves. She expects that the batterer will retaliate. That expectation is grounded in the fact that there have been verbal or physical threats about what would happen if she left, or there has been such behavior when she attempted to leave before, or there is knowledge regarding what the batterer did when his previous partner left him. Even when she does leave her batterer, she has the very real fear of having to continue to interact with the batterer as he attempts to maintain coercive control over her through custody and visitation maneuvers regarding her children.[19]

Because of emotional conditioning, cues such as yelling, drinking heavily, and particular facial expressions can become aversive and fear provoking.[20] Fear conditioning is now known to cause neurological alterations in the brain.[21] For all of these reasons, family violence researchers have suggested that "victim fear" distinguishes battering from some of the other forms of intimate partner violence.[22]

Economic Resources

Often a lack of economic resources is the major reason why a woman remains in an abusive relationship. Without transportation, a place to stay, or money to buy food, clothing, child care, and health care, it is nearly impossible for a woman to leave. Essentially, without help, a battered woman who lacks economic resources has a choice between being homeless or returning to her violent partner. Two early studies supported this observation. In one, 58 percent of the abused women in the study did not leave because of economic needs,[23] and in another study 30 percent stayed for that reason.[24]

Lack of employment or problems finding employment further complicate a woman's economic issues and her ability to leave the batterer. A study of almost three thousand women who were victims of domestic violence found that unemployment and assault had a cyclical pattern. Victimization increased a woman's risk for unemployment, reduced income, and divorce, and women who were recently assaulted were more than twice as likely to be unemployed at the end of the study.[25] Another reason why women who are victims of battering have problems finding and maintaining employment is that their abusers often use physical force, threats, or control tactics to keep them from active participation in the workplace. In one study of battered women, it was found that 55 percent missed work, 62 percent were late or left work early, 24 percent lost their jobs, and 56 percent were harassed by their batterers at work.[26] However, on a positive note, the results of this study also indicated that ending the abuse enabled nearly half of the women to return to employment or school.

Children

Children are an important reason why battered women stay with their batterers. Victims often believe that it is of paramount importance to provide their children with two parents and the opportunities afforded by a greater income. Many women believe that economic deprivation will have such a detrimental impact on their children that it is the lesser of the evils to keep the family together. And then there is the issue of custody and visitation rights. Women who have no real likelihood of obtaining custody of their children face the dilemma of staying in the relationship to protect their children or of being unable to protect them if the batterer were to receive custody of the children or visitation rights.[27]

Societal Influences

How many times has a battered woman been told to "stand by your man," or to "give him one more chance," or even to "pray for him" in order to hold her marriage together? The answer to that question is "far too many times"! These are some of the societal influences that keep women emotionally connected or attached to men who abuse. There are also those religious influences that instruct women to honor their marriage vows and to stay in an abusive situation "through thick and through thin, until death do us part." Such influences help to create emotional connections that are not easily broken. A woman who has difficulty leaving an abusive relationship is not attached to the battering behavior. Rather, the woman is attached to the previolent person with whom she fell in love, the father of her children, and the person with whom she planned her life. She always hopes that the batterer will change and the relationship will return to its previolent status. Society needs to understand that when violence enters a relationship, these types of cultural influences hinder the battered woman from making decisions that are in the true interest of safety for her and her children. We need to help the battered woman overcome these influences that underlie her strong emotional connection to family she envisioned and to the batterer.[28]

PSYCHOLOGICAL EFFECTS ASSOCIATED WITH BATTERING

After years of being abused by my husband, I lost hope that anything would ever change. At first I believed that somehow if I were just a better, stronger woman my marriage would survive and my husband would stop the violence. However, there came a point where I just did not care about anything anymore. My family practice doctor prescribed medication to help me sleep with the advice that it should only be used intermittently. However, that was the only way I could fall asleep and soon I needed a few glasses of wine to augment the effect of the sleeping pill. I became depressed. Every task of daily living became a struggle. I began drinking more. At least that way I had some escape from the pain . . . some type of anesthesia. Then one day I just did not feel like showing up for life. I felt helpless, worthless, and just wanted not to be in pain. I contemplated suicide many times but always came back to the realization that if I were dead, the only caretaker my children would have was the man who beat me. The thought of that horrific outcome kept me alive and I got help.[29]

Being a victim of domestic violence can result in serious and long-lasting psychological consequences. The initial emotion reported after a battering incident tends to be helplessness. Over time, most women become fearful, anxious, angry, and depressed. As in the case of victims of sexual assault, many battered women develop PTSD.[30] The duration of the abuse and the victim's history of prior abuse impact the severity of the symptoms she may experience.

Learned Helplessness

During the 1970s, Lenore Walker suggested that a response known as "learned helplessness" might explain why battered women did not free themselves from their abusers. Learned helplessness (LH) is often defined as a condition in which an individual does not attempt to escape from a painful situation after learning from a previous, similar situation that escape is not possible.[31] According to this perspective, battered women come to believe that they are unable to take action to free themselves from their abusers, so they resign themselves to the belief that abuse is inevitable. As a result, the victims attribute their abuse to things over which they have no control.[32]

Although the concept of LH was helpful in explaining why a battered woman stayed with her abuser, some experts in the field argued that this concept blamed the women and did not take into account the many help-seeking activities that women undertake to leave their abusive environments.[33] A battered woman averages six help-seeking behaviors (seeking out clergy, calling police or a crisis center) before she enters a shelter.[34] Moreover, the results of another study indicated that, among the women they studied, 38 percent sought help from the police, 32 percent applied for restraining orders, and 31 percent obtained medical care but 41 percent did not access any services. The factors that were related to individuals who did not seek help included higher income, no children in the house, employment, homemaker or school activities, higher educational attainment, nonminority racial status, and youthfulness.[35] Finally, some researchers have suggested that LH may not be a learned response, but rather an accurate reflection of reality for victims of domestic violence.[36]

Problem-solving and Coping Deficits

There is disagreement regarding whether battered women have lowered problem-solving and coping abilities. Sometimes when such deficits have been noted, they are found to be situation specific. Some victims may be poor problem solvers, because they have sustained head injuries as a result of the battering or as a result of distorted thought processes associated with PTSD.[37] Other researchers have suggested that being a victim of domestic violence diminishes a person's effective coping skills. One study found that the coping strategies of placating or resisting that women initially used most often in their relationships to avoid violence were the least effective.[38] When we compare victims of domestic violence with nonvictims, victims seem to be less likely to use active coping strategies, such as seeking support, and are more likely to use passive coping strategies, such as avoidance and emotional distance. Moreover, the latter two styles of coping seem to be associated with feelings of depression.[39] It appears, however, that after a woman leaves her abuser, emotional reactions decrease while problem-solving skills increase, thus enhancing her ability to make more effective decisions.[40]

Self-Blame and Depression

It is common for battered women to believe that they provoked the violence or that they should have been able to prevent it by changing their behavior.[41] In part, this is because the batterers contribute to this belief by holding their partners responsible for relationship violence. In one study of victims of intimate partner violence (IPV), the women reported that they regretted isolating themselves from sources of support and regretted their failure to seek knowledge and take care of themselves.[42] The results of another study found that a larger proportion of battered women who were still involved with their abusers blamed themselves for causing the violence (53 percent) as compared to women who were no longer in abusive relationships (35 percent).[43]

Similarly, almost without exception, researchers have documented that battered women are quite likely to suffer from depression. In fact, depression and suicide attempts were four times more likely in IPV victims than in nonvictims.[44] IPV victimization is considered a major risk factor for depression.[45]

Substance Abuse

Battered women are at an increased risk for developing a substance abuse problem for a number of reasons. Alcohol or other drugs can be used to help them cope with their victimization. Even if the effects are only temporary, alcohol and drugs can reduce feelings of anxiety, depression, and sleeplessness. As seen in the previous vignette, a battered woman may be given medications by her physician in response to complaints of anxiety or insomnia. The physician may be unaware that the patient is in an abusive relationship. Then, over time, with continued use of drugs that are capable of inducing tolerance and dependence, the woman develops a substance abuse problem.

Some women are coerced into using substances with their batterers and do so to reduce the risk of violence. Some battered women with histories of childhood physical or sexual abuse may have used drugs and/or alcohol since a young age to numb the effects of victimization. Unfortunately, the use of drugs or alcohol as a coping mechanism may also numb the battered woman to the risks of violence and reduce her ability to protect herself and her children. In an even more dangerous scenario, the use of alcohol or drugs may increase a woman's sense of courage and reduce her inhibitions, thus enhancing the likelihood that she may try to fight back against her batterer despite the high risk of doing so.[46]

Trauma Effects, PTSD, and Stockholm Syndrome

Being battered by one's partner definitely constitutes a traumatic event. Typically the response to a traumatic event entails fear, helplessness, and horror. The greater the frequency and severity of the assaults, the greater the likelihood that a victim will develop trauma-related symptoms, PTSD, or Stockholm syndrome. Moreover, the effects of trauma are cumulative. There are many symptoms that occur as a result of traumatic experience. They include depression, aggression, physical illness, identity problems, guilt, shame, and difficulties in interpersonal relationships.[47]

With respect to PTSD, it can occur when a person is confronted with an event such as actual or threatened death or physical injury or a threat of harm to oneself or others.[48] When a traumatic event causes an acute, prolonged emotional reaction in a victim, clinicians designate the disorder as PTSD. Symptoms associated with PTSD include the reexperiencing of painful recollections of the traumatic event, flashbacks, nightmares, sleep difficulties, memory and concentration problems, numbing of emotions, exaggerated startle response, and avoidance of stimuli reminiscent of the trauma. Data suggest that 40 to 60 percent of battered women develop PTSD[49] and that even psychological abuse or "mild" IPV can result in PTSD. Moreover, the extent and severity of the IPV correlates with the severity of the symptoms of PTSD[50] and is a predictor of future mental health issues. For example, when battered women with PTSD were compared with those who did not have PTSD and with non-abused women, the women with PTSD showed more impaired physical health and social functioning.[51]

Another explanation for some of the traumatic effects of battering is derived from the observations of instances where hostages who have been severely threatened begin to identify with their captors. In these cases, the captives may praise their captors, deny that abuse has occurred, and blame themselves for the abuse. This phenomenon is known as Stockholm syndrome or *hostage syndrome*. Dee Graham, Edna Rawlings, and Nelly Rimini first noticed that this behavior was very similar to the attachment that a battered woman often has for her batterer. It is thought that such an attachment can develop from the batterer's threats to kill the victim coupled with the victim's perception that he has the capacity to do so, an inability to escape that fosters the victim's dependency on the batterer for survival, isolation that narrows her external reality to the abuser, and occasional kindness from him.[52] The captor alternates threats with kindness. Captives come to believe that the only way to survive is to align themselves with the captors. Sometimes they will even begin to believe that they love or admire their captors. The development of this type of captor/captive existence can result in severe symptoms of trauma in a victim and make leaving the relationship even more difficult.

As you can see, there are a wide array of consequences that can occur as a result of battering. Not all women develop the same symptoms. Factors such as the duration and severity of the violence correlate with the numbers and intensities of the symptoms reported. The sooner a victim can leave the situation, the sooner healing can and does occur. No one has to be battered, and remaining in the situation never makes it better.

MONETARY COSTS OF INTIMATE PARTNER VIOLENCE

Not only does IPV devastate the lives of women and children, but it also incurs great costs to society as a whole. The National Center for Injury Prevention and Control (NCIPC) estimates that the annual cost of IPV for the United States is $5.8 billion.[53] Researchers have begun to determine how much IPV costs society with respect to health care, homelessness, and the processing of domestic violence cases through the criminal justice system.

Victims of IPV utilize health care services more often than nonvictimized women.[54] Data from the NVAWS indicate that of the 1,451 women who were victims of battering, 41.5 percent were injured. Of those injured, only 28.5 percent received medical care. Of those receiving care, 78.6 percent received hospital care, 51.8 percent received physician's care, 14.9 percent received ambulance/paramedic care, 9.5 percent received dental care, and 8.9 percent received physical therapy. The price tag for the medical and mental health costs due to IPV is estimated to be $4.1 billion annually.[55]

Moreover, family violence is one of the major causes of female homelessness. It has been estimated that 21 to 64 percent of women in homeless shelters are there because of IPV. Given that it costs social service agencies approximately $68 per day per person to provide housing and services for clients in shelters, it is apparent that billions of dollars are expended on housing homeless battered women and their children.[56]

Although the police, court, probation, and prison costs associated with battering are difficult to estimate, New York City has attempted to determine the cost of domestic violence. They had 12,724 IPV arrests in one year. Each arrest cost $3,241. When the police costs, court costs, and detention costs were considered, it was determined that IPV cost the city $41 million! In 1991, a federal survey of correctional facilities found that 20,170 inmates were incarcerated for harming their partners. At an annual average cost of $15,513 per inmate, incarceration of batterers costs taxpayers more than $300 million every year. If we then consider the court costs incurred by batterers, the total expenditures are even higher. It is estimated that court costs for each batterer are approximately $158 plus another $86 for each incremental review. Probation costs, which are paid by taxpayers, total about $130 per batterer, whereas a 30-day sentence in jail costs about $2,000 per batterer.[57]

Hence, these data support the notion regarding the critical need for the prevention and elimination of IPV. Not only does domestic violence negatively impact the lives of women and children, its financial impact on society is staggering.

CONCLUSION

Domestic violence is a major problem for women and children in the United States. Indeed, it may occur in nearly one-fourth of our households. Its consequences wreak havoc on the lives of its victims. Additionally, the costs to every member of our society are enormous. Those of us who are not in a battering relationship must become part of the solution to this problem. Services and support for victims need to be increased so that women can liberate themselves and their children from their batterers. Volunteers are always needed at women's shelters. Hotline workers are needed as are victim advocates. Reach out. Help your local crisis center. If you are a battered woman, you deserve a violence-free life. Access the resources in your community. Let the people who want to help you do so. You do not have to be beaten.

Chapter 5

Sexual Abuse of Women

Camille N. Ward
Paula K. Lundberg-Love

The sexual assault of women and children in the United States is a crime of major proportions. This type of attack literally turns the victim's world upside down. During the aftermath of sexual assault, the victim may experience a wide array of psychological symptoms. It takes time and therapeutic intervention to recover from such a violation of body and spirit. The purpose of this chapter is to provide a detailed review of both child sexual abuse (CSA) and sexual assault (SA) in adulthood. Issues pertaining to sexual assault, including the definitions of sexual abuse, the estimates of its incidence and prevalence, possible signs of sexual abuse, the effects of abuse, and some characteristics of perpetrators will be discussed. The first half of the chapter will address CSA and the latter segment will focus on adult SA.

CHILD SEXUAL ABUSE

Emma, age 7, was the younger of two children. Her 15-year-old brother, Joshua, baby-sat for her every day after school. One day he asked her if she wanted to play "house" with him. He said that he would be the daddy and she would be the mommy, and he informed her that they would do the things that parents were supposed to do. Each day after school they would kiss each other on the cheek, ask how the other's day had gone, and watch television together.

Joshua slowly and subtly became more affectionate with her. They began to cuddle on the bed together. The kiss on the cheek transformed into one on the lips. The touches and holding became more intimate. The kisses grew longer. Joshua soon began fondling Emma's genitals and ordering her to undress and lay with him. She was overwhelmed with feelings of confusion, fright, and discomfort. When she expressed resistance, her brother reassured her that it was just a game and told her to stop acting like a baby. She thought she should tell her parents, but she did not want Joshua to get in trouble, or worse, stop loving her. He attempted vaginal penetration on two occasions, but discontinued when Emma cried for him to stop.

One afternoon their mother found them undressed together. Law enforcement was contacted and Joshua was court-ordered to live with his grandparents for an indefinite period of time. Emma did not fully grasp why her brother was sent away and felt responsible for what happened, further intensifying her shame and anguish.[1]

DEFINITIONS OF CHILD SEXUAL ABUSE

Definitions of CSA differ among various studies. They include a broad range of illegal behaviors.[2] The unavailability of a single, clearly stated definition of CSA provides a unique challenge. Criminal statutes for CSA also vary from state to state, causing additional confusion and ambiguity. One of the earliest definitions of CSA was published by the National Center on Child Abuse and Neglect in 1978. According to this definition, CSA is:

> contacts or interactions between a child and an adult when the child is being used for sexual stimulation of the perpetrator or another person. Sexual abuse may also be committed by a person under the age of 18 when that person is either significantly older than the victim or when the perpetrator is in a position of power or control over another child.[3]

This definition integrates several components that are common in many of the present legal and research definitions of CSA. First of all, most definitions allow for the inclusion of abuse both by non-family members (extrafamilial) and by family members (intrafamilial or incestuous). Definitions also encompass situations involving both physical contact and noncontact experiences.[4] Forms of contact sexual abuse include fondling, oral sex, and penetration of the vagina, anus, or mouth. Showing pornography to children, using children to create pornography, exposing private parts to children, and forcing children to participate in sexual acts with one another are all examples of non-contact CSA.[5] Another crucial component involves the adult's use of authority and control over the child to obtain sexual gratification. It is assumed that children are incapable of consenting to sexual relationships with adults, because they lack the ability to fully understand to what they are consenting and the repercussions that are likely to follow. Last, the age disparity between the victim and the offender is taken into account. Many definitions of CSA restrict the age difference to five years or more, whereas other definitions consider multiple factors such as the size, sex, and status, in addition to the age differential.[6]

INCIDENCE AND PREVALENCE

Although the actual percentage of girls and women that have been sexually abused is unknown,[7] the number is high. Several early studies found CSA to be more common than expected, but the results were viewed with skepticism and did not receive much public attention. However, in the latter part of the twentieth century, there was a dramatic increase in the number of reported sexual abuse cases, which sparked a renewed interest in the study of CSA and a demand to uncover the true scope of the problem.[8]

Due to the absence of any national reporting system for crimes committed against children, official statistics on CSA lack reliability and precision.[9] Child Protective Services (CPS) and other government agencies have attempted to gather information on annual rates of CSA.[10] These studies provide data regarding incidence, defined as the number of cases that occurred within a specific time frame, typically a 12-month period.[11] According to the American Association for Protecting Children, 50,714 cases of CSA were reported to CPS agencies during 1986. In 1997, this figure increased to 223,650 reported cases.[12] However, the accuracy of these numbers is highly questionable, particularly because most cases of CSA are never brought to the attention of the authorities. Many cases remain undetected for a variety of reasons, including the fact that children are reliant on parents or other adults to provide their basic needs, and the nature of the offense is secretive and stigmatizing.[13] Indeed, the reluctance of victims, their family members, and professionals to report CSA substantially contributes to recurring underestimates of abuse.[14]

The most dependable statistics regarding CSA are derived from epidemiological retrospective studies in which adult populations are asked whether they have been victims of CSA. The primary focus of these studies is on the prevalence of CSA, which refers to the percentage of individuals who have been victimized at some time during their lives. However, inconsistencies exist among study results, primarily due to variations in the methods used to conduct the research. For example, differences in the nature of the people questioned, the manner in which they are questioned, the definitions of sexual abuse used, and the type and number of screening questions impact the reported numbers of sexual abuse. Furthermore, studies using self-report methods are frequently found to underestimate the actual frequency of abuse history.

Two recent studies that consisted of adults with documented histories of sexual abuse discovered that over 30 percent of the respondents did not report their early abuse experiences.[15] Thus, even when conducting prevalence studies with adult populations, we cannot be certain how many participants either deliberately (due to an unwillingness to disclose) or unknowingly (due to an unconscious repression of abuse memories) fail to report instances of sexual abuse.

A 1992 review of college student and community studies found prevalence rates of CSA ranging between 7 percent and 62 percent for women and between 3 percent and 16 percent for men.[16] Such wide variations exemplify the ongoing challenge to establish precise estimates of sexual abuse in children. The most valid statistics are derived from the results of studies that use the soundest experimental procedures. Descriptions of the results from several of these studies follow.

Diana Russell conducted a study in which 930 females residing in San Francisco were interviewed one-on-one with a trained interviewer. Sixteen percent of the women in this study reported at least one experience of incestuous abuse prior to 18 years of age, and 31 percent reported one or more experiences of extrafamilial abuse before age 18. Because some women experienced both forms of abuse, when the two categories were combined it was found that 38 percent of the women reported one or more experiences of sexual abuse prior to age 18.[17]

In his review of retrospective prevalence surveys conducted in both the United States and Canada, David Finkelhor concluded that at least 20 to 25 percent of women and 5 to 15 percent of men have been victims of contact sexual abuse at some time during their lives, and many other studies have revealed similar results.[18] For example, the Gallop Organization sponsored a 1997 telephone survey involving a national random sample of 1,000 adults who were asked two questions about their personal childhood experiences of sexual abuse; 23 percent of the participants reported experiences of sexual abuse prior to 18 years of age.[19] These findings, which are modest at best, offer a shocking example of the pervasive and insidious nature of CSA in our society.

VICTIM CHARACTERISTICS

Increased public awareness and the need to recognize children who may be at risk for CSA have prompted researchers to try to identify factors associated with CSA. However, identifying risk factors is a difficult task. Because large numbers of CSA cases go unreported, the associated risk factors remain uncertain. Risk factors that are similar among victims who are brought to the attention of authorities may not be the same for victims whose abuse is kept secret. Community surveys, which uncover many cases of previously unreported abuse, allow researchers to retrieve the most accurate information on victim vulnerability.[20] Most studies have focused on the demographic characteristics and the family and social factors thought to influence a child's susceptibility to sexual abuse.[21]

Research results indicate that children between the ages of 8 and 12 are at greatest risk for CSA, and there is a slightly lower risk for children at the upper and lower ends of the age spectrum. The outcomes of virtually all studies suggest that children under age seven may be less likely to experience CSA.[22] However, small children may be less likely or less capable of reporting abuse, and adults who are surveyed may not recall early sexual abuse experiences. Overall, the evidence suggests that an increased risk for CSA occurs in middle childhood.

It is widely accepted that the majority of CSA victims are female. Girls are approximately three times more likely than boys to be sexually abused. However, some experts believe that boys are subjected to sexual abuse more often than the data indicate. Possible factors contributing to the underreporting of male CSA may stem from the fact that boys believe that they should be strong enough to prevent such assault, and, if the perpetrator is a female, some boys do not even consider the events abuse. Also, many people believe that boys commonly engage in sexual experiences at an early age. Because boys are more likely to be abused by male perpetrators, they may fail to disclose the abuse for fear that people will think they are homosexual.[23] Even though more research aimed at addressing CSA issues in males is needed, girls unquestionably remain at a greater risk for CSA than boys.

Certain family characteristics also increase a child's vulnerability to CSA. These include living without one or both biological parents at some time during childhood, having a poor relationship with one or both parents, parental discord and/or violence, and the presence of a stepfather in the home. In fact, stepfathers are more likely to commit more severe forms of abuse.[24] Other risk factors are having a mother who is employed outside the home, living with a parent who is disabled due to physical illness, having a parent who abuses drugs or is emotionally disturbed, and having a parent with a prior history of sexual abuse.[25]

Additionally, children with psychological or cognitive vulnerabilities seem to be at greater risk for CSA. For example, the incidence of sexual abuse in children with disabilities is 1.75 times the rate of children with no disability.[26] The evaluation of other variables including social isolation, ethnicity, and socioeconomic status has generated varying results.[27] It is clear, however, that CSA is a ubiquitous problem and no child regardless of age, sex, ethnicity, socioeconomic class, or family circumstance is immune to such victimization.

PERPETRATOR CHARACTERISTICS

Common stereotypes portraying child sex abusers as "dirty old men" or strangers who prey on children in school yards and playgrounds are simply false. There is absolutely no offender profile, perpetrator checklist, or other detection device available to warn potential victims or their families of impending abuse. In fact, research data indicate immense perpetrator diversity. The following information highlights what we know about CSA offenders regarding age, sex, and relationship to the victim.

Research suggests that CSA perpetrators vary greatly with respect to age. The mean age of incest offenders in the Russell study was 33 years. Only 20 percent were over the age of 46.[28] Recent evidence suggests that juveniles may represent up to 40 percent of the offender population and that most sexual perpetrators acquire their aberrant sexual interests before reaching adulthood.[29]

At least 75 percent of CSA offenders are men. In fact, between 4 percent and 17 percent of men surveyed in a study using a national random sample admitted to having had sexual relations with a child.[30] Equally astonishing, 21 percent of the male undergraduates surveyed in another study reported having feelings of sexual attraction to children, and 7 percent expressed some likelihood of having sex with a child if they knew for certain that they would not be caught.[31] These numbers, which represent at least one perpetrator or potential perpetrator in any random sampling of 25 men, demonstrate that such offenders are relatively prevalent in the population.

The prevalence of female offenders may actually be higher than existing data suggest. For example, inappropriate sexual contact may be disguised by routine child care.[32] It has been established that women are more likely to abuse boys than girls, and women are implicated in 40 percent of the reported cases of sexual abuse in day care facilities.[33] Most female offenders are accomplices to male perpetrators, lonesome and isolated single parents, teenage babysitters, or adult women who cultivate romantic relationships with young boys, such as the case involving 36-year-old Mary Kay Letourneau and her 13-year-old former student. The two engaged in an eight-month sexual relationship before their secret affair was uncovered.[34]

Sexual offenders are typically classified into one of two groups: those who commit extrafamilial abuse and those who commit intrafamilial abuse. Intrafamilial abuse is more common among cases reported to the attention of authorities. In contrast, most CSA victims responding to general population surveys report accounts of extrafamilial abuse.[35] According to survey results, between 6 percent and 16 percent of CSA is perpetrated by a parent or stepparent, whereas abuse by any relative constitutes over one-third of cases.[36] In Russell's study, 11 percent of the victimizations involved fathers or stepfathers, 20 percent involved other relatives, 45 percent involved acquaintances or friends of the child or family, and 11 percent involved strangers. Although extrafamilial abuse appears to be more common than intrafamilial abuse, in most cases the perpetrator is, at the very least, familiar to the child victim.[37]

EFFECTS OF ABUSE

Claire was first abused by her teenage baby-sitter at age 11. The sitter ordered Claire and her younger sister to act out scenes that he showed them from pornographic videotapes. When they refused, he tied them up, made them watch him while he masturbated, and then locked them in the bathroom as punishment. The abuse ended after several weeks when the girls told their mother what he was doing to them.

At age 14, Claire was sexually abused by her uncle who was staying with her family while he was out of work. She and her uncle were home alone and he was drinking heavily. He had the radio blasting and playfully asked Claire if she wanted to dance. They were having fun until he tried to kiss her. When she resisted, he became angry and aggressive. After slapping her and pulling her by the hair, he pinned her on the floor, and raped her. He threatened to kill her if she ever told anyone. Out of fear she remained silent.

Fifteen years after the second assault, Claire still harbors feelings of betrayal, disempowerment, guilt, shame, and rage. She suffers from depression and has seen a therapist for the past two years. Sometimes flooded with overwhelming distress and anxiety, she cuts her wrists and arms. The cutting provides temporary relief followed by increased guilt and self-hatred. Any reminder of her abuse experience, such as a song, the smell of beer, or exposure to pornography, can trigger intense flashbacks. Claire cannot wear bracelets because they induce the sensation of being tied up. She says she has a hard time relating to other people and socializes very little. She distrusts everyone, but especially men. Her romantic relationships have been brief and unfulfilling. Claire has almost no desire to have sex, which she finds dissatisfying, and at times painful.[38]

The majority of research indicates that a variety of psychological, behavioral, physical, and cognitive problems are more common among CSA victims than nonvictims. Sexual abuse can be an excruciating experience characterized by fright, confusion, self-blame, and humiliation. Such painful events may hinder normal developmental progression and increase the likelihood of disturbances in adulthood.[39] Studies have revealed myriad acute and long-term consequences of CSA.

Initial Effects

Symptomatology varies from child to child and depends on factors such as the severity of abuse, the child's relationship to the abuser, the amount of physical force involved, the age difference between the victim and the perpetrator, and the duration of abuse.[40] Different symptoms also may occur at different developmental stages (i.e., preschool, school-age, and adolescence). Depression, anxiety, decreased self-esteem, and suicidal behavior are more likely among CSA victims compared to nonabused children. Other common emotional disturbances include nightmares, obsessions, guilt, fear, anger, and aggression.[41] Additionally, over one-third of sexually abused children meet the diagnostic criteria for PTSD, a trauma-induced disorder characterized by persistent reexperiencing of the traumatic event, avoidance and numbing behaviors, and increased autonomic nervous system arousal. Studies suggest that CSA victims are diagnosed with PTSD more often than children who experience other forms of abuse.[42]

Sexually abused children also exhibit more behavioral problems than other children. Increased sexual behaviors associated with intercourse, such as mimicking sexual acts and inserting objects into the vagina or anus, are more prevalent in victims of sexual abuse. In fact, sexualized behavior may be the best behavioral indicator of CSA. Additional sex-related behavioral effects include sexual preoccupation, precocious sexual knowledge, seductive behavior, sexual language, sex play with others, genital exposure, and promiscuity.[43] During adolescence, girls are more likely to engage in promiscuous behaviors, whereas boys are more likely to engage in genital exposure or sexual coercion. Teenage victims are more likely than nonvictims to run away, use drugs, drop out of school, and engage in other delinquent behaviors. Sexually abused children often view themselves as being different from other children and display a general mistrust of their surroundings. They tend to be less socially competent and exhibit poor peer relations, social withdrawal, and other interpersonal difficulties.[44]

Various physical symptoms and somatic complaints such as stomachaches, headaches, sleep disturbances, and eating disturbances indicative of heightened anxiety are quite common. Children may experience genital pain, bleeding, itching, and/or odors, as well as problems walking or sitting. Furthermore, older girls may become pregnant as a result of sexual abuse.[45]

Sexual abuse also can impact cognitive functioning. Overall, sexually abused children are lower academic achievers in comparison to their nonabused peers.[46] Common school-related problems include learning difficulties, impaired concentration and attention, and declining grades.[47]

Long-Term Effects

CSA is a major risk factor for numerous problems later in life. Although some survivors report little or no abuse-related effects, others exhibit considerable symptomatology in many aspects of their lives. Depression is the most commonly reported symptom in adults who were sexually abused as children. As a result, they also are more likely to engage in suicidal behaviors. Other widely noted emotional disturbances include chronic anxiety, anger, and symptoms of PTSD.

CSA victims have more difficulties in their interpersonal relationships as well. Female survivors are more likely to remain single. If they do marry, they are more likely to divorce or separate. They commonly report poor relationship satisfaction and have fewer friends. Survivors of sexual abuse also report sexual maladjustment more frequently than nonabused adults. Typical sexual problems include sexual dysfunction, sexual preoccupation, fantasies of forced sexual contact, or superficial and short-lived sexual relationships.[48] A significant number of women also experience revictimization in adulthood. It appears that many victims learn how to survive, but they remain at risk for sexual abuse.[49]

Survivors of sexual abuse report higher rates of alcohol and substance abuse, self-mutilation, and eating disorders. Victims may engage in these self-defeating behaviors in an attempt to reduce their unbearable pain and restore an inner balance.[50] Adults with a prior history of sexual abuse also are more likely to report physical problems such as headaches, insomnia, gastrointestinal complaints, and pelvic, abdominal, or back pain.[51]

SIGNS OF CHILD SEXUAL ABUSE

Although CSA victims do not respond to sexual abuse in a uniform manner, certain behaviors may serve as warning signs of either present or past abuse experiences. Inappropriate or excessive sexual behavior, sleep problems (e.g., nightmares), depression, withdrawal from family or friends, suicidal behavior, and uncharacteristic aggression can be signs of abuse. Other indicators can include refusal to attend school, engagement in delinquent behaviors, secretiveness, or demonstration of features of sexual maltreatment in drawings, games, or fantasies. Victims may make statements that their bodies are dirty or damaged, or they may fear that something is wrong with their genital area. Physical symptoms such as genital pain or bleeding and subsequent problems walking or sitting also may indicate sexual abuse. However, physical signs may be absent or difficult to detect, necessitating a thorough medical examination.[52]

SEXUAL ASSAULT

Kate, a 21-year-old college student, was at a bar with friends when a guy she recognized from campus approached her and introduced himself. He bought Kate a couple of drinks, and asked her if she wanted to go with him to a party. She was flattered by the invitation, and she agreed to go with him. He told her that he needed to make a quick stop by his apartment to get beer for the party and asked her if she wanted to come in to meet his roommate. When they got inside, there was no one else home. Kate began to feel uneasy. After making small talk for a few minutes, Rob began making sexual advances. Kate politely asked him to stop, but he persisted. He got up, locked the door, grabbed her by the hands, and escorted her forcefully to his bedroom. She was petrified and said that she was feeling ill in an attempt to leave. He clasped her upper arms, told her to relax, and leaned to kiss her neck. When she fought back, he just tightened his grasp and threw her on the bed. He said he knew she wanted him and proceeded to take off her clothes. She screamed and struggled to get away, but his strength was overpowering. He held her down with his body weight and forced her to have sex.

After he had finished, he went into the bathroom. Kate dressed quickly, left, and used her cell phone to call a cab. She was scared and confused, yet infuriated by what he had done and how he had violated her. At her apartment, she took several hot showers in an attempt to cleanse herself, but she continued to feel unclean. She eventually crawled into bed and cried herself to exhaustion. She told no one about her assault, fearing that they would not believe her or would blame her for using poor judgment and "setting herself up" for the attack.[53]

DEFINITIONS OF SEXUAL ASSAULT

In legal practice, SA is synonymous with rape.[54] However, in much of the literature, SA refers to any form of unwanted or forced sexual activity, such as forced exposure to pornography (either forcing a person to pose for pornographic pictures or to look at pornography), genital exposure, sexual harassment, unwanted sexual touching, and attempted or completed rape.[55] Even though we will limit this discussion to the topic of rape, it is important to recognize that other sexual offenses may cause significant psychological trauma and should not be trivialized. In fact, there are many similarities between the response to rape and other forms of SA.[56] Information also will be presented on dating violence (DV), which includes SA as well as other types of aggression in dating relationships.

The traditional offense of common-law rape is defined as "carnal knowledge of a female forcibly and against her will."[57] Carnal knowledge refers solely to penile-vaginal penetration, excluding other sexual offenses. This exceedingly narrow definition of rape was adopted by the FBI in compiling its UCR and in previous years by the BJS in its NCVS. The FBI has broadened its definition to include "homosexual rape"; however, this term implies that men who rape men are always homosexual, which is certainly not the case.

Rape is actually not a federal crime. Instead, rape statutes are written at the state level and vary accordingly.[58] Feminist legal scholars and women's groups have made great strides in their efforts to reform these laws in recent years. The reformed statutes are much more inclusive with respect to gender, form of penetration, and level of force applied during the assault. Current statutes typically define rape as nonconsensual sexual penetration of an adolescent or adult obtained by physical force, by threat of bodily harm, or at such time when the victim is incapable of giving consent by virtue of mental illness, mental retardation, or intoxication.[59] Sexual penetration may take the form of "sexual intercourse, cunnilingus, fellatio, anal intercourse, or any other intrusion, however slight, of any part of the person's body, and emission of semen is not required."[60]

TYPES OF RAPE

The act of rape may vary in a number of ways. Many rapes involve a single perpetrator, whereas others involve two or more perpetrators (also referred to as gang or "party" rape). Rapes also differ according to the interpersonal context in which they take place. In the case of *stranger rape*, the victim and perpetrator do not recognize or know one another prior to the attack. *Acquaintance rape* involves persons who know each other such as relatives, neighbors, friends, co-workers, or fellow students. *Date rape* refers specifically to SA within a dating relationship. Finally, *marital rape* occurs when the victim and offender are spouses. Rapes may be premeditated, partially planned, or completely spontaneous. Unplanned assaults are often influenced, at least in part, by the use of drugs or alcohol. Some rapes are reported to the police, but many remain unreported and thus hidden from public knowledge. Rapes go unreported for numerous reasons. Some victims recognize their experience as rape but fail to report the incident for a variety of reasons, such as fear of a damaged reputation or lack of support from family and friends. Others do not realize that their assault meets the legal requirements of a crime.[61]

INCIDENCE AND PREVALENCE

Rape incidence data are obtained from two federal sources, the UCR and the NCVS. The UCR is a collection of yearly figures of rape and other crimes based on the number of complaints reported to local police authorities. It is widely believed that rape is one of the most underreported crimes of personal violence. Because so many rapes go undetected, the UCR fails to provide a comprehensive estimate of the true scope of rape. The NCVS, conversely, is a nationwide household-based survey designed to obtain a more accurate crime rate estimate by including both reported and unreported cases. However, the NCVS has been strongly criticized for numerous methodological problems in past years that also result in inaccurate rape estimates.

Many studies have flaws that can adversely affect their results. First of all, survey interviews conducted in the presence of family members may ensure confidentiality, which often inhibits full disclosure. In addition, interviewers who do not receive special training to handle sensitive issues and who are not matched to the victim for ethnicity and gender may be less capable of building rapport. Poor wording of survey questions can confuse respondents and inhibit their disclosure. Furthermore, inaccurate results are obtained when studies use a very narrow definition of rape or when they exclude repeated attacks by a single perpetrator from rape estimates. Because multiple incidents tend to involve intimate partners, such data can inflate the proportions of rapes attributed to strangers as well as rapes committed across racial boundaries.[62] To overcome methodological obstacles, the BJS launched a 10-year project to revise the NCVS questionnaire and survey procedure. The transformation resulted in a 44 percent increase in the reported number of personal crimes and a 157 percent increase in reported rapes.[63]

A few specialized studies on rape incidence have also been conducted using nationwide samples. Results from all studies suggest a much higher rate of rape than indicated by federal estimates. For example, Koss and colleagues administered 10 sexual victimization screening questions to a nationally representative sample of women students at 32 colleges and universities across America. Six questions probed for experiences of attempted and completed rape but described behaviorally specific scenarios rather than using the word *rape*. Example items include: "Have you ever had sexual intercourse with a man when you did not want to because he used some degree of force such as twisting your arm or holding you down to make you cooperate?" or "Have you had other sexual acts with a man such as oral or anal intercourse or penetration with objects when you did not want to because he used some degree of force . . . or threatened to harm you to make you cooperate?" Using the UCR definition of rape, Koss found that 76 per 1,000 college women experienced attempted or completed rape within a 12-month period. The incidence doubled to 166 per 1,000 women when a more comprehensive definition of rape was used. Overall, the study estimates were still approximately 10 to 15 times higher than NCVS estimates during the same year.[64] One in four women surveyed were victims of attempted or completed rape, 84 percent knew their attacker, and 57 percent of the rapes occurred on dates. Such figures make acquaintance and date rape more common than left-handedness, heart attacks, or alcoholism.[65]

Because incidence is restricted to a preceding 12-month period, a woman who was raped 13 months ago would not be considered a victim for the purposes of incidence estimates. Yet, the physical and emotional effects of rape may persist for months or years after the assault, and some victims never fully recover. Therefore, prevalence estimates present a more complete picture of the true scope of rape over the lifetime.[66]

Results from the Koss study indicate that approximately 1 in 3.6 college women has been a victim of rape or attempted rape in her lifetime. Fifty-four percent of the women experienced unwanted contact such as fondling, kissing, or petting against her wishes. Most rapes occurred off campus and were equally as likely to take place in the man's house or car or the woman's house or car. Victims reported that the perpetrator used a significant amount of force such as twisting their hand or holding them down. Hitting or beating only occurred in 9 percent of the incidents. Eighty-four percent of the women tried to escape harm by reasoning with the offender, and 70 percent engaged in a physical struggle. Fewer than 5 percent reported the assault to the police, and nearly 50 percent told no one at all. Only 5 percent visited a rape crisis center in response to their attack.[67]

Several other studies have assessed prevalence estimates in adult women. In Russell's San Francisco study, 44 percent of the participants reported experiences of attempted or completed rape. Of the 644 women who had ever been married, 14 percent reported that her spouse had physically forced her to engage in penile-vaginal, oral, or anal sex.[68] Another study by Wyatt compared the lifetime prevalence of rape between African American and white women. The findings indicated that one in four African American women and one in five white women reported at least one incident of rape or attempted rape since the age of 18.[69] Thus, research suggests that a large number of adolescent girls and women experience rape and other forms of SA during their lives, and the majority are assaulted by people they know, including friends, relatives, and dating partners. These findings may be hard for many to fathom, because they are inconsistent with the common notions of rape. The goal of the upcoming section is to review the most common rape myths and replace those misconceptions with accurate facts about rape in contemporary society.

DISPELLING RAPE MYTHS

Rape myths are molded by the world in which we live. Such false beliefs distort the true reality of rape and contribute to society's ignorance of a problem affecting millions of women worldwide. First of all, many believe that rape is committed by psychotic strangers, when in fact most women are raped by "normal" acquaintances. A second myth is that women who get raped deserved it, particularly if they agreed to go to a man's house or get in his car. However, no one ever deserves to be raped, and being in a man's house or car does not equal sexual consent. Others believe that women who do not fight back have not been raped. Actually, rape involves being forced to have sex against one's will, whether or not a physical struggle occurs. Another myth asserts that a gun or knife must be present for the act to constitute rape. On the contrary, rape is rape whether the perpetrator uses a weapon, his fists, verbal threats, drugs or alcohol, the weight of his body, or any other tactic to overpower his victim. Some people believe that a woman has not been raped if she is not a virgin at the time of her attack. However, rape is rape regardless of a woman's past sexual experiences, even if she willingly engaged in sex with the man previously. Another false belief is that a woman owes a man sex if she allows him to buy her dinner, drinks, or a movie ticket. In reality, no one owes sex to anyone else, no matter how expensive the date might have been. Many also believe that agreeing to kiss or "neck" with a man means that the woman has consented to have intercourse with him. Everyone has the right to say no to sexual activity no matter what has preceded it and to have their wishes respected. Some people contend that when men become sexually excited, they cannot control themselves from forcing sex on a woman or else they will incur some adverse effect (e.g., "blue balls"). Men actually are perfectly capable of controlling their behaviors, even when they are sexually aroused, and they will not suffer harmful consequences if they do not have sex. A final myth asserts that women lie about being raped, especially if accusations involve a date or acquaintance. Investigations show that only a very small percentage of alleged rapes are not factual.[70]

VICTIM CHARACTERISTICS

Women constitute the vast majority of rape victims, although as many as 10 percent of victims reporting to rape crisis centers are men (almost all from male-against-male rapes). Results from the Koss study indicated that rape victims generally did not differ from nonvictims in terms of personality or background characteristics. However,

they were somewhat more likely to have experienced childhood abuse, to have lived without their mothers for some time, and to have run away from home.[71] Past victimization in childhood or early adolescence, in particular, has been consistently linked to adult revictimization. Psychological disturbances and various health consequences such as promiscuity and substance abuse may heighten the risk for revictimization.

The available data suggest that women who frequently date, have multiple sexual partners, and engage regularly in consensual sex are more likely to be raped.[72] Alcohol or drug use is an additional risk factor. Women in the Koss study reported that 73 percent of their assailants were under the influence of drugs or alcohol, and 55 percent admitted that they, too, were intoxicated. Alcohol consumption and multiple sexual partners are thought to increase a woman's exposure to risk. Women placed in situations where they meet more men and are more likely to become drunk give potential offenders a greater opportunity to act out their sexual aggression.[73] Also, if a man perceives a woman as being "loose" or "easy," he may consider her a fair target for victimization.[74] However, given that 41 percent of the women in Koss's study were virgins and 45 percent were sober, situational variables are only one type of risk factor.[75]

Young women who are of dating age are at the greatest risk for SA. More than half of acquaintance rapes involve victims between the ages of 16 and 24, and almost 80 percent of all acquaintance rapes happen to women who are between the ages of 16 and 34.[76]

Women raped by acquaintances are sometimes referred to as "safe" victims, because the perpetrators know that these women are less likely to strongly resist an attack or report the incident to the police. Experts believe that information conveyed to girls by parents, teachers, friends, and other media teach women to be "safe" victims. For example, girls are taught that it is unladylike to act assertively and that they should rely on men to provide them with physical and financial security and provide them with sexual pleasure in return. However, they are also taught to limit the distribution of these pleasures so as not to "devalue" their marketability or appeal.

In the face of rape, many women react with denial as well as dissociation from the experience, both of which are psychological coping mechanisms. Self-blame is also common. Victims may blame themselves for not fighting back, for getting drunk, or for misjudging a man's character or their level of safety before the rape. Because they blame themselves, victims also expect others (e.g., family, friends, medical personnel, police officers) to blame them. For all of these reasons, many women fail to report their experiences of SA, which increases the likelihood that women will be "safe" victims.[77]

PERPETRATOR CHARACTERISTICS

Rapists do not differ significantly from other men with regard to race, social class, or residential area. They tend to be seen as "regular" guys or "average Joes." However, differences do exist between men who rape and men who do not. Men who witness or experience family violence and whose fathers endorse sexually aggressive behaviors are more likely to commit sexual offenses. A number of investigators also have correlated sexual abuse and other early sexual experiences with later assaultive behavior. Additional predictors of SA include delinquent peer-group association, lower academic aspirations, poorer school performance, and a lack of religious affiliation or commitment.

Perpetrators of SA tend to adhere to traditional gender-role stereotypes, especially with respect to the acceptance of male dominance, acceptance of rape-supportive myths, acceptance of interpersonal violence as a means of conflict resolution, and hostility toward women.[78] These beliefs develop at an early age and come from many sources, usually other men. The extent to which men adhere to such beliefs is sometimes termed the *hypermasculinity factor*.[79]

Men who rape are more likely to find aspects of sexual aggression attractive and arousing. They may possess certain personality traits such as antisocial tendencies, poor socialization, irresponsibility, impulsivity, and nonconformity.[80] In fact, evidence suggests that sexual aggressors possess characteristics typical of the "common" criminal, and many have criminal records for drug arrests and other convictions.[81]

DATE RAPE DRUGS

Date rape drugs exhibit pharmacological properties that act rapidly to sedate a woman. They also cause significant memory impairment. Even though these drugs are potent and dangerous, rapists use them to incapacitate their victims and thus eliminate the possibility for sexual nonconsent. Two of the most widely used date rape drugs are Rohypnol (flunitrazepam) and gamma hydroxybutyrate (GHB).

The possession or manufacture of Rohypnol, also referred to as roofies, circles, mind erasers, and Mexican Valium, is illegal in the United States. However, it is legally prescribed for insomnia in 80 countries. Effects occur approximately 30 minutes after ingestion, and last for about eight hours. Rohypnol produces muscle relaxation, slowing of psychomotor performance, lowered blood pressure, sleepiness, and amnesia. Side effects include headache, dizziness, drowsiness, slurred speech, loss of balance, and unconsciousness. When taken with alcohol or other drugs, the consumption of Rohypnol can be fatal. The drug is typically odorless, tasteless, and colorless and readily dissolves

in any fluid, making it very difficult to detect. Recently, the drug manufacturing company that markets Rohypnol has reformulated the tablets so that they will color the drinks in which they are dissolved blue, thus increasing the likelihood of detection.[82]

The effects of GHB, also called scoop, cherry meth, easy lay, and super-G, are similar to Rohypnol and occur typically within 5 to 15 minutes after ingestion. GHB may cause confusion, sleepiness, dizziness, weakness, memory loss, nausea, vomiting, and unconsciousness. Other effects include difficulty focusing the eyes, hallucinations, tremors, seizures, heart and respiratory depression, and coma. Most symptoms subside within three to six hours, but drowsiness and weakness may last for several days, and confusion may persist for a few weeks. Like Rohypnol, the interaction between GHB and alcohol or other drugs can result in death. GHB overdoses are quite common, particularly because most available GHB is manufactured illegally. It is typically distributed in a clear or syrupy liquid, which can be carried in an eye- or nose-dropper bottle and easily squirted into the drink of an unknowing victim. The drug's unpleasant taste and odor can be disguised by putting the drug into a sweet or fruity drink. Rohypnol can only be detected in urine for up to 72 hours, and GHB only remains in the urine for a maximum of 12 hours. If a woman suspects that she was drugged, it is important for her to go to an emergency room immediately and get tested.[83]

EFFECTS OF RAPE

Gabrielle was 15 when her close friend Cameron had an overnight party for his friends at his parents' lakeside house under their supervision. Two big tents were pitched near the water, one for the boys and one for the girls. The teens had little prior experience with alcohol, but one boy managed to provide beer through his older brother, and everyone was drinking. Around midnight, one girl decided she did not want to "rough it" in a tent and called her sister to pick her up. The sister arrived and invited the other girls to leave as well. The girls piled in, but there wasn't enough room for Gabrielle, who didn't think staying alone in the tent would be a problem.

After going to sleep alone in the girls' tent, she awakened drunk and disoriented into a nightmare. Her friend Cameron was pulling down her pants and forcing himself inside her. Confused and shocked, she describes the experience: "I was completely limp and paralyzed. I could not even speak out loud. It was as if my whole body had gone into some sort of shock and I had lost all control. At some point, I remember feeling a strange detachment from my body, as if it were happening to someone else." When it was finally over, she laid there with her eyes closed and tried to pretend that nothing had really happened. Minutes later, she was forced to relive her terror once more, but this time she was raped by another boy at the party.

Ten years later, she still has only split-second flashbacks of the assault. "I guess that the pain is just too much to bear. I was violated and humiliated. They stole my virginity, which I valued very much. Even worse, I lived in a small town and the entire school found out about it. Rumors and various versions of the story were rampant, and in most of them I was portrayed as a slut and a whore who asked for it."

Gabrielle's rape had a profound and long-lasting impact on her life. She never reported the incident. She was anxious and panic ridden. Significant mood swings, irritability, and insomnia prevailed. She blamed herself for using poor judgment and for not fighting back. Currently, she suffers from chronic anxiety, panic attacks, and bouts of depression. Other symptoms include sleep disturbances, fear of being alone with men, recurrent flashbacks, and nightmares of the assault.[84]

Several features of the vignette are common to many acquaintance rapes. The victim and her attackers were all white, upper middle-class teenagers. The perpetrators were popular, good looking, and respected by their peers. Gabrielle never anticipated that anything like this would happen, especially with people she knew and trusted. Typically, alcohol consumption and a lack of supervision precipitated the event. Although the rapes occurred concurrently, many women are raped simultaneously by more than one attacker. In the Koss study, 26 percent of the men who committed attempted or completed rape participated in episodes involving two or more attackers.[85] Gang rapes are often initiated by cohesive male groups such as college fraternities or athletic teams. However, individual rapes remain much more common.

There is no such thing as a typical rape or a typical rape victim. Consequently, the responses of victims differ in many ways. However, rape responses often unfold in a sequence, and rape survivors may be faced with similar challenges in their journey toward recovery. The effects of rape trauma generally arise immediately after the assault and may persist for months or even years to come.

Initial Effects

Contrary to what one might expect, the level of psychological impact experienced by victims of stranger rape (where assaults are often more brutal and life threatening) is no greater than that experienced by victims of acquaintance rape. Women who are raped by men they know may actually recover more slowly, in part because they are less likely to recognize their experience as rape and seek counseling or other forms of support. In a society that strongly adheres to rape myths, they often receive little sympathy from others and may be blamed for their victimization.[86]

The most predominant symptoms during and following rape are usually fear and anxiety, especially fear of personal safety.[87] Acute stress responses such as shock, disbelief, confusion, and crying often occur immediately after the incident.[88] Depression is very common, and research suggests that 17 percent to 19 percent of rape victims attempt suicide. In addition, victims are often diagnosed with PTSD and suffer from symptoms such as intrusive thoughts or avoidance of trauma-related stimuli.[89] Initial symptoms also may include anger, self-blame, guilt, embarrassment, irritability, and fluctuating mood.

Victims of SA may sustain a variety of bodily injuries such as soreness, bruising, and vaginal or rectal bleeding.[90] Other chief medical concerns include the possibility of becoming pregnant or contracting a sexually transmitted disease. Many women also report feeling that they will never be able to get clean again, and they may take a series of hot baths or showers in an effort the cleanse themselves.[91] Typical physical symptoms include headaches, fatigue, sleep disturbances, eating disturbances, stomach pains, and nausea.[92]

Rape also can alter a victim's perception about the world. Everyone and everything in a woman's immediate environment is a potential threat, for she now realizes that she has limited control over her personal safety and well-being. Victims may view themselves as helpless and become dependent on family or friends. To feel safer, they may acquire an unlisted phone number, relocate, change jobs or schools, withdraw socially, or discontinue activities that may be too "risky," such as walking their dog in the park or shopping alone. Victims also may change their style of dress or appearance to maintain a low profile.

Sexual dysfunction is another common consequence of rape. Sex may produce a sense of anger or repulsion, which leads to sex avoidance. Some victims engage in sex more frequently, because they feel "devalued" by their assault and believe that there is nothing left for them to protect.[93] Although sexual satisfaction tends to decrease initially, sometimes it can improve as early as three months after the assault.[94]

Sexual victimization also can negatively impact relationships with family and loved ones. Telling a boyfriend or a spouse about the sexual assault is a difficult task, and his response may or may not help the recovery process. For instance, revenge-seeking, victim-blaming, and guilt-ridden behaviors due to his inability to protect his significant other can make the situation worse. Also, some men want to resume sexual activity quickly, while others are unable to have sex at all. Some relationships simply cannot withstand the additional stress accompanying SA. Many factors influence the reactions of both family and friends including religious, cultural, and social values. Indeed, it is not uncommon for people close to the victim to provide little support or empathy in the event of acquaintance rape. If, for example, a woman is raped by a man who is attractive, successful, and respected in the community, even a close friend may react with denial because accepting the truth would mean that she too could be in danger.[95]

Long-Term Effects

PTSD is a common long-term effect, and, in fact, rape survivors may be the single largest group of individuals suffering from this disorder. According to one large community survey, the lifetime prevalence of PTSD in rape victims was 57 percent, and symptoms may not actually appear until years after the assault. Long-term sexual dysfunction may also occur. Many victims experience depression, diminished self-esteem, and fear of being alone long after having been raped.[96] Repressed feelings of anger, rage, and guilt may emerge years after the rape.[97] Victims may also experience long-term impairment in marital, family, social, and leisure functioning. Research suggests that despite the amount of time that has elapsed since their assault, rape victims view their current health as less favorable than nonvictims, and they report more harmful health habits such as drinking alcohol, smoking, overeating, and driving without seat belts.[98]

DATING VIOLENCE

DV is a serious problem among our youth, and it has been conceptualized as a training ground for violence in future relationships. Definitions of DV vary, creating confusion as to what behaviors and types of social interactions fall under the DV umbrella.[99] DV involves the perpetration of physical, emotional, or threat abuse by at least one member of an unmarried dating couple. This definition is broad enough to encompass dating couples who may or may not be sexually active, as well as heterosexual and homosexual couples. SA and stalking also are subsumed under this definition, although they are often addressed independently. As defined by the Office for Victims of Crime, stalking involves "the willful or intentional commission of a series of acts that would cause a reasonable person to fear death or serious bodily injury and that, in fact, does place the victim in fear of death or serious bodily injury."[100] Stalking behaviors include harassing, following, and communicating in various ways with the victim.

Like other forms of interpersonal violence, the private nature of DV discourages victims from disclosing it and camouflages its detection. In addition, ambiguous and incompatible definitions as well as other methodological shortcomings hinder precise data collection and con-tribute to inconsistencies in the literature.[101] Despite limitations, the data indicate that DV is at least as common as violence in marital rela-tionships. Empirical reviews suggest that over one-fourth of both men and women are involved in DV at some time during their lives. Research also shows that a higher level of relationship commitment is linked to a greater likelihood of abuse.

Studies regarding victim and perpetrator characteristics have pro-duced equivocal results. Some data suggest that women exert violence against dating partners about as often as their male counterparts. How-ever, the veracity of this conclusion is somewhat questionable.[102] For example, these findings do not account for the perpetration of SA or stalking, in which the vast number of assailants are men. In addition, men are more likely to inflict serious bodily injury or harm. It is possi-ble that men are more likely to lie about or minimize self-reported acts of violence and that some violence perpetrated by women is in fact a mechanism of self-defense. Nevertheless, DV appears to be more gen-der neutral compared to other forms of intimate violence.

Perpetrators of DV are more likely than nonviolent men to have a criminal record and to possess antisocial personality characteristics. They may be more accepting of traditional sex-role attitudes or have witnessed or experienced family violence during childhood. High lev-els of hypermasculinity, feelings of helplessness, and a strong need to control others are additional factors that influence DV perpetration. Poor relationship satisfaction, high levels of relationship stress, ineffec-tive communication between dating partners, and alcohol consumption also are associated with violence in dating relationships. Members of fraternity and athletic organizations, as stated earlier, are often associ-ated with higher levels of DV perpetration. Indeed, male athletes often exhibit violence both on and off the field, and fraternities have a repu-tation for engaging in aggressive behaviors and heavy alcohol con-sumption.

Victims of DV may sustain a host of emotional and physical injuries, many of which were described in the section on SA. Bodily injuries may include cuts, bruises, broken bones, or more serious consequences such as brain injury or death. Chronic headaches, depression, suicidal ideation, self-blame, substance abuse, and eating disorders are possible results from DV.

Mounting evidence suggests that DV is a widespread phenomenon, and a unified effort is needed to effectively reduce violence in dating relationships and in other arenas. Prevention programs, which are increasing in number, have many purposes such as providing clinics for DV victims and at-risk daters and challenging sexist- and violence-supportive attitudes. Programs may promote anti-drug and alcohol misuse campaigns, provide information on date rape drugs, and teach anger management, problem-solving skills, and stress-reduction techniques to young people.

Schools also are becoming more involved in intervention and prevention efforts. Some universities have incorporated violence prevention programs into freshman orientation seminars or other routine admissions procedures. Although early college prevention programs focused primarily on the woman's responsibility to take the proper precautions to avoid danger, current efforts have shifted attention toward male prevention and education programs. Community collaboration and the promotion of DV education to the public also are critical in the fight to end aggression and abuse. Finally, medical and mental health providers must screen teenagers and young adults for problems associated with DV to provide proper treatment interventions and prevent future violence.[103]

Chapter 6

Adult Survivors of Child Sexual and Emotional Abuse

Paula K. Lundberg-Love

The impact of childhood physical and sexual abuse on my life is profound and pervasive. In fact, there are few areas of my life that are unaffected. Fear seems to dominate my life. Whether it is fear of intimacy, fear of conflict, fear of being angry, fear of receiving gifts or affection, or the greatest fear, fear of not being in control, fear permeates my life. Even positive feelings are often scary because I know they are fleeting and it is only a matter of time before the fear returns.[1]

CSA can fundamentally alter the human psyche in profound ways. After sexual abuse, one's world is no longer a safe place. After sexual abuse, one's ability to trust other people and to trust one's instincts is compromised. During the horror that is sexual abuse, victims are rendered physically and/or emotionally powerless. As a result, they often fear for their lives. Such fear can give rise to a lifelong struggle to avoid the experience of ever being made powerless again. Additionally, the trauma of CSA can poison the experience of intimacy, sexual or otherwise. An experience that might have been one of the most beautiful, instead becomes defiled.

Although it is impossible to know the precise number of women in the United States who have been physically, sexually, and emotionally abused during childhood, we know the number is quite large. Often the numbers reported in the media vary greatly. This is usually because the numbers vary depending on the population that was studied.

Some researchers have used *community samples*, meaning that large numbers of women in the general population have been asked about their histories of child abuse. Other researchers have studied women who are in therapy, psychiatric hospitals, or emergency rooms. These types of studies are said to utilize *clinical samples*. It is important to have some reliable estimate of the number of women affected by this type of victimization so that society can be aware of its magnitude and the impact it has on the lives of the women affected. It is also important to know its frequency in the population so that health professionals can screen for this history to treat those women effectively.

PREVALENCE OF WOMEN WHO WERE ABUSED IN CHILDHOOD

The prevalence rates of childhood abuse found in women from community samples in the United States vary widely.[2] A multinational study of the prevalence of CSA in women from 21 countries reveals that 20 percent were sexually abused as children.[3] With respect to the prevalence rates of child physical abuse (CPA) found among various community samples, the numbers range from 10 to 20 percent.[4] Often the differences obtained in prevalence rates are due to the differences in the definitions of abuse used by the researchers. Definitions can vary in terms of whether the study included cases of contact and noncontact (e.g., exhibitionism, voyeurism) abuse, the age at victimization, the age of the perpetrator, and the degree of severity of abuse (e.g., physical violence, force, aggression). However, when definitions are narrowed to match each other as closely as possible, the prevalence of CSA in women based on community sample data is between 11 and 13 percent.[5] In the results of studies based upon clinical samples, larger prevalence rates are found, probably because a history of childhood abuse is associated with some difficulties in life. The rates of CSA range from 13 to 70 percent but cluster at around 42 percent, while the rates of CPA range from 31 to 74 percent and also cluster at around 42 percent.[6] Therefore, the data indicate that the numbers of women who have been victimized during their childhoods are significant and that over 40 percent of women who have health/mental health issues also have a history of child sexual or physical abuse.

CONSEQUENCES OF CHILDHOOD ABUSE

When one reviews the literature on the adult survivors of childhood abuse, it is apparent that there is not a short, concise list of consequences that are related to childhood abuse. Most experts discuss the various realms of behavior that are affected, whereas others discuss the types of psychiatric and/or medical diagnoses that survivors of CSA and CPA receive. Also, it is important to understand that the majority of studies have investigated women with histories of sexual abuse or multiple forms of abuse. This chapter will focus on summarizing those results. The behavioral categories of effects that have been associated with CSA include effects on emotions, interpersonal relations, social functioning, sexuality, and health.[7] The diagnostic categories of symptoms associated with CSA include depression, anxiety disorders, dissociative disorders, substance abuse disorders, and eating disorders.[8] This chapter will focus primarily on the diagnostic entities that have been associated with childhood abuse.

Depression

> Depression is a constant companion. It is particularly intense during holidays when I realize that I do not have, and never did have a family that truly loved me. I feel alone and isolated, not just from my family, but from most of humanity. I long to be like other people. It is as if I have been shoved off the continent on a tiny life raft. Hopelessness at times gives way to thoughts of suicide, an option that I refuse to relinquish.[9]

One of the psychological symptoms initially identified in adult survivors of CSA was depression. High frequencies of depression have been noted in CSA survivors, and it is probably the symptom most commonly reported. In fact, it has been suggested that survivors of CSA may be more than four times more likely to develop depression when compared with nonabused women, and this is true whether the study is based on community or clinical samples. Feelings of stigmatization, alienation, and isolation tend to coexist with depression. When those feelings are also coupled with a sense of chronic betrayal, disempowerment, guilt, hopelessness, and low self-esteem, it is not surprising that CSA survivors report suicidal thoughts. In some studies of women in therapy, it was found that those with a history of childhood abuse were twice as likely to have attempted suicide as their nonvictimized peers. Even in a large community sample, 16 percent of women with a history of sexual abuse had attempted suicide as compared with only 6 percent of women who lacked such a history.[10]

An association between CSA and depression is important, because it has a profound impact on human health. It is the fourth most common cause of early death and disability in the world and is second only to coronary artery disease in the industrialized countries.[11] It has been found that the presence of depression impacts the course of cardiovascular disease and affects immune response. Patients who had a heart attack and developed depression, even if the depression was mild, were three to four times more likely to experience an increased risk of cardiac mortality. Depression can have as much negative impact on people with heart problems as coronary artery disease itself.[12] Depression can also suppress the immune system, because it is associated with greater secretion of a substance called *cortisol*. Cortisol is a chemical secreted by the adrenal gland. Elevations of cortisol have many physiological effects, one of which is to reduce certain types of white blood cells that are important to maintaining health. Studies of people who are HIV-positive and depressed have shown that the depressed individuals have lower levels of a number of subsets of white blood cells, which can last for years. Even negative moods that do not qualify as a major depressive disorder can suppress the levels of a certain antibody, immunoglobulin A, which is considered the first line of defense against the common cold.[13]

Depression is also associated with a number of health-related behaviors. Negative mood has been correlated with poor eating habits, the use of tobacco, the abuse of alcohol and drugs, and even the increased consumption of chocolate. People often report that they engage in these behaviors as a way to cope with their depression, despite the fact that none of them are effective. In a study of male and female college students, depression was associated with not eating breakfast, irregular sleep hours, lack of physical activity, and not using a seat belt. In women, depression was associated with smoking, including increased nicotine dependence, not eating fruit, and not using sunscreen.[14]

Anxiety Disorders

> We were driving down a road and grandfather pulled over. He started touching me, putting his hands in between my legs under my clothes. He started kissing me on the mouth. He stuck his fingers in my vagina. He kept saying, "I love you . . . I love you." I just stared at him. Then he said, "I only do this because I love you." He played with himself and he put my hands on his penis. He ejaculated all over my hands. I opened the door of the truck, got out, and threw up. I got back into the truck. He put his clothes on and I put mine on. Then we went to the auction. Whenever he abused me, my mind would shut itself down. I guess you'd call it a safe place where nobody could hurt me. It was like I would go into this hole, like a tunnel. The further I'd go, the darker and smaller I'd get until I could fit into a space the size of your fist. I could see and hear what was going on, but he couldn't hurt me again. He could touch my body, but he couldn't touch me.[15]

Anxiety is a symptom that is related to the internalization of traumatic experience. Adult CSA survivors are five times more likely than non-abused women to develop various types of anxiety disorders such as panic disorder, obsessive-compulsive disorder, generalized anxiety disorder, and certain phobias. Studies of college students with histories of sexual abuse have found that they have greater levels of anxiety and sleep disturbance. Anxiety can also manifest itself as a preoccupation with an overreaction to real and perceived danger. Chronic arousal of the nervous system of CSA survivors is associated with more headaches, gastrointestinal problems, muscle tension, back pain, and chronic pelvic pain.[16]

Perhaps the anxiety disorder most often reported by adult survivors of CSA is PTSD. PTSD can develop when a woman is exposed to an event that threatens to result in death, serious injury, or damage to the physical integrity of herself or others. Typically an individual's response to the event involves intense fear, a sense of helplessness, or horror. Subsequently, over weeks, months, and even years, the traumatized individual may reexperience the event. She may notice that she avoids things, places, and people that remind her of the traumatic event and that she has persistent symptoms of nervous system arousal. Some of the reexperiencing symptoms include recurrent, intrusive recollections, thoughts, or images of the event; recurrent distressing dreams of the event; and a reliving of the trauma (flashbacks). The avoidant symptoms associated with PTSD can also include the inability to recall aspects of the trauma, a markedly diminished interest in activities, feelings of detachment from others, a restricted range of mood, and a sense of impending doom.[17] In some studies, as many as 36 percent of adult CSA survivors reported symptoms of PTSD. In other studies, if the abuse involved vaginal penetration, the frequency of PTSD rose to 66 percent. PTSD is often experienced as feelings of not having personal control and being powerless and of needing to avoid all anxiety-provoking stimuli.[18]

Judith Herman, one of the first women to research and write about incest, has proposed that a new diagnostic entity be created and called *complex posttraumatic stress disorder*. This diagnosis is intended to encompass the extremes of suffering that may occur in adults who experienced the most severe forms of child abuse.[19] Complex PTSD encompasses seven categories of symptoms:

1. problems regulating emotions such that one can enter into an extreme emotional state and be unable to calm oneself;

2. flashbacks, dissociation (spacing out) under stress, and emotional numbing;

3. alterations in self-perception that include self-blame, guilt, a sense of alienation, and self-hatred;

4. alterations in the perception of the perpetrator as idealized or all-powerful;

5. alterations in relationships with others that include distrust, isolation, and a search for a rescuer;

6. alterations in nervous system activity that result in exaggerated startle response, chronic hyperarousal, excessive vigilance, and numerous physical symptoms; and

7. alterations in one's system of meaning that include hopelessness, no sense of a future, and a sense that life has no meaning.

The results of preliminary studies of complex PTSD suggest that women with a history of CPA, CSA, or both are at risk for developing complex PTSD.[20]

Just as depression has a long-term effect on the physiological response to stress and can affect parts of the brain, PTSD also has a biological impact upon the physiology of the nervous system. PTSD appears to result in a dysregulation of the body's normal stress response. In a normal response to stress, the levels of the hormone cortisol and of the neurotransmitter norepinephrine act in concert. In PTSD, the levels of cortisol and norepinephrine operate separately. Individuals with PTSD tend to have abnormally low levels of cortisol and abnormally high levels of norepinephrine. One of the functions of cortisol is to modify the activity of other stress hormones. When cortisol levels are low, the levels of other stress hormones cannot be appropriately maintained; this can result in overactivity of the sympathetic nervous system, which appears to underlie some of the symptoms of PTSD. High levels of norepinephrine have been associated with the intrusive thoughts of PTSD and other more severe symptoms. Low levels of cortisol immediately after a stressful event can predict the risk of developing PTSD. PTSD has been shown to have an impact on brain development. When the magnetic resonance images (MRIs) of abused children are compared to those of similar children who were not abused, it is found that certain areas of the brain are smaller in volume. Certain brain parts involved in learning and memory may also be affected. They include the hippocampus, the amygdala, the locus ceruleus, and the sensory cortex. When the MRIs of adults with PTSD are compared with those of adults without a child abuse history and without PTSD, the volumes of the hippocampus are smaller in those with PTSD, which may explain some of the memory problems reported by people with PTSD. A reduced volume of the hippocampus also was observed in patients with histories of severe physical or sexual abuse. Studies found no differences in the sizes of the amygdala, the caudate nucleus, or the temporal lobe of the brain. However, even a particular neurotransmitter site, the NMDA glutamate receptor, has been shown to be involved in the formation and retrieval of traumatic memories.[21]

Dissociation

When I was in graduate school, I was taught that Multiple Personality Disorder, now known as Dissociative Identity Disorder (DID), was a very rare disorder and that it was unlikely that I would ever see such a case. Then in 1987 a woman was referred to me. She was a very soft-spoken, elegant lady who had been raised in a traditional Southern family. She and her husband were in marital therapy with another therapist due to sexual difficulties in their marriage. During the first year of therapy, I learned that her father had sexually abused her when she was four or five years old. Treatment for PTSD aided her recovery significantly. However, one day I asked her a question and suddenly she responded in a coarse, angry tone of voice. I then explained that I did not understand her answer and asked her to repeat it. In her typical tone of voice, she responded that she did not know what I was talking about. It appeared as if she had no knowledge of what she had just said. On that occasion, I just thought that perhaps I had misunderstood her or that perhaps I had been working too hard and needed a vacation. But then over the next six months, it happened on three more occasions. The utterances were longer and more detailed, and the client clearly had no recollection of what had just occurred. That was when I realized that this might be my first case of DID and began to read everything that was available on the topic. It turned out that she did have DID and over the course of the next five years she came to learn much about her past of which she had been unaware. She recovered completely. She successfully raised three fabulous, talented children and remains a brilliant, creative educator.[22]

Dissociation is a psychological process that helps a child to cope with a traumatic event by providing a mechanism for defending against overwhelming emotion. Dissociation is a coping mechanism that separates, segregates, and isolates certain aspects of experience from one another. It compartmentalizes traumatic experience so that it does not become associated with other experiences. Braun has characterized dissociation as the separation of an idea or thought process from the mainstream of consciousness.[23] There are a number of dissociative disorders including dissociative fugue, dissociative amnesia, depersonalization disorder, and dissociative identity disorder (DID). Dissociative fugue usually entails a sudden, unexpected travel from home or workplace with the inability to recall the past. Persons may be confused about their past or even create a new identity. Dissociative amnesia consists of episodes of the inability to recall important personal information, often of a traumatic or stressful nature, that is too extensive to be explained by ordinary forgetfulness. Usually dissociative amnesia does not occur independently of PTSD or DID. When individuals have persistent or recurrent episodes of feeling detached from their mental processes or bodies (e.g., feeling as if they are an outside observer of their behavior or as if they are in a dream), they are diagnosed with depersonalization disorder. In contrast, DID is characterized by the presence of two or more separate and distinct identities or personalities, each of which can take control of the person's thoughts and behavior. This results in an inability among personalities to recall information that is too extensive to be explained by ordinary forgetfulness.[24] DID appears to result from problems integrating memory, affect (emotional feelings), and cognition (thinking). One model of DID, called the *BASK model*, suggests that DID can impact four components of human personality, including behavior, affect, sensation, and knowledge.[25] Another model of DID proposes that consistent dissociation in response to traumatic experience becomes DID when the parts of self become separate enough to form distinct personalities that can alternately emerge and take control of behavior.[26] However, when one reviews the theories of the origin of DID, most researchers and clinicians agree that repeated childhood trauma enhances the capacity for dissociation, which may provide the basis for the creation and elaboration of alternate personalities over time.[27] Many individuals who have DID have a childhood history of sexual abuse (85 percent), physical abuse (80 percent), or both. However, DID can also develop when young children are victims of extreme neglect or witness extreme violence and/or trauma.[28]

Individuals with DID typically do not come to therapy with knowledge that they have the disorder. However, they may report a history of a number of psychological, medical, and even neurological symptoms that may have been resistant to treatment. The various psychological symptoms often reported by individuals with DID include depression/ suicide attempts, anxiety/phobias, substance abuse, voices inside their head, times when they physically harm themselves (self-mutilation), periods of catatonia, and transvestism or transsexualization. Frequently reported medical symptoms are headaches (often migraine-like), seizures, fainting, sensory and visual disturbances, cardiac and respiratory symptoms, gastrointestinal disorders, gynecological disorders, rashes and other dermatology symptoms, unexplained fevers, and odd, unexplained reactions to various types of drugs. It is not uncommon for women with DID to have seen many physicians and received many diagnoses.[29] Treating clients with DID is like completing a jigsaw puzzle using pieces of behavior, feelings, and memories over time. Because many individuals with DID are bright, talented people, early identification can facilitate their therapeutic progress.

Substance Abuse

When I was four years old, my grandfather gave me a cigarette as a reward after he sexually abused me. When I was in the fourth grade, one of my friends introduced me to marijuana. I enjoyed marijuana, because it numbed me out and it remained my drug of choice from age 10 to 18. I never liked alcohol, because it made me do stupid stuff and whenever I was around a man who was drunk he wanted to beat the hell out of me. At age 18, I began injecting methamphetamine (crank) and by age 19 I was also doing cocaine on a daily basis. It was the only way I could deal with the sexual abuse. I had nightmares all of the time. When I went to sleep, I would dream about my grandfather and I would feel him touching me and I could do nothing to stop it. So crank and cocaine kept me from sleeping. If I didn't sleep, I did not have nightmares. I remember when he died. I thought, "Thank God, it cannot happen anymore. He can no longer hurt me."[30]

A number of research studies involving a variety of samples of women have identified a link between CSA and substance abuse. In a national survey of nearly 1,100 women in the United States, those who had been sexually abused were more likely to report drinking to intoxication, associated drinking-related problems, symptoms of alcohol dependence, and lifetime abuse of prescription and illicit drugs when compared with women who had not been sexually abused.[31] Women who were patients in primary care medical settings with a history of sexual abuse were compared with those who did not have such a history. It was found that women with a history of victimization were more likely to abuse drugs and to report that they needed to reduce their consumption of alcohol. They also were more likely to use recreational and intravenous drugs and to report heavy drinking. Additionally, childhood abuse was associated with a greater likelihood of dropping out of drug and alcohol rehabilitation programs as a result of problems with authority and problems with interpersonal relationships.[32] In a study of patients coming to a psychiatric emergency room, it was found that sexual abuse survivors were 10 times more likely to have a history of drug addiction and 2 times more likely to have been alcoholics.[33] A study of African American sexual abuse survivors found that multiple sexual victimizations were associated with heavy drinking and binge drinking. Victimization at younger ages predicted greater binge drinking, perhaps as an attempt to block a specific trigger or memory of the abusive experience. The multiply victimized women who were first assaulted at a somewhat older age were more likely to become chronic heavy drinkers. These women were more likely to have intrusive memories, and heavy drinking may have been their attempt to numb the feelings associated with the sexual assaults.[34]

Researchers have speculated on why adult survivors of sexual abuse might be prone to misuse drugs or alcohol. Some have suggested that the use of alcohol and drugs is a means of self-medication to block painful memories or to reduce anxiety. Others have speculated that alcohol and drug use can temporarily boost low levels of self-confidence or relieve social anxiety. Some survivors use substances because it gives them a sense of power and control, even though it may be fleeting. Drugs and alcohol also reduce guilt feelings and can relieve anxiety about having sex.[35] However, there also may be some biological explanations for vulnerability to drug and alcohol abuse in adult survivors of sexual abuse. There is a particular pathway in an area of the brain known as the *ventral tegmental area* that contains nerve cells that secrete a neurotransmitter known as *dopamine*. Activation and sensitization of this pathway is common to all types of drug abuse. This is what keeps users compulsively taking drugs even when their lives are collapsing around them. Sensitization of the brain can result from exposure to past traumatic events. Susceptibility to addiction seems to be related to both genetic factors and emotional experiences that disrupt normal function in the hypothalamus of the brain, which, in turn, affects the pituitary gland and the adrenal gland. This results in prolonged secretion of various hormones that are released in response to stress.

Eating Disorders and Obesity

> Alexis is a 38-year-old woman who has battled anorexia and bulimia since the age of 18. While she has had some periods in her life when she has not binged and purged or restricted her eating, she has continued to relapse. Food and her weight have controlled her life in spite of the fact that she has lost relationships, a marriage, and even left her position with a successful attorney because she could not tolerate being around the food that was ever present in the office. Now in her second marriage, she has been unable to become pregnant as a result of the effects of the eating disorder on her menstrual cycle. What appears to have complicated her recovery is the fact that she was sexually abused by the husband of her day care worker when she was around four years old. Her parents learned that this was happening to their child as well as others and removed her from the day care facility but believed that the best way to deal with the situation was to never talk about it again. Thus Alexis never received any therapeutic intervention during her childhood and although she had a very vague memory of the man fondling her, it wasn't until she was in young adulthood that she came to the realization that the sexual abuse had affected her relationships with men and was related to her eating disorder. Nevertheless, each time Alexis has attempted to participate in trauma-focused psychotherapy to address her issues, she has been unable to allow herself to revisit the past and decides to just focus on her eating disorder.[36]

Another issue that faces some adult CSA survivors is disturbed patterns of eating. Three of the most common of these patterns are obesity, anorexia, and bulimia. Although many people with eating disorders do not have a history of CSA, CSA survivors do appear to be at increased risk for developing an eating disorder. In one study, women who were sexually abused in childhood were on average 40 percent over their ideal body weight.[37] Some researchers became interested in the connection between CSA and obesity when they noticed that women who failed to lose weight in a weight control program also had a history of CSA. Of the women who were 50 pounds overweight, 60 percent had a history of incest as compared to only 28 percent of women who had no history of CSA. Similarly in the group of women who were 100 pounds overweight, 25 percent had histories of CSA as compared to 6 percent of women without that history.[38] In another study of women enrolled in a hospital-based weight loss program, the sexually abused women lost significantly less weight, had more trouble sticking to their weight loss plan, and had lower feelings of being capable than the nonabused women.[39]

The National Institute of Mental Health (NIMH) estimates that 1 percent or less of all women suffer from anorexia nervosa, 1 to 3 percent have bulimia nervosa, and as many as 4 percent may have a binge-eating disorder.[40] In comparison studies of women with eating disorders who have a history of sexual abuse and those who do not, it has been found that the CSA survivors reported more disturbed eating patterns such as eating too little, eating too much, and making themselves vomit. They also were more likely to think they were too fat, to report at least one symptom of anorexia, and to have had a sudden weight change. Additionally, the CSA survivors were more likely to report interpersonal distrust and score higher on measures of the drive for thinness, body dissatisfaction, and ineffectiveness.[41]

Experts have speculated that a history of sexual trauma may sensitize the body and increase concern regarding body issues in general, which in turn may heighten awareness of and dissatisfaction with body shape and size. It also appears that sexual trauma can impact a number of neurotransmitter systems in the brain, including serotonin, norepinephrine, dopamine, and the endorphins, which can underlie disturbances in eating behavior. Serotonin levels, in particular, are associated with feelings of being satisfied after eating a meal. Drugs that enhance brain serotonin levels such as the selective serotonin reuptake inhibitors (SSRIs) decrease food intake somewhat and have been helpful in treating bulimia. Administration of such a drug reduced the numbers of binge episodes in bulimics. Some researchers have suggested that impaired central nervous system serotonin pathways may contribute to or maintain disordered eating patterns in women with bulimia.[42]

Obesity and other eating disorders have a serious impact on health. People who are overweight are at greater risk for the development of heart disease, stroke, diabetes, elevated levels of cholesterol and triglycerides, hypertension, and gall bladder disease. Dietary fat intake is also related to cancers of the breast, colon, prostate, and lung. Although obesity has not received as much attention as the other eating disorders with respect to its link to a history of sexual victimization, it is more common than all of the other eating disorders combined. Although sexual abuse is only one explanation for obesity, research should probably look more closely at that link.[43] Anorexia and bulimia also have serious health consequences. Anorexia can lead to osteoporosis, cardiac arrhythmias, hypotension, hypothermia, infertility, depression, suicide, and death.[44] Consequences of bulimia include erosion of tooth enamel, cardiac arrhythmias, rupture of the esophagus or stomach, aspiration of stomach contents, and heart and kidney problems due to blood chemistry imbalances such as low levels of potassium. Not all CSA survivors develop obesity or other eating disorders, but there is a substantial proportion of them who are more vulnerable to these disorders than is the general population, and this can have a serious impact on their health.[45]

TREATMENT OF ADULT SURVIVORS OF CSA

> During the course of treatment, I have conquered fear and pain, perfectionism, inflexibility, and an obsession with achievement. I no longer needed to prove to myself that I was worthy to be alive and that I was not invisible. It took some time and persistence, but now my life continues to be full of times of real joy, peace, and strength, which were unavailable to me until I resolved the issues surrounding my childhood sexual abuse.[46]

After reading this chapter, you might think that recovery from CSA is difficult and that perhaps a victim never truly recovers from sexual trauma. That would be inaccurate. The powerless can regain their power, tragedy can lead to triumph, and a victim of abuse can develop healthy relationships and sexuality. Even though CSA can devastate people, appropriate therapy can greatly reduce its effects. Victims do become survivors with the aid of trauma-focused therapy. They do overcome overwhelming barriers to their successful development. All they need is the appropriate assistance. At times, this requires that the therapist be a bit of a teacher, a bit of a coach, a cheerleader, a mentor, and a role model. People often ask me how I am able to treat adult survivors of CSA without becoming depressed. The answer to that question is that, in using the appropriate therapy, I find that victims not only survive such trauma but go on to thrive in their ongoing development. I have had the wonderful opportunity to watch survivors of CSA rise from the ashes of traumatization to become nurses, school counselors, teachers, therapists, physicians, dancers, entrepreneurs, and, most important, wonderful parents.

Most experts in the field agree that CSA survivors need trauma-focused therapy in order to recover. Although different therapists might execute these interventions in different ways, there are some fundamental issues that must be addressed. People often ask, "How does talking help?" Talking helps because human beings need to make sense of their lives, and talking helps them do that. Clients need to tell their stories. They need to recount what happened and what they did to try to protect themselves. They need to sort out their thoughts and feelings about the events and then come to understand how all of this influences the ways in which they think and behave. The healing process of therapy occurs when clients are able to make sense of their experience using words in the presence of another human being who understands and confirms their understanding of the trauma and its aftermath.[47]

In seeking a therapist, it is important to understand what the therapist's role is and is not. Ethically, the therapist cannot be a friend. Neither should the therapist share a spiritual journey with the clients. Therapy is not a form of re-parenting, so a therapist should not be a substitute parent. Therapists are not blank slates upon which clients project their fantasies. Therapists cannot replace the clients' inner void with endless caring. Most important, however, therapists do not heal their clients. Clients heal themselves. Therapists can help clients detect and identify problematic emotions, thoughts, and behaviors and aid them in the development of new coping strategies. In addition to focusing on what the client says, the task of the therapist is to analyze how it is being said and how it is being recalled and to note the multiplicity of emotions that are expressed. Clients need to be given knowledge about the topic of sexual abuse and its emotional and physiological consequences. They also should be informed of the possible psychiatric diagnoses, the treatment options available, and the risks and merits associated with each option. A therapist must remember that a client is a human being with a past, a racial and gender identity, and a sexual orientation who has been shaped by cultural, ethnic, and social forces.[48]

Judith Herman, who was mentioned earlier in this chapter, was one of the first authors to identify a series of 10 steps that assist survivors in their recovery from CSA. These steps are a good general model for what one might expect in the journey to recovery, and they are described below.[49]

Step 1: Readiness—Not all survivors are necessarily ready to begin the therapeutic process of healing. There are three types of potential clients: visitors, complainants, and customers. *Visitors* include clients who do not think that they have a problem and have been brought to therapy by a worried spouse or relative or clients who have been court-ordered to go to treatment. *Complainants* may be aware that they have a problem, but they may not think of it as their problem. Rather, they may view their problem as existing outside of their control and thus may seek solutions to their problem in the external environment. The *customers* are the clients who realize that they do have a problem and that they are the ones who will have to do something about it.

Step 2: Believe—The therapist must create an environment in which clients understand that what they say is believed. At the same time, the therapist's task is to remain neutral, neither confirming nor denying any particular recollections. Just the fact that the therapist knows that what clients are saying could be true creates a form of nonverbal permission for continued exploration.

Step 3: Safety—The therapist's office needs to be a safe haven where clients can feel relaxed. Also, true healing cannot begin if the clients are still battling daily with traumatizing events and occurrences. Supportive friends and family of the clients are very helpful, because they provide an opportunity for lifelong support.

Step 4: The story—Clients need to tell their story in their own way and as they are ready. Indeed, clients will need to revisit their story many times as the process of therapy unfolds. Therefore, it is critical for all mental health professionals to understand how to listen and to hear and understand with sensitivity, because every client needs to be able to tell sympathetic others about what has happened.

Step 5: Anger and sadness—For the clients, emotion has come to represent an unpredictable source of deep pain that must be avoided at all costs. Clients tend to feel that they are abnormal, because they have somehow missed knowing what, it appears to them, others magically understand: how to relate to others, how to be happy, and how to be at peace. A childhood of trauma and terror prevents survivors of CSA from being able to express many emotions, particularly those of sadness and anger. If anger is not expressed in a healthy manner and remains suppressed, it can lead to deep depression. Moreover, grief tends to be stored up, gaining power year after year until survivors feel they will burst with the pain. So, a therapist must introduce clients to the language of emotion, the range of emotional possibilities available for expression, and the rules by which they are governed. Then a therapist should encourage the clients to express their anger and other emotions in ways that will keep them and the people they care about safe.

Step 6: Mourning the losses—Not only have survivors of CSA lost much during their lives but they also have lost a particular kind of hope that is associated with the dreams of what might have been. Mourning the death of hope is usually the most painful step for clients. However, as they proceed through this stage of therapy, they tend to hold on to the faint chance that somehow, some way, the past can be made right. The therapist is not able to do much to ameliorate the pain of the clients as they goes through this process. The task of the therapist is to be emotionally present for the clients and accompany them through this process.

Step 7: Telling a new truth—During this stage of therapy, the clients replace the dead hopes of the past with new hopes for the future, and they become ready to face some truths. Those truths include the fact that no one is coming to rescue them. No one can make this better for them. Life is not fair, and their past cannot be changed, only their future. Sometimes at this point, clients may struggle because they strongly desire justice or even revenge. But eventually, they face the fact that they must move forward, because every step toward a new life must be taken by them and only them.

Step 8: Defining a new self—Now the clients begin to ask who they are and what they want. The task of the therapist is to support the clients' healthy process of self-discovery and introspection by giving them substantial time to explore those important questions without imposing views upon them. The therapist needs to teach the clients to use sentences that begin with the word "I."

Step 9: Social and spiritual reconnection—During this phase of treatment, clients take what they learned in therapy and practice it. As clients begin to strengthen their sense of self and become more adept at maintaining healthy boundaries and keeping safe in relationships, they become more capable of connecting with others in healthy, positive ways. The task of the therapist is to support the development of positive relationships. The therapist should also explore the topic of spirituality, helping the clients find activities or beliefs that nurture their essence.

Step 10: Saying good-bye—Although growth and development are lifelong pursuits, therapy is not. The topic of the process of termination of therapy should be discussed at various periods of the therapeutic process. However, as the end of therapy approaches, it is helpful for the therapist to reduce the frequency of sessions to help the clients adjust to life after therapy. It is also important for the therapist to let the clients know that, as they move through the various developmental stages of life, there may be some "bumps in the road." If this happens, they can return for some "booster" sessions. Often clients are comforted when they are reminded that the end of therapy is similar to other transitions in life, such as graduation from school. It may seem bittersweet, but most clients move forward and enjoy embracing their futures.

Although this is not the only approach to treatment, it addresses the fundamental issues that most survivors of CSA encounter. However, the reader is also encouraged to review the treatment program created by the author of this chapter[50] and the approach of Briere.[51] Every survivor who seeks therapy should be knowledgeable about what to expect as he or she completes the therapeutic journey. Therapy works!

CONCLUSION

The purpose of this chapter has been to acquaint the reader with the numbers of women who are survivors of CSA, the various types of health and mental health challenges that they may face, the reasons why they should seek treatment, and what to expect from the therapist. It is important to understand that most people recover from the consequences of CSA. Some complete the journey rather quickly. For others, it takes more time. Recovery is not a race. It certainly is not a test. It is a path of human maturation in which each individual must travel along his or her unique pathway. Often when I meet with a new client who is an adult survivor of CSA, she will ask me if the pain of facing the trauma that she has worked so hard to bury is worth the effort. My answer to her is, "Absolutely. It is like living in color instead of black and white. It is about fully participating in life instead of going through the motions. It is about moving from feeling powerless to feeling powerful. It is about becoming whole again rather than being defined by the experience of abuse. But most of all, it is about being free, at last."

Chapter 7

Legal Issues in Intimate Partner Violence

D. Karen Wilkerson

THE MOST IMPORTANT THINGS YOU NEED TO KNOW

Whether you are reading this text for a college course or simply for your information, please plan to share what you learn with others who may desperately need to know what to do. If, however, you are a victim of intimate violence of any type and are seeking information to assist you in escape, be aware that you are facing a difficult and often dangerous, but not impossible, task. Hundreds of thousands of women have taken the steps necessary to escape a violent relationship and succeeded in improving the outlook for themselves and their children. You can, too. Take courage, and read on.

The process of ending violence in intimate relationships requires first recognizing it, then developing a plan for escaping it. The simple act of obtaining information is empowering, but the legal procedures necessary to achieve freedom from a violent relationship can present an almost overwhelming tangle of requirements. Furthermore, although current federal law makes uniform the recognition of orders for protection from battering, sexual assault, stalking, harassment, and other types of intimate violence, the application and enforcement of those laws in all jurisdictions of the United States is often not uniform.[1]

Virtually all professionals who work with battered women agree that the preparation of a safety plan is perhaps the most important first step. (A sample safety plan is available in Appendix 1.) Developing a network of trusted confidants, making financial and credit arrangements, and sometimes creating an entirely new identity to permit a covert existence away from the batterer will take quite a bit of time and forethought.[2] The various protections offered through legal avenues also require time, not only for court hearings and consulting with civil attorneys, criminal district attorneys, or law enforcement personnel, but also for gathering necessary evidence, filing pleadings, serving subpoenas, and scheduling court appearances. For victims who have adequate means and stable psychological support, these tasks are daunting; for victims in a state of shock after years of abuse or horrific trauma, the experience of trying to organize such plans can be paralyzing.

What a victim says to authorities and professionals who help her *can be used against her*. Although discussions with physicians, attorneys, counselors, and ministers are generally considered privileged (cannot be compelled as court testimony), intimate violence situations present a unique circumstance.[3] For example, a victim of marital rape must disclose significant personal information to law enforcement and medical authorities, some of which may come back to haunt her in subsequent divorce or child-custody proceedings. Evidence and allegations of marital abuse or suspected abuse of children submitted during a divorce or custody case may, in some cases, not be utilized in seeking a protective order at a later date. The tendency for victims to keep abusive relationships secret from others may be a huge hindrance when they seek a protective order, because there may be few witnesses to the abuse and little admissible evidence for use in the courtroom. Del Martin, whose 1976 text *Battered Wives* is commonly considered the catalyst for the battered women's movement, wrote:

> From one point of view, the battered wife in her secrecy conspires with the media, the police, the social scientists, the social reformers, and the social workers to keep the issue hushed up. We can picture a very thick door locked shut. On the inside is a woman trying hard not to cry out for help. On the other side are those who could and should be helping, but instead are going about their business as if she weren't there.[4]

The situation has changed somewhat in recent years, but the practice of keeping "family matters" outside the view of friends, family, and professionals continues among many victims. This has unfortunately fueled prevalent misconceptions that victims of intimate violence are masochistic, unstable, weak, stupid, or in some way to blame for their misery, namely, the "why does she stay" argument. The truth, however, is that victims of battering have also been victims of a double standard, as described by Donna Ferrato in *Living with the Enemy*:

Despite widespread changes in police policy, many officers still don't view the batterer as a criminal, although they'd arrest him in a minute if he did to a stranger in the street what he does to his wife at home. It used to be that if a man roughed up his wife a little, the police would advise her go downtown to police headquarters and lodge her complaint. But realistically, how could a woman leave her home, round up the kids, and find some way to get downtown, with little or no money, no means of transportation, and no concrete proof of her husband's brutality? The criminal justice system required evidence, and if you didn't have it you weren't going to get anywhere with your complaint. The judicial system ultimately discouraged women from seeking ways, within that system, to fight their husbands' abuse.[5]

The same attitudes described in law enforcement have also been observed among prosecutors, judges, counselors, ministers, and others in positions of authority and assistance who are normally contacted by victims fleeing intimate violence. These ways of thinking, although incorrect, are persistent, and they may be encountered even today by victims of intimate violence.

OPTIONS FOR THE VICTIM ESCAPING A VIOLENT SITUATION

In most states, there are three distinct avenues available through the judicial system for victims who need assistance in fleeing safely from an abusive relationship: *family law* (divorce or separation), *civil law* (protective and restraining orders), and *criminal law* (prosecution of individual acts such as assault, sexual assault, stalking, or kidnapping).[6] Although the use of one type of legal remedy does not preclude the use of another in these cases, each remedy is somewhat unique, both in the standards of evidence which must be presented and in the various channels of their administration within the judicial system.

Most victims of intimate violence do not stay in an abusive relationship. Unfortunately, many studies concur that about one-third of battered women who are forced to seek assistance from a shelter (and who often have limited financial and emotional resources) will eventually return to their abusers.[7] For these victims, the law may offer little protection. Victims who leave their partners permanently and who are financially able may file for divorce or separation at the time or soon after they move away from the abuser. Although the process of maintaining independence is complicated by joint custody of minor children, laws in many states now allow judges to modify custody orders when intimate violence is an issue. In an effort to manipulate a partner's behavior, one partner may threaten violence toward children or imply plans to remove the children from the other partner's possession, especially when separation or divorce is an issue. Family courts sometimes prepare orders of protection (also known as restraining orders, injunctions, no-contact orders, or stay-away orders) to accompany divorce decrees or custody documents. However, such orders are not enforceable in criminal court, that is, violations must be addressed through civil contempt of court proceedings. Violation of an order of protection constitutes contempt of court and may be overlooked, stimulate a verbal reprimand from the judge, or be punished by a fine and/or jail time, generally of short duration.

CIVIL PROTECTIVE ORDERS

Although most of the acts comprising intimate violence are crimes, for many years family law offered the only practical protection to most victims.[8] Orders for protection may be issued by either civil or criminal courts. The process takes several weeks, on average, due to requirements that the offender be given advance notice of court hearings and pleadings. Filing for protective orders in civil court offers two advantages to victims: the victims control the initiation of action against the battering spouse, and the level of proof required in civil court is easier to achieve.[9] Depending on state law, a protective order may also be available to victims of dating violence, live-in intimate partners, and victims of sexual assault, where the relationship of the offender to the victim may be unknown. Once a final protective order has been issued by a court, the "full faith and credit" provision of the VAWA requires its enforcement in all states, territories, and tribal nations, regardless of where the order was originally issued.[10] Additionally, permanent protective orders must be registered in each state and thereby become accessible to all law enforcement and court officers through the National Crime Information Center (NCIC), a division of the FBI. In some states, a victim, a law enforcement officer, or others acting upon the victim's behalf may request an emergency protective order at the time of arraignment following an arrest for an act of family violence.

In Texas, for example, a Magistrate's Order for Emergency Protection (MOEP), which may only be issued at an arraignment hearing, becomes effective immediately and remains enforceable for 31–61 days. The MOEP is available to any victim of family violence or stalking, including persons living in the same household or those who have or have had a romantic or intimate relationship with the victim; in fact, it is *required* in every case involving arrest for aggravated assault against a family member in Texas.[11] An additional benefit of the Texas MOEP is that it is criminally enforceable, as is a final protective order. At the time a victim files for a final order, a request is routinely made for a temporary *ex parte* protective order. The temporary *ex parte* order requires only the applicant's statement of abuse and does not require notice to nor court appearance of the batterer, but it is not criminally enforceable in Texas. Like orders joined with many family law decrees, the only remedy available for violation of a temporary *ex parte* order is through a civil contempt case. Therefore, for the period between the initial hearing and a final hearing to obtain the protective order, a victim in Texas may not be fully protected if the batterer decides to violate the temporary order protecting her unless she previously obtained an MOEP.

In any state, victims are often encouraged to seek shelter or alternative housing during the period between hearings due to the explosive reaction of some batterers.[12] Once a final protective order is granted, the criminal and civil prohibitions within it are enforceable in all states under provisions of VAWA. Violations of criminal prohibitions may result in the immediate arrest of the offender, whereas failure to heed civil requirements may result only in contempt proceedings. In addition, federal law prohibits anyone who has ever been convicted of a misdemeanor family violence assault or who is a respondent in a protective order from possessing a firearm or ammunition.[13] Many states have enacted laws against possession of firearms by persons who have committed acts of family violence.

Bear in mind that state laws about protective orders undergo constant change and vary from state to state. In addition, state laws differ in many ways, from application and nomenclature to the degree of safety they confer on victims. It is critically important to understand the laws that currently apply to intimate violence in the state in which a victim resides and to seek knowledgeable legal support. (A comprehensive list of state coalitions and legal resources providing assistance to victims of domestic violence, sexual assault, and other violent acts is located in Appendix 4.)

CRIMINAL CHARGES

There is no lack of crimes committed upon intimates for which criminal charges may be filed. State-level charges that may be brought against a person who commits an act of intimate violence include murder (first or second degree); manslaughter; criminally negligent homicide; unlawful restraint; kidnapping; aggravated kidnapping; assault; aggravated assault; sexual assault; aggravated sexual assault; injury to a child, elderly, or disabled individual; deadly conduct; terrorist threat; criminal trespass; robbery; obstruction or retaliation; interference with emergency telephone call; harassment; stalking; unlawful possession of a firearm; and violation of a protective order or magistrate's order.[14] Additionally, federal charges enacted under VAWA make it unlawful to commit domestic violence crimes across state, territorial, or tribal lines; these laws also cover stalking and protective orders.[15]

Assaults

Put simply, *assault* is the threat or attempt to strike another person and cause bodily harm, provided that the target is aware of the danger. In some states, the victim need not be aware in cases where a deadly weapon is used; in some cases, a threat or offensive touch may suffice for a charge of assault, particularly if the intended victim is an elder, child, or disabled person. Several levels of assault intensity are recognized under most state law, from offensive touch to serious injury. *Serious bodily injury* is defined as an injury that involves substantial risk of death, disfigurement, or impaired function of a body member or organ or mental faculty.[16] The term *aggravated assault* bears no relationship to the emotional state of either the victim or the assailant; it means that a deadly weapon is used or displayed during the assault or that a serious bodily injury resulted from the assault.[17]

In practical terms, assault charges can stem from pushing, slapping, shoving, scratching, hair-pulling, grabbing, beating, or hitting another person, as well as making a threat to perform any of those acts. Women are five times more likely than men to be the target of intimate partner violence, and the overwhelming proportion (83.6 percent) of criminal acts committed against both men and women by their intimate partners are simple and aggravated assaults.[18] Punishments for assaults range from a misdemeanor (fine and/or jail time of generally less than one year) to a felony, which typically results in a prison term.

Taken to the most horrific extreme, assaultive behavior results in the death of the intended victim. Murder, manslaughter, and criminally negligent homicide are typical labels for different "degrees" of this crime; the serious *first degree* murder is usually reserved for a killing that is deliberate and premeditated. Deaths resulting from the commission of other crimes, including arson, rape, or armed robbery; with more than one victim; using certain weapons, particularly guns; or in which certain persons are the victim (such as children or law enforcement officials) also carry first degree status in many states. *Second degree* murder (sometimes called *manslaughter*) results from an assault that could possibly have caused the death of the victim but that lacks the planning and intentionality elements; such a situation applies to the "sudden passion" bedroom murder case that often receives significant press coverage. Second degree murder charges may also be brought against an intoxicated person who inadvertently causes a death during the commission of a nonfelony crime. Criminally negligent homicide charges result from an unintended death—one which is due to an act or omission, that is, without criminal intent. Included in this category are deaths due to self-defense, hunting accidents, and automobile accidents. In most states, all murders are considered felonies, but the degree will determine the punishment that may be assessed, from a fine and/or jail time up to life in prison or, in some states, execution.[19]

Sexual Assault

In *The War Against Women*, Marilyn French states, "The United States has one of the highest, if not the highest, rate of rape in the world, counting only those that are reported."[20] The old "stranger danger" myths about sexual assault simply do not bear up under scrutiny; victims are quite likely to know their perpetrators. The BJS shows that, of an estimated 240,980 violent sexual offense victimizations in 2001, almost twice as many incidents of rape, attempted rape, and sexual assault were committed by nonstrangers (i.e., family members, intimates, and friends) than by strangers.[21]

Susan Brownmiller, whose book *Against Our Will* was among the first significant explorations of the subject, acknowledged the use of rape since prehistoric times as a "conscious process of intimidation by which *all men* keep *all women* in a state of fear."[22] Rape has long been recognized as a crime, dating to Babylonian, Hebrew, and Greco-Roman legal codes. However, with few exceptions, rape was primarily considered a property crime in which a man's property (his wife or daughter) had been defiled. Women who had been raped often were not considered victims; some were forced to marry their attackers or were put to death, especially if they were married women and therefore considered adulterous. Rarely was any protection under the law given to prostitutes. During the Middle Ages, the law began to consider rape a crime against the individual and identified four elements of proof: violence, abduction, intercourse, and lack of consent. Early statutes in the American colonies followed what is known as the common-law definition of rape, which required that the sexual assault took place by force against the woman's will.[23] The level of a victim's resistance and ability to consent continue to shape modern interpretation of rape laws. One current definition of rape is found in *The People's Law Dictionary*: ". . . the crime of sexual intercourse (with actual penetration of a woman's vagina with the man's penis) without consent and accomplished through force, threat of violence or intimidation."[24]

"Date rape" as a significant social issue began to gain attention in the United States during the late 1980s, when a study conducted on college campuses by the National Institutes of Health (NIH) cited the incidence of rape at 15 percent and attempted rape at 12 percent.[25] Although date rape is significantly more prevalent than sexual assault by a stranger, it is less likely to be reported to police, prosecuted in court, or considered rape by mental health counselors.[26] Alcohol ingestion has long been a tool of perpetrators intent on diminishing their date's resistance to sexual activity, as well as the likelihood the sexual assault will be reported. The more recent use of date rape drugs (including Rohypnol, GHB, and other substances, whether acquired by prescription or illegal means) placed secretly in an intended victim's drink at a party or bar has facilitated sexual assaults worldwide. These drugs frequently result in unconsciousness and memory loss, making a victim's ability to recall and report evidence of the sexual assault more difficult, if not impossible.[27]

Note that the subject of marital rape has not been mentioned; indeed, it was not illegal, except in a very few cases, until quite recently. The marital rape exemption can be traced to statements by Sir Matthew Hale, Chief Justice in England during the 1600s. Hale wrote, "The husband cannot be guilty of a rape committed by himself upon his lawful wife, for by their mutual matrimonial consent and contract, the wife hath given herself in kind unto the husband, which she cannot retract."[28]

Marital rape was not even recognized as a criminal act under U.S. state laws, nor were many studies of its incidence conducted, until a few decades ago.[29] Although early women's rights activists discussed the subject of women's sexual rights in the mid-1800s, it was not until the emergence of the modern feminist movement in the 1960s and subsequent social research that the legal response to sexual assault within a marital relationship began to change.[30] One researcher, speaking before a state legislature, is quoted as having testified, "When you are raped by a stranger you have to live with a frightening memory. When you are raped by your husband, you have to live with your rapist."[31]

As of July 1993, marital rape became a crime in all 50 states;[32] however, in many states the degree of violence committed by the husband or the ability of his wife to give consent determines whether the rape is prosecutable.[33] The historical lack of legal condemnation unfortunately does not mean that marital rape did not occur. Recent studies indicate that between 10 and 14 percent of married women are raped by their husbands; the incidence of marital rape soars to one-third to one-half among clinical samples of battered women. Many researchers estimate that sexual assault by one's spouse accounts for approximately 25 percent of all rapes committed. Women at particularly higher risk for marital rape include pregnant women, those recently discharged from hospitals due to illness, and those who make an attempt to leave their abusers, either by fleeing or instituting divorce proceedings.[34] Criminal charges of sexual assault may also be triggered by other acts, which may include genital contact with mouth or anus or the insertion of objects into the vagina or anus, all without the consent of the victim. Each state's laws regarding criminal charges of sexual assault and/or rape differ greatly, but in most states they are considered felonies, which qualify for significant prison sentences. There also are a host of sexually aggressive behaviors that could result in criminal charges, were they committed by strangers, but which often go unprosecuted within an intimate relationship, including voyeurism, exposure to exhibitionism, undesired exposure to pornography, intentional touching of a victim's body against her will, coercion, intimidation, and pressuring for sexual compliance.[35]

Assaults on Children

Virtually all imaginable types of assaults, both physical and sexual, are committed upon children on a regular and daily basis. John E. B. Myers, noted authority on the investigation and litigation of child abuse and neglect, called it "a scourge on children that inflicts incalculable suffering." He went on to say that, although society has begun to take the issue more seriously since the mid-1960s, it has not been eradicated nor will it ever be without coordination of the legal and helping professions to improve the protection of children.[36] A series of studies on the incidence of child abuse and neglect conducted by the U.S. Department of Health and Human Services reveals some extremely troubling trends:[37]

- The total number of children seriously injured and the total number endangered quadrupled from 1986 to 1993.
- Between 1986 and 1993, the estimated number of physically abused children in the United States increased by 97 percent; sexually abused, up 125 percent; emotionally abused, up 183 percent; physically neglected, up 163 percent; and emotionally neglected, up 188 percent.
- Children of single parents were at increased risk of almost all types of abuse and neglect (except sexual abuse); family income was significantly related to increased risk of harm in nearly every category of maltreatment.
- The proportion of cases investigated by CPS decreased significantly from 1986 to 1993, even though the total number of cases has risen, possibly indicating that the CPS system may have reached its capacity to respond to this issue.

Early reports from similar studies conducted in 2000 revealed that the trend continues to increase, with an estimated three million reports of child maltreatment.[38] Although these numbers are staggering, two things must be kept in mind. First, these figures are based upon reported incidents and likely represent only the tip of the proverbial iceberg regarding the violence and maltreatment of children. Second, much of what is reported may be relatively minor in scope (i.e., although harmful and emotionally painful, the incident may not have resulted in serious injury or death to a child) or may remain unsubstantiated by authorities. The law has traditionally allowed parents wide latitude in what is considered reasonable corporal punishment. However, three-quarters of parents surveyed in 1985 admitted to at least one act of violence with a high probability of injury against their child, the most common being slapping or spanking. Another study in 1998 revealed that one-half of parents said they had engaged in severe physical assault of their children at some point during parenting; reported behaviors included "hitting the child with an object such as a stick or belt, slapping the child on the face, hitting the child with a fist, kicking the child, and throwing/knocking down the child."[39]

Sexual abuse of children, abhorred during the Victorian era, went essentially unnoticed by law and popular culture from the early 1900s until the 1970s. Victims were held accountable, while offenders went unpunished. As one author wrote, "For most of the 20th century, when child victims were not viewed as liars, they were labeled as sex delinquents."[40] One complicating variable is the age of consent (the age at which an individual is legally capable of consenting to sexual contact); most states place the age of consent somewhere between 14 and 18 years old, although they also define incest as illegal regardless of the age of the victim. The difference in age between victim and perpetrator may also be an issue of prosecutability, as many states consider sexual activity between children near the same age to be "sex play," which is not considered an offense under the law.[41]

The true prevalence of child sexual abuse is not known, because most cases still are not reported to authorities; as many as 75 percent of adults who are told by children of the sexual assault fail to report it.[42] Several reviews of investigations into false reports of sexual abuse of children conclude that very small proportions, probably between 2 and 10 percent, are totally fictitious allegations. Even among cases reported in the course of couples divorcing, when such allegations are more prevalent and also likely to be dismissed as irrelevant, one study revealed that about three-fourths of the reports were deemed reliable.[43] Some authorities place the estimated number of child sexual abuse cases at around 300,000 per year, although only a fraction are reported and prosecuted.

All abusive behavior toward children, whether physical or sexual, assault or neglect, is reportable as a criminal act in all 50 states. In fact, most states mandate reporting of suspected abuse or neglect to CPS, especially by teachers, medical professionals, counselors, child care providers, law enforcement officers, clergy, and others who come into contact with children. State laws vary as to who must make the report, what level of suspicion triggers a mandatory report, and by what means the report must be made.[44] Failure to report suspected abuse or neglect can result in loss of professional licensure and/or criminal charges in some cases, as well as liability under civil law for abdicating one's responsibility to protect children from harm. Criminal charges have been brought in a few cases against nonoffending parents who failed to intervene on behalf of their child.

Children are defenseless in the battle between adults in a violent relationship. Simply witnessing the violence in such households has an enormous negative effect on children, altering their educational achievement, emotional well-being, and potential for using violent behavior themselves.[45] Some research indicates that male children from homes where domestic violence occurred are more likely to become batterers, having learned that intimate violence against women is acceptable.[46]

Criminal charges for assault, aggravated assault, murder, negligent homicide, sexual assault, and aggravated sexual assault committed against children carry the same, if not enhanced, status as when the offenses are committed upon adults. In fact, several types of molestation behaviors (touching, exposure, taking photographs, and inducing acts between children) are singularly applied when victims fall below the age of maturity. It is sad, however, that verdicts for offenses against children generally result in shorter sentences, or even probation, than would offenses against adults or non-family members.

Kidnapping, Stalking, and Other Crimes

Kidnapping is defined as "the taking of a person against his/her will (or from the control of a parent or guardian) from one place to another under circumstances in which the person so taken does not have freedom of movement, will, or decision through violence, force, threat or intimidation."[47] Many captures also involve the commission of other crimes, particularly sexual assault. Although the situation in which a parent takes and hides a child in violation of a court order is considered kidnapping, refusal to follow agreed-upon custody orders by not surrendering a child to the other parent does not usually satisfy kidnapping criteria but is instead typically handled in family court. Kidnapping is considered a criminal felony (state jail or prison sentence); but when bodily harm to the victim occurs, the charges may be accelerated to capital crimes, which are death penalty offenses in some states. If state lines are crossed in the commission of a kidnapping offense, the FBI will be involved in investigating the crime, now a federal offense. Lesser but related charges include false imprisonment, unlawful restraint, taking due to irresistible impulse, and similar acts.

Stalking is a term for engaging in a course of conduct directed at a person that serves no legitimate purpose but seriously alarms, annoys, or intimidates that person; it is a pattern of willful and repeated following or harassing that causes the person who is stalked to fear injury or death because of express or implied threats.[48] In the context of intimate violence, stalking and harassment may take the form of threatening harm to the victim or the victim's children, family, or household or threatening damage to personal property or pets. Unfortunately, stalking tends to escalate from seemingly harmless acts to more obsessive and potentially lethal behaviors.[49] Some acts committed by stalkers may seem innocuous, but they have sinister meaning when evaluated in terms of the relationship history. For example, placing notes on car windshields, making phone calls and leaving messages on telephone answering machines, or sending flowers to a workplace may mean a batterer has discovered the new location of a woman who fled and making this discovery known sends a strong message of danger to the victim. Stalking behavior was previously considered by legislators, law enforcement, and courts as a potential crime, not a completed one, such as assault or rape. However, stalking creates a "climate of fear and harassment that actually harms victims by causing them extreme emotional distress and limiting their social and workplace movements."[50] Stalking is now considered a felony in most states; the Violent Crime Against Women Act of 2000 amended VAWA to add cyber-stalking to the list of federal domestic violence offenses.[51] *Harassment*, a misdemeanor charge, is often applied to lower intensity actions of a systematic and continued nature that may include obscene telephone calls, E-mails, faxes or written communications, demands, threats of inflicting harm, and other efforts to annoy, alarm, or embarrass the intended target.[52] Both stalking and harassment require considerable record keeping as evidence for prosecution, partly because law enforcement authorities in many jurisdictions continue to hold outmoded views of stalking as merely a possibility and therefore not a crime.

WHY THE VIOLENCE AGAINST WOMEN ACT IS IMPORTANT

The VAWA of 1994 was enacted decades after most states legally recognized domestic violence and other intimate violence and began to write legislation specifically designed to protect victims. Soon after, several problems in the application of those laws became apparent, often surrounding state differences in handling protective orders. VAWA offered broader remedies than before for those suffering intimate violence. For the first time, the acts of abuse, neglect, and terrorism committed by a spouse or intimate partner were recognized as criminal activities in many states.[53] VAWA provided the funding for the National

Domestic Violence Hotline (1-800-799-SAFE). It also created a civil rights remedy to permit victims of gender-motivated crime the right to sue in either federal or state court for monetary damages, including medical and mental health expenses, job retraining, loss of property and assets, and other losses suffered as a result of intimate violence. However, the civil rights provision of VAWA was struck down by the United States Supreme Court in 2000 (*U.S.* v. *Morrison*), reserving these areas to over-sight by state courts.[54]

Equal Enforcement

As late as the 1970s, if a victim was granted a protection order in one state and then moved to another state, there was no assurance that the order would be enforced as the issuing state intended or would even be considered valid. Add to this the general reluctance of law enforcement to deal with intimate violence as a criminal matter and the inability of officers in one jurisdiction to verify court orders issued by other states. Obviously, no state could pass laws to compel other states to enforce their orders nor were they under any obligation to provide enforcement of orders written under laws not valid in their states. Because this situation served to create an abridgement of an individual's rights to equal protection under the law and her right to safely enjoy interstate travel, the Congress passed VAWA. Referred to as the Full Faith and Credit Provision, this section of VAWA requires that all states, territories, and tribes enforce a protective order as vigo-rously and completely as they would enforce one of their orders, even when the issuing state's laws offer protections not available in the vic-tim's current residence.[55] VAWA also mandated the entry of protective order information in the NCIC database maintained by the FBI, which permits access to this information by law enforcement and court offi-cers all over the United States.

Criminal Acts Across State Lines

A state's laws can address only crimes committed within that state's borders, as is the case with Native American tribes and U.S. territories. There was no effective response to crimes that were committed across jurisdiction lines, such as stalking, harassment, kidnapping, and similar acts. New federal crimes have been created under VAWA, all based on the interstate travel clause: (1) the commission of an act of domestic vi-olence across state, territorial, or tribal lines; (2) violation of a protec-tive order in the course of crossing those boundaries; (3) stalking across state lines or within special federal jurisdictions; and, in 2000, (4) cyber-stalking.[56]

Gun Ownership Provisions

Firearms pose a significant threat to victims of intimate violence; although they are used in only a tiny proportion of family violence incidents, those incidents are the most lethal. In 63 percent of spouses and 47 percent of dating partners murdered by their intimates in 2002, firearms were the weapons used by the offender.[57] Congress amended the Gun Control Act in 1994 and 1996 to prohibit firearm or ammunition possession by persons subject to certain types of protective orders or those convicted of certain types of misdemeanor domestic violence crimes. Specifically, the gun control provisions apply to cases where there is a "credible threat" to the victim protected by the order or in cases where the protective order specifically bars the offender from using, attempting, or threatening use of physical force against an intimate. Law enforcement and military personnel are exempt from this provision while on duty. Transferring a firearm or ammunition to a person subject to a protective order addressed by these laws is also a federal crime; this section would apply to gun shops and private sellers who know or have reasonable cause to believe that the buyer is under a protective order.[58]

VAWA was reauthorized and some of its provisions expanded by Congress in 2000. Among the important provisions within the 2000 revision are the following:

1. prohibits notification of the offender that the original protective order has been registered in another state;
2. provides funds for civil legal assistance to victims of domestic violence, stalking, and sexual assault;
3. requires grantees providing civil legal assistance to certify that they will not require mediation or counseling of offenders and victims together;
4. provides funds for transitional housing assistance for victims; and
5. provides monies for supervised and safe exchange during visitation with children under custody orders when interpersonal violence is an issue.[59]

VAWA was signed into law January 5, 2006.

CHANGING YOUR NAME AND/OR SOCIAL SECURITY NUMBER

For a person fleeing from a violent relationship, the level of safety that secrecy permits is often difficult to obtain. Offenders are often able to find their victims through court records, medical records, financial and credit reports, children's school records, and property documents. One option that may be helpful for victims in avoiding pursuit is to change their name and social security number. Consultation with an attorney is recommended, particularly if children subject to a custody agreement are involved.

A name change is fairly simple, although it does require a court order and, in most cases, a small classified ad in the newspaper to serve as legal publication of the change. In cases where intimate violence of any type has been an issue, some courts permit publication without the inclusion of any information regarding the new name or new address, or they may require the inclusion of the name-changer's attorney or other contact in the ad to facilitate location by creditors. Special arrangements may be made through the courts to permit direct notification of creditors and others who have a right to know of the name change, thereby avoiding publication requirements altogether.[60]

In 1998, prompted by Al Gore, former vice president of the United States, the Social Security Administration changed its policies to permit issuing new social security numbers to victims of intimate violence.[61] A victim must present evidence documenting harassment or abuse along with documents establishing the original identity (old social security number, driver's license, passport, etc.) and documents showing the name change. When the issuance of new numbers is requested for children, evidence of custody of those children must also be supplied. This process can be accomplished at any Social Security Administration office. More information can be accessed on the Social Security Administration Web site at http://www.socialsecurity.gov.

In addition to these identity changes, other records may need to be altered as well; these include driver's license, passport, voter registration, bank, credit card, physician, insurance, state and federal tax bureaus, investments, retirement plans, auto registration, employer, schools, clubs, and other memberships. Anyone changing his or her name may need to update wills, health care proxies, living wills, trusts, power of attorney documents, and any contracts or deeds.

WORKING WITH LAW ENFORCEMENT

As is clearly documented throughout this book, intimate partner violence is a major public health and criminal justice issue in our country, with an estimated 3.5 million violent crimes committed against family members annually. About half of these incidents continue to go unreported, most commonly because they are considered private or personal matters or because female victims fear retaliation from the offender. One ray of hope in this horrid picture is an apparent trend since 1993: the estimated incidence of violent crimes committed by intimate partners has decreased while the percentage of cases reported has increased.[62] Certainly, reporting and prosecuting an offense makes a difference in an individual case, although doing so may be difficult and fearsome.

Reporting the Offense

We teach our children, even as toddlers, how to obtain emergency assistance: dial 911. The same advice holds true for any person who experiences an assault, a sexual assault, or any other criminal act at the hands of an intimate. Even though law enforcement authorities generally agree that the family disturbance call is one they dread, it is also among the most important. Because the risk of injury to an officer is thought to be greater in this situation than at any other time, special training in handling the domestic violence incidents is routine in most police departments today. Many jurisdictions have mandatory arrest policies in cases where the officer has reason to believe an assault has occurred, even though the officer did not witness the violence.[63] Some encouraging studies have shown substantial decreases in aggression and reoccurring offenses after mandatory arrest policies are instituted.[64] Whether or not an arrest is made, officers may take separate statements from each party in the home, photograph the scene and any visible injuries, obtain other available evidence, and provide information to the victim regarding legal rights and personal safety. Officers may also offer the victim transport to crisis centers, battered women's shelters, or medical facilities when necessary.

Although the incidence of intimate partner violence is somewhat higher in African American households, among low income families, in urban areas, and among younger couples, no one is immune.[65] Concerns over what the neighbors may think upon seeing police cars or ambulances in the driveway may be one factor in these crimes not being reported. Embarrassment may be unpleasant, but it is not lethal and it does not leave physical and emotional scars that last a lifetime.

Evidence That May Be Gathered in an Investigation

After intimate violence began to be considered a crime against an individual, many victims refused or were afraid to file complaints or were later pressured by their batterers into requesting nonprosecution of the crime. Likely a consequence of fear and intimidation, victims' reluctance to pursue criminal complaints added to the difficulty the courts and law enforcement faced in addressing intimate violence. Many local jurisdictions have what they call a "no-drop" policy, that is, the state will pursue prosecution of the case regardless of the victim's wishes or objections.[66] The practice of considering these acts "crimes against the state" has encouraged law enforcement to make arrests and to collect sufficient evidence to prosecute offenders upon the sheer facts, relying less upon a victim's testimony or even presence in court. If you are a victim, this means that your home and your body have now become crime scenes; your experience may become part of a court record. This may be unpleasant and shocking, but it is a necessity if criminal acts are to be prosecuted successfully. Useful evidence includes:

- Law enforcement officers' notes from interviews with the victim, the offender, and witnesses (neighbors, children in the home);
- Written and photographic documentation of the condition of the crime scene, particularly broken items and damage to or disarray of the rooms;
- Photographs of the victim's and the suspect's visible injuries (both at the time of the incident and after a day or two if additional bruises or injuries become visible);
- Photographs or actual confiscated weapons, torn/bloody clothing, and other evidence obtained at the scene of the attack.

In sexual assault cases, medical professionals (usually a specially trained nurse and an emergency room physician) will administer a special type of examination and obtain specific types of evidence (called a *rape kit*) to be used in prosecuting the crime. In these cases, it is vitally important that the victim not shower or change clothing prior to the examination. Special investigators from law enforcement, medical, and counseling disciplines may interview and examine children who have been victims of assault, sexual assault, or neglect. It is important not to question children or coach their answers beforehand, as this may compromise prosecution of any offense committed against them.[67]

Difficulties Sometimes Encountered with Law Enforcement

As discussed earlier, violence within the context of an intimate or familial relationship has historically been largely ignored, because of both the lack of legal underpinnings for prosecution and the cultural bias against interference in "family matters." Certainly, this has had a significant effect on the recognition of abuse as a criminal act by law enforcement and may still be a factor in some locales. Prior to the "discovery" of wife abuse in the last few decades, police departments tended to treat family violence incidents as "trivial, non-criminal, non-injurious, inconsequential and primarily verbal 'spats.'"[68] Unfortunately, a double standard still persists in many cases where an act against an intimate goes unpunished that, had it been committed against a stranger, would otherwise have resulted in immediate arrest. The situation is improving, however. Law enforcement officers are now routinely informed about changes in the law as well as trained to exhibit increased sensitivity to victims of physical and sexual assault, so that the crimes will be identified properly and the victims will be less likely to feel blamed, humiliated, or intimidated by police comments.[69] As noted earlier, mandatory arrest procedures based upon probable cause guidelines (instead of turning a blind eye to apparent signs of abuse) have had a positive impact in reduction of violence within intimate relationships. It cannot be denied that the effect of VAWA in directing registry and equal enforcement of protective orders across the country, combined with pressure from women's advocates, has improved attitudes and increased victim assistance from law enforcement.

WILL YOU FOLLOW THROUGH?

Even though many jurisdictions now have pro-arrest policies in domestic violence situations that warrant immediate action to protect the victim, many cases either do not meet the attention of law enforcement or are handled without any arrest being made. A victim's initial goal may be not to have the offender arrested but instead to scare, embarrass, inform, or pressure the offender in hopes of stopping the behavior. In cases where it remains the victim's prerogative to file, or not to file, a criminal complaint against an aggressor, the willingness of the victim to stay the course all the way through prosecution has been a major issue among police and prosecutors. Court and law enforcement personnel must wonder whether the efforts they expend on behalf of victims are really worth the effort when one-third to one-half of cases involving intimate partner violence continue to be dismissed from the courts.[70] Some states assume the duty of prosecuting these offenses, even though the victim withdraws support for pursuing the case.[71]

Issues in the Courtroom

It should be clear that there are vast differences in the legal redress available to victims of intimate violence through criminal courts, civil courts, and family law courts. Many victims utilize more than one means of achieving freedom from abuse and sometimes must repeat the process more than once to accomplish permanent security. One principal difference between the criminal justice system and the civil law courts is the level of proof required; proving a violation of civil law requires a "preponderance of evidence" commonly approximated by a greater than 50 percent probability, whereas criminal law requires the much higher standard of "beyond a reasonable doubt." Recall also that jail sentences and fines are reserved for those guilty of criminal charges or any civil charge whose violation results in contempt of court charges. The remedies offered under most civil and family law include a prohibition of certain behaviors, a command to perform certain acts, or a monetary payment to the victim. In civil cases, both parties must hire their own attorneys or obtain the assistance of legal aid services; in criminal cases, the prosecutor (usually a county or district attorney) represents both the state and the victim. Unless charges are brought by the state, civil or family court will provide the only recourse for victims of intimate violence. Patience and persistence are essential to success in legal matters; particularly in family law, the lack of access to legal representation and inadequate financing can sometimes present major obstacles to pursuing a case to its conclusion.

Attitudes Prevalent among Judges and Attorneys

There are some notorious examples of conduct in the courtroom that creates bias against female victims of interpersonal violence of all types. It is easy to minimize an assault after the bruises have faded and broken bones have healed. This is one reason that photographic evidence is so useful in prosecution, as are witness statements and 911 tapes. Other defense techniques include blaming the victim, using the "why does she stay" argument, or pointing to a lack of prior medical or police records (which could attest to a pattern of brutal attacks) as general denial that any abuse ever occurred. Many times the victim and, perhaps, the children are the only witnesses to the true level and history of danger within the household. In these cases, the courtroom scene becomes a "he said–she said" battle, which is unlikely to reveal the truth to a judge and jury. Not only do defense attorneys blame the victim and play down the level of severity of the attack suffered, but some judges have been guilty of ill-informed utterances in the courtroom. In one notable case, a judge sang "you light up my wife" from the bench following testimony about a batterer who had set fire to his lighter fluid–soaked wife.[72] A California state senator has also been widely quoted for his statement, "But if you can't rape your wife, who can you rape?"[73]

It is hoped that these examples are the exception rather than the rule in most jurisdictions today, due to improved training of judges and continuing education programs that are conducted in large part through continuing pressure from women's advocacy groups beginning in the 1970s. To find an attorney who understands the dynamics of interpersonal violence, consult a local battered women's shelter or sexual assault crisis center or contact the state coalition for referrals in your area.

Red Flags in Any Case

Several practices that are often recommended by well-intentioned law enforcement, court, and counseling professionals appear, at least on the surface, to offer the potential benefit of reducing violent behaviors within a relationship. However, because they have been shown to have little positive effect and, in some cases, may create a more dangerous situation, these practices should be considered "red flags" during court proceedings by any victim of abuse.

1. Mutual orders for protection: This is a single agreed-upon protective order that usually prohibits both parties from committing violent acts, being in the vicinity of the partner's home or workplace, or harassing the other partner. The difficulty for law enforcement is discovering which party is the primary aggressor; in some cases neither party will be arrested.[74] In these situations, the only recourse is to seek a civil contempt issue and not a criminal justice response (arrest). Mutual orders for protection are now discouraged in many states, as they typically are not enforceable. They offer no protection for the victim.

2. Anger management classes (also called *batterer's intervention* or *community intervention programs*): These are designed to reduce interpersonal violence by reeducating the offenders, usually men, in small weekly groups using standardized lesson plans for three to six months. Many judges, upon finding that abuse has occurred within a relationship, require the offender to attend a series of classes when available in their locality; in many places, support is simultaneously provided to the offenders' victims or partners. In some cities, separate groups are also available for batterers of certain ethnic groups, same-sex batterers, and women who commit interpersonal violence against male partners. So long as a batterer remains under the control of a court, his or her compliance and attendance at treatment sessions can be compelled. Although this sounds like an excellent plan, follow-up studies have shown that these programs are only partially successful, particularly in men with history of childhood abuse, substance abuse, and personality or mood disorders.[75] One review of batterers' intervention programs shows successful outcomes of 53 to 85 percent,[76] whereas another reported that 35 percent of partners battered their wives within 6 to 12 months following treatment.[77] Recidivism rates do decrease in many

cases, however, and doing something to address the issue is preferable to nontreatment, particularly in programs with approved curriculum, coordination with community supervision offices (sometimes still called probation), and long-term follow-up of offenders.

3. Orders for mediation or couples' counseling: These are often added in family court in divorce, custody, and visitation documents when there have been allegations of abusive behavior. Successful mediation is based on the premise that both parties have equal power under the law, which is definitely not the case if interpersonal violence has occurred. As a result, the National Council of Juvenile and Family Court Judges has recommended that no judge mandate mediation in such cases.[78] Similarly, huge obstacles to mutually beneficial couples' counseling exist any time there is power inequality, the potential for victim blaming, and a failure to assign responsibility to the batterer for the abuse. Many victims suffer from the effects of their traumatic experiences, which makes it difficult for them to stand up for themselves in a joint session or even to recall the important details of what happened. This obviously would make joint counseling difficult, if not impossible. Counseling either party from a violent relationship requires specialized training; clients who seek counseling are well advised to inquire about a therapist's experience and credentials in this area. It should also be noted that joint counseling presents an additional risk for victims: Information revealed in these sessions is not protected under confidentiality rules and may be of benefit to the batterer in an ensuing divorce or custody case. Many state coalitions for battered women therefore deem traditional couples' counseling, family therapy, and mediation inappropriate when intimate violence has been present in a relationship.[79]

CRIMINAL CASES: STATE VS. THE ABUSER

Once police make an arrest, with or without a warrant, the case is automatically entered into the criminal justice system. The arrested suspect is usually booked at the local jail, where photographs and fingerprints are taken. Some suspects are released by law enforcement immediately after booking, while others remain in jail until an arraignment or bail hearing before a local magistrate, who is often a justice of the peace or municipal judge. (Recall that it is at this hearing that a victim may have the sole opportunity to obtain an MOEP.) The amount of bail is determined on the basis of several factors, including the nature of the offense, the future safety of the victim and the community, and the likelihood that the defendant will show up for trial. In the event bail is ordered, the defendant typically pays 10 to 20 percent of the amount of the bail as a nonrefundable fee to a bail bond company. Some defendants are released with no payment of bail on "personal recognizance," which presupposes they will appear for trial because they are sensible and law abiding. In either event, the offender is now out on the street; sometimes victims have only enough time to leave the house with absolute necessities before the offender returns. This underscores the need for comprehensive safety planning.

The Prosecutor's Office

In cases where no arrest is made, but the victim files a criminal complaint, the local prosecutor (sometimes called the county attorney or district attorney) will determine which criminal charges, if any, will be filed. Although the arresting officer may have determined initial charges, a prosecutor may subsequently adjust the charges against the defendant based upon the evidence available and the probability of obtaining a conviction.

In misdemeanor cases, no preliminary trial or grand jury hearing is generally necessary after the prosecutor's accusation; instead, an arraignment is held to permit a defendant to make a plea before a trial judge. Upon a guilty plea, the defendant may be sentenced; if the defendant pleads not guilty, a trial is scheduled in the appropriate court.

Felony cases are handled differently. In some states, evidence is first presented by the prosecutor to a grand jury who makes the decision whether to proceed to trial. If sufficient evidence to proceed is found, an indictment or formal accusation is issued against the defendant; if not, the case is said to be "no-billed," and the defendant is released. In other states, a preliminary hearing or arraignment before a judge will be held at which the accused is formally identified and some evidence of the felony is given by prosecution witnesses before a trial is set.[80]

Pretrial hearings may be held to file a variety of motions, often to limit what evidence may be introduced at trial or to determine the degree of strain to which a witness (particularly children) may be subjected in a courtroom appearance. A defendant may file a motion requesting that charges be dropped in return for participation in a batterer's intervention program, substance abuse rehabilitation program, or similar class; such an approach may result in pretrial diversion of the criminal charges, provided the offender completes the agreed-upon regimen. A plea bargain may also be negotiated at this point between a defendant and his or her attorney and the prosecutor's office in which the offender will agree to plead guilty, often to a lesser charge, in return for a lighter or probated sentence, thus saving the court and the victim the onerous and often emotionally difficult task of proceeding to trial. It is estimated that between 70 and 90 percent of all criminal cases are disposed of through plea bargains.[81]

If the Case Goes to Trial

A defendant has the right to request a bench trial, held before a judge only, or a jury trial, held before a panel of citizens. In states that decide sentencing separately from the guilt–innocence phase, the defendant may waive his or her right to a jury trial on either or both of the issues of guilt or sentence. Evidence is presented in court through the witnesses called by both the prosecution and the defense during trial. Typical witnesses may include police officers and detectives involved in the case, medical and counseling personnel, neighbors, employers, close friends and family members, the victim, and any other person with knowledge of the facts at hand. In some states, a wife may be compelled to testify against her husband in a criminal case involving intimate violence.

All witnesses offer sworn testimony under questioning by whichever side called them to the stand, and then they must be cross-examined by the opposing side. In many cases, the pretrial discovery and deposition process permits both sides access to evidence that will be presented at trial; there are, therefore, few surprises reminiscent of Hollywood courtroom scenes. Testifying in court may appear confusing and nerve-wracking on television and movie enactments, but it is often quite orderly and private, although adversarial. Many hearings take place without a courtroom full of onlookers, because of requests for a closed courtroom by the attorneys involved in the case, and witnesses are often not permitted to discuss the case with anyone but the prosecutor or their own attorney during trial.

When all evidence has been presented and each side's closing arguments have been heard, the judge sends the jury out to deliberate on a verdict after giving instructions about the law pertinent to the case. In cases where no jury was requested by the defendant, the judge will recess to consider a verdict. If a guilty verdict is returned, the defendant's case is set for sentencing.

Some states permit juries to assess the sentence, whereas others entrust only judges with sentencing decisions. In either event, evidence may be gathered regarding the appropriate punishment, including past history of violent behavior and assessment of continuing risk factors (alcohol or other substance abuse, mental health issues, other criminal history) for presentation at a presentencing hearing or during the sentencing phase of the trial. Again, states differ somewhat in these courtroom procedures. Sentencing is often discretionary to some degree, with guidelines often being set by individual state legislatures. Sentencing can include a combination of jail time, fines, and community supervision (or adult probation). In some cases, a court may stop just short of a guilty verdict and instead place an offender on deferred adjudication that, upon the completion of community supervision or probation requirements, will result in removal of any record of the criminal conviction.

Considering the fact that the state provides a prosecutor to present the facts of the case, thereby attesting to the victim's suffering and need for protection from the defendant, one might wonder whether any necessity exists for a victim to obtain additional legal representation or advice on his or her own. Certainly it cannot hurt in cases where the victim has little familiarity with the criminal justice process or when the risk of further abuse is high. In cases involving disabled victims or children, who may be either the primary victim or offspring of the adult victim or offender in the case, many courts appoint a special attorney (*guardian ad litem*) to look out for the best interests of their clients. In addition, many prosecutor's offices, rape crisis centers, and domestic violence shelters can provide advocates to assist in the support of any crime victim during court proceedings.

Many expenses are incurred by victims of intimate violence for which they have limited opportunities to obtain any financial recovery. Many victims are forced to move great distances and to start over with only the possessions they could carry. They may have experienced significant medical and psychological trauma that requires treatment. Under the Victim of Crime Act of 1984 (VOCA) certain fees and penalties collected from state and federal offenders are utilized to make payments to victims for medical care, counseling, lost earnings, and other expenses directly resulting from a crime. Over $5 billion has been deposited into the VOCA Crime Victims Fund for distribution to state and federal victim assistance programs since its inception. Major changes were made to this act under the USA Patriot Act in 2002, and the current administration has further recommended rescission of the fund by fiscal year 2007, which would leave the fund with a zero balance.[82]

CIVIL CASES: THE RESTRAINING ORDER PATH

As discussed earlier in this chapter, civil orders for protection, also sometimes called *restraining orders*, offer some safety to persons fleeing a dangerous relationship. Available in all 50 states and the District of Columbia, the documents typically command that all abuse, harassment, and threatening behavior by the offender cease. Depending upon applicable state law, persons eligible to obtain an order may include spouses, former spouses, parents, children, siblings, in-laws, common-law spouses, dating partners, a sexual assault victim, unmarried co-parents, foster parents, or foster children. These civil court orders may also contain provisions for:

- Prohibiting contact with the victim at home, school, or work-place;
- Exclusion of the batterer from the home;
- Child custody and visitation;
- Child and spousal support;
- Payment for a victim's expenses (medical, legal, moving);
- Payment of court costs; and
- Participation of the batterer in educational sessions, counseling, or substance abuse treatment.[83]

Many states waive the collection of any court fees for providing protective orders, but private attorneys generally charge a fee for preparing them. A form of protective order often accompanies a divorce or custody suit, particularly when abusive acts have occurred in the marriage. In some states, victims can request orders directly from the court without the aid of an attorney through a *pro se* ("for self") appearance. The process is tedious, but fairly simple, and many courts and organizations assisting abuse victims can assist in preparing the documents necessary for filing an application for a protective order. Filing for a protective order soon after the last abusive incident is a good idea, since evidence is readily available and the imminent risk of danger is credible.

In many states, the process of obtaining a permanent protective order includes a preliminary hearing, at which only the victim (and his or her attorney, if any) appears. A temporary protective order (sometimes called an *ex parte* order) may be issued by the court at this hearing. Notice must be given to the batterer to appear at court for a final hearing on the matter, often set within several weeks; the batterer is by this notice also informed of the allegations made by the victim and is encouraged to seek legal representation. Service of notice may be difficult, as some offenders habitually move frequently in an effort to evade law enforcement officers. At the final hearing, testimony or written affidavits of the victim and witnesses and other credible evidence is offered that a permanent order for protection of the victim is necessary. If the judge finds that intimate violence has occurred, an order will be issued; in some states, the orders are good for up to two years and may be renewable under circumstances of continued danger.

Violations of the criminal provisions of a final protective order are punishable by criminal law, requiring immediate arrest and possible jail sentence. Violations of civil provisions must be handled through civil contempt of court actions, which may also result in eventual arrest. Under VAWA, these remedies are available in all states, tribal areas, and territories and may be also available through military law. A protective order presents a significant disincentive to violent intimate partners, and in many cases the violent behavior ceases as a result. However, it should be remembered that protective orders are pieces of paper, not bulletproof armor or invisible force fields, and they are not accompanied by bodyguards. The importance of arrangements to improve security and preparations for emergency safety procedures cannot be overemphasized.

FAMILY LAW CASES

Family law is perhaps the most difficult route to navigate because there is rarely much evidence as to what actually goes on within a household that is usable in the courtroom. Furthermore, this area of law is laden with emotion on both sides of the dispute, particularly when the couple has children. Family law also varies most broadly from state to state and often permits significant discretionary power to family court judges. As a result, no two family law cases are identical, which makes for uncertain outcomes and anxious parties to each suit. At best, both sides are able to agree upon orders that are fair and offer the hope of more peaceful lives in the future. At worst, these cases can become very contentious and unpleasant. Attorneys often remark that two things you never want to watch being made are sausage and family law. Nonetheless, in cases where the parties are married or when one victim of the violence has children, a family court will be involved.

Like criminal and civil law, family law has gradually evolved over the past 30 years to recognize the imbalance between parties when intimate violence is involved. Change has been slow, and no uniformity in the law exists from state to state. Unfortunately, the same can often be said in regard to the application of law from one judge's court to another. Skilled legal representation is the key to obtaining suitable relief, but this comes at significant cost; some attorneys who provide family law services charge fees of up to several hundred dollars per hour, and a contested case can easily cost in excess of $50,000 to pursue to a close. Legal aid services at nominal cost are often available only for pressing matters, such as protective orders, immigration, or criminal defense cases; in many localities, these organizations are not permitted to represent clients in family law cases at all. This creates an enormous inequality for victims of ordinary means and those who live in areas without legal aid services for family issues. VAWA and VOCA initially provided limited relief in these situations, but little to no money is currently set aside under these federal programs for individual legal aid service.

Provisions in Divorce Agreements

Clauses that may be written into divorce decrees include those ordering separation of assets, spousal support (alimony), child support, and agreements to continue payment for some benefits that were enjoyed by parties to the marriage or their children, such as medical insurance or educational expenses. If there are children, orders will also be written regarding custody, visitation, and other issues relating to the children's daily lives. For most couples obtaining a divorce or legal separation, the standard applied is what is "fair and reasonable" to both sides. For couples with a history of intimate violence, however, this standard can hardly be appropriate. Many state legislatures have altered their family law codes to reflect the power inequality and fear of retaliation that pervades relationships involving violent behavior. Similarly, family law courts have changed their policies by not requiring mediation in cases with domestic violence and by removing suggestions for joint counseling, discontinuing mutual protective orders, and generally taking more interest in and responsibility for ensuring a safe parting of the couple.

Custody, Visitation, and Moving

Changing the courts' views toward parental rights in these cases has been slower. Placement of children with their mothers under the "tender years" doctrine progressed to the common 1970–1980s joint custody doctrine based on the "best interest of the child" principle, which presumed that people who were unable to make their relationship work would somehow manage to co-parent.[84] Again, the law is based upon what is fair and reasonable to parties on equal footing. Battered women's coalitions and social scientists soon recognized not only the inability of some victims to minimize further violence in their children's lives and the effects of that violence, but also the failure of the family law system to fully protect their children. In many cases, marital separation changed nothing; contact between the two households to arrange visitation and transfer of children created the prospect of constant friction. Further complications often arose when the nonviolent parent felt the need to move in order to gain protection from continued threats of abuse, thereby denying the batterer the free exercise of visitation rights. Under joint custody, some courts denied parents who wanted distance from a batterer that right. In some cases, the victim's choice boiled down to staying in the proximity of the batterer or losing custody of the children.

In the late 1990s, some state legislatures began to adopt the Model Code on Domestic and Family Violence of the National Council of

Juvenile and Family Court Judges. The provisions within that code recognize that there is "a rebuttable presumption that it is detrimental to the child and not in the best interest of the child to be placed in sole custody, joint legal custody, or joint physical custody with the perpetrator of family violence."[85] Other sections of the code suggest significant changes to custody agreements, such as suggesting children reside with the nonviolent parent, even if he or she chooses to move to another state. Further, with consideration given to a child's distress and the inherent conflict and danger, the code suggests limits on a parent's visitation based upon prior violent acts, past violations of visitation terms, and any threats to harm or flee with the child. Supervised visitation centers have been developed in many localities to provide a safer environment for visitation and transfer of children.[86] It remains to be seen how many states will incorporate these ideas in their family court decrees and what effects the application of these principles will have upon the children of families torn by violence.

IS LEGAL RECOURSE WORTH THE EFFORT?

There is no simple answer to this question. Certainly, if no legal means of ending the violence is ever attempted, the odds are heavily against any improvement; indeed, people who use violent behavior rarely change without significant cause. However, many advocates who work with victims of intimate violence agree that the use of every legal avenue available to end the violence accomplishes two important goals: first, it sends a clear signal to a victim's abuser, as well as to other batterers, that the violent behavior will not be tolerated; and second, it restores to the victim a sense of power that has long been absent. Once the process of restoring power to a victim begins, it can lead to significant healing and progress in rebuilding a shattered life.

Chapter 8

Therapeutic Interventions for Survivors

Carol Ann Broaddus
Melinda S. Hermanns
Bobbie K. Burks

SEXUAL ASSAULT INTERVENTIONS

One in six women and 1 in 33 men in the United States have been victims of sexual assault or attempted sexual assault during their lifetimes, and 8 out of 10 victims knew their perpetrators.[1] Sexual assault is a largely underreported crime, making it difficult to accurately count the number of cases. A national study of women documented that 84 percent of women in their sample did not report their assaults to the police.[2] A major reason for the nondisclosure is the sociocultural mores and myths that stigmatize and blame victims for their assaults.

Many myths exist about sexual assault. Some of the more prevailing myths are that women lead men on, sometimes women are just asking to be raped, women cannot be raped against their will, anyone can stop rape if they really want to stop it, women often make false accusations of rape, and rape is committed by strangers.

The National College Women Sexual Victimization Study estimated that between one in four and one in five college women experienced completed or attempted rape during their college years.[3] According to the Youth Risk Behavior Surveillance System (YRBSS), a national survey of high-school students, approximately 9 percent of students reported having been forced to have sexual intercourse against their will and female students (11.9 percent) were more likely than male students (6.1 percent) to report having been sexually assaulted.[4] Overall, 12.3 percent of African American students, 10.4 percent of Hispanic students, and 7.3 percent of white students reported forced sexual intercourse.[5]

Sexual assault has abrupt and long-standing consequences that can have devastating biological, psychological, social, and interpersonal health responses. Recovery requires a multidisciplinary approach that focuses on the immediate crisis and exposure to the overwhelming stress of the event. Stress of the assault modifies the personal adjustments and systems of worth for the victim. The consequences of these psychobiologic modifications influence mental and physical health, social adaptation, secondary revictimization experiences, and parenting abilities. Trauma overwhelmingly disturbs the survivors' capacity to direct emotional familiarity by causing them to under- or overreact. These unhealthy responses affect the survivors' ability to construct and sustain healthy relationships.

There are counseling strategies at both basic and advanced intervention levels. Most communities provide a basic level of counseling in the form of 24-hour hotlines for survivors. Hotlines provide information, referral services, and an introduction to a personal contact for future telephone counseling. Although most survivors are able to resume their previous lifestyles, many bear constant emotional trauma such as flashbacks, phobias, nightmares, fear, and other symptoms associated with posttraumatic stress. A severe emotional or psychotic episode may require hospitalization as well as long-term individual psychotherapy.

Factors That Affect Therapy Success

There are numerous and varied personal, event, and environmental factors that have the potential to affect the sexual assault survivor's response and recovery processes. These may include the age and developmental maturity of the victim; her or his relationship to the offender; the ability of the victim to identify and make use of available social support; the response to the attack by police, medical personnel, victim advocates, and loved ones; the frequency, severity, and duration of the assault(s); the setting of the attack; the level of violence and injury inflicted; the response by the criminal justice system; community attitudes and values; and the meaning attributed to the traumatic event by the sexual assault survivor.[6]

The physical consequences associated with sexual victimization include premenstrual syndrome, chronic pelvic pain, gastrointestinal disorders, and a variety of chronic pain disorders such as headache, back pain, and facial pain.[7] Sexually transmitted infection occurs in 4 to 30 percent of patients.[8] Pregnancy results from between 1 and 5 percent of sexual assaults, for approximately 32,000 pregnancies per year.[9]

Sexual assault has immediate and long-term psychological consequences. The immediate impact, comparable to that experienced by victims of war and natural disaster, can exhibit as overt or controlled behaviors. Overt reactions include smiling, tension, agitation, withdrawal, or hysteria, whereas controlled reactions include shock, numbness, disbelief, confusion, indecision, or subdued or masked faces. Somatic reactions during this acute phase may include nausea, anorexia, insomnia, bruises, soreness, or headache. Some of the emotional reactions would be fear, denial, self-blame, anger, guilt, embarrassment, and low self-esteem.

Long-term impact is often experienced in the form of a cluster of symptoms: sleep disturbances, flashbacks, emotional detachment, increased motor activity, intrusive thoughts, violent dreams, fears, and phobias. Those symptoms are usually referred to as PTSD and may be present immediately after the incident. Many victims maintain an abnormal awareness of environmental stimuli, marked by symptoms of frequent nightmares, repetitive anxiety, dreams, insomnia, and intrusive disturbing thoughts. This condition is referred to as *hypervigilance*.

Additional long-term effects often experienced by the victim are depression, alienation, sexual dysfunction, substance abuse, nervousness, anxiety, sleep disturbances, distrust, and suicide. The victims may relive the assault in their minds. Women reporting forced sex are at a significantly greater risk of depression and PTSD than those who have not been abused.[10] Women with a history of sexual assault are more likely to attempt or commit suicide than other women.[11]

Current research suggests that victims experience a multiplicity of debilitating physical and mental health effects from sexual assault, including, but not limited to, posttraumatic stress symptoms (Table 8.1). In addition, survivors may be overwhelmed with the reactions of family, friends, and intimate partners to the assault. Practitioners must be cognizant of the array of diverse behaviors and responses survivors may portray in treatment.

Therapists who work with survivors may experience emotions similar to those of their clients. These emotions are called *secondary traumatic stress, compassion fatigue,* or *vicarious traumatization.* These emotions are more frequently encountered among therapists who have a large number of sexually traumatized clients. Self-care techniques are imperative for persons who provide therapy for the survivors. These persons should also address their acknowledged barriers (lack of appropriate training, unfamiliarity with the issues) and unacknowledged barriers (therapist's personal history, survivor who is unlikable or difficult) to

Table 8.1.
Possible Victim Effects from Sexual Assault

Possible Physical Effects of Sexual Assault
Pain
Injuries
Nausea
Vomiting
Headaches

Possible Emotional/Psychological Effects of Sexual Assault
Shock/denial
Irritability/anger
Depression
Social withdrawal
Numbing/apathy (detachment, loss of caring)
Restricted affect (reduced ability to express emotions)
Nightmares/flashbacks
Difficulty concentrating
Diminished interest in activities or sex
Loss of self-esteem
Loss of security/loss of trust in others
Guilt/shame/embarrassment
Impaired memory
Loss of appetite
Suicidal ideation (thoughts of suicide and death)
Substance abuse
Psychological disorders

Possible Physiological Effects of Sexual Assault
Hypervigilance (always being "on your guard")
Insomnia
Exaggerated startle response (jumpiness)
Panic attacks
Eating problems/disorders
Self-mutilation (cutting, burning, or otherwise hurting oneself)
Sexual dysfunction (not being able to perform sexual acts)
Hyperarousal (exaggerated feelings/responses to stimuli)

Note: Reprinted, by permission of the publisher, from The National Center for Victims of Crime (2004).

providing therapy for these clients, because these issues can influence the effectiveness of the therapy.

The therapist should incorporate the following strategies when counseling sexual assault victims: listen without judging; let them know the assault(s) was not their fault; let them know they did what was necessary to prevent further harm; reassure them that they are cared for and loved; encourage them to seek medical attention; encourage them to talk about the assault(s) with an advocate, mental health professional, or someone they trust; and let them know they do not have to manage this crisis alone.[12]

Moreover, the therapist needs to establish an environment of mutual empathy and mutual respect to engender a trusting rapport and healthy empowerment. The therapist must guide and direct the victims' emotions by actively identifying with and understanding their situation, feelings, and motives. In addition to mutual empathy and respect, constructive "client-professional relationships have a number of necessary components: clear communication, permeable boundaries, authenticity, and accountability."[13]

A safe physical, social, moral, and psychological environment must be ensured to promote healing and encourage disclosure. Psychological safety refers to the ability to be safe in risking self-disclosure, whereas social safety is the ability to be safe in group settings and with other people. Moral safety addresses a value system that consistently supports human growth. Barriers to disclosure may include shame, guilt, fear of retaliation, and insensitive therapist responses. The therapist must provide compassion and understanding without blame and criticism. The therapist must give the survivor hope.

The survivor will exhibit many emotions that are destructive or objectionable. However, these overwhelming and uncontrollable emotions are the survivor's only coping methods. Because the survivor has experienced helplessness, isolation, confusion, anger, powerlessness, and frustration, the therapist must focus on empowerment as one of the most important coping mechanisms for the client to use in overcoming those emotions. Additionally, the therapist must encourage and allow the survivor to grieve. As grief accompanies any significant traumatic event, unresolved grief postpones the recovery process.

Depression and suicidal ideations are common sequelae of sexual assault. Any stimuli that trigger the survivor's memory of the traumatic event may activate a reliving of the traumatic state. Depression is far more common in persons who have not disclosed the assault to others. Nondisclosure may be due to the legal, social, cultural, or personal implications.

PTSD is the expansion of characteristic attributes that follow an extreme traumatic stressor, which involves a personal encounter with actual or threatened physical injury or death. The victim may be a bystander, but he or she can still perceive the threats of death or injury as being real. Although the lifetime prevalence of PTSD in the United States is estimated at 7.8 percent, the occurrence may vary according to the intensity of the trauma.[14] Women are twice as likely as men to develop PTSD. The most traumatic events for women are sexual assault, sexual molestation, physical childhood abuse, and physical assault with or without a weapon.[15] Thirty-one percent of all sexual assault survivors develop PTSD during their lifetime, and 10 percent of these survivors still have persistent symptoms of PTSD.[16] There appears to be a positive correlation in individuals who develop PTSD following a trauma and have a family history of PTSD, anxiety, depression, or antisocial personality. Although there is no known cure for PTSD, treatment includes a variety of psychotherapeutic techniques, such as cognitive-behavioral therapy, group therapy, and exposure therapy, as well as psychopharmacological agents.[17] Regardless of the treatment technique, therapy should always encourage disclosure of the traumatic event.

Psychometric assessment instruments are available that measure the severity of sexual assault outcomes and can be used initially and in subsequent sessions. These instruments include the Clinical Trauma Assessment (CTA), Impact of Event Scale, Rape Aftermath Symptom Test (RAST), Rape Trauma Syndrome Rating Scale (RTSRS), and Sexual Assault Symptoms Scale (SASS). The CTA assesses the immediate aftermath of sexual assault and is completed by the clinician. The Impact of Event Scale assesses symptoms of intrusion and avoidance of the previous week. The RAST measures the survivor's level of distress from a particular item. The RTSRS assesses the degree of symptoms of the trauma. The SASS is a self-report used immediately after the assault. Assessments should be conducted prior to therapeutic interventions to ascertain a baseline of cognitive functioning and provide a direction for the type of therapy.

Stages of Recovery

Although there are many descriptions of the emotions and behaviors that victims experience after a sexual assault, victims have a predictable set of responses to recovery.[18,19,20,21,22,23,24,25,26,27] Koss and Harvey best summarize these responses as anticipatory, impact, reconstitution, and resolution.

The *anticipatory stage* encompasses the victim's initial interaction, which illuminates a potentially dangerous state. Victims "report the use of defense mechanisms such as disassociation, suppression, and rationalization to preserve their illusion of invulnerability."[28] The *impact phase* is the actual crime coupled with the experience outcomes. The victim "of a sudden, unexpected attack of violence will initially respond with shock, numbness, and disbelief . . . the reaction of fear is so profound and overwhelming that the victim feels hopeless about getting away."[29] Extreme guilt may accompany the aftermath, because the victim perceives that he or she was ineffective in handling the assault. The victim may present in either of two behavior styles during the impact phase. According to Burgess and Holstrom, the controlled style is covert, which may present as a calm and subdued appearance or one of shock and disbelief, whereas the expressed style displays open verbal and nonverbal behaviors such as crying, restlessness, smiling, and anger. There may be a compound reaction that accompanies the impact phase due to unresolved social and emotional issues. This is particularly true if the victim has not resolved a prior sexual abuse issue. Within the first several weeks of the impact phase, somatic reactions to the physical trauma will present as skeletal muscle tension, gastrointestinal, and genitourinary complaints. Victims who were assaulted in their bed are particularly distressed with insomnia.[30]

In the *reconstitution phase*, the victim has a superficial and mechanical adjustment to the return to basic activities of daily living. This phase may resemble "the denial encountered by an individual going through the grieving process."[31] The length of this phase is dependent upon whether the victim chooses to press charges against the perpetrator. "Reconstitution cannot take place until the prosecution process has been completed."[32]

Resolution is the final phase and is usually accompanied by intense anger, which may be inappropriately directed to therapist, friends, and family. This phase is highly dependent upon the degree of resolution the victim has achieved with the assault.

Methods of Therapy

Cognitive-behavioral therapy (CBT) can be effectual in reducing immediate postsexual assault fear and anxiety indicators. Didactic techniques serve to educate survivors about the myths of sexual assault and the techniques of anxiety reduction. CBT encompasses many forms of therapy (flooding, prolonged exposure treatment, desensitization, stress inoculation training), but these approaches entail systematic exposure to the traumatic memories and cognitive reinterpretation of the actions. Continued exposure to the feared events may help to gradually lessen the clients' short-term anxiety and fear-related behaviors. Clients should be encouraged to challenge automatic thoughts to discount the guilt, fear, and anxiety emotions. This cognitive technique helps to instill more positive self-talk, which will empower the clients to decrease their degree of self-promoting causation.

Feminist therapy (FT) helps the survivor focus on the longer term symptoms of guilt, shame, and self-blame, while learning that sexual assault is a global societal issue and not an individual one. Although additional research is necessary in the area of application of FT and its effect on survivors, available data propose that FT may be an effectual technique.[33] A critical component of feminist analysis in therapy is the cultural context in which the sexual assault exists and the identification of gender roles in intimate associations. The prevalence of sexual assault is a compilation of myths, power disparities between sexes, and gender role socialization.[34] FT attempts to create an egalitarian therapeutic model relationship and empower the clients to displace helplessness. Clients are encouraged to discern the way in which their power was taken from them and to reestablish healthy control and outcomes in their lives.

Group therapy is recommended as an avenue for survivors to process self-blame following the assault and to thwart stigmatization. A support group setting allows survivors to share experiences, breaking the isolation that many of them experience and allowing them to develop new supportive relationships. However, if a survivor has a preexisting psychological issue, group therapy may be inappropriate. Adjunctive techniques that may assist in anxiety reduction, self-awareness, and empowerment may include journaling, meditation, yoga, dancing, painting, music, biofeedback, self-defense or assertive training, guided imagery, and survivor groups. Trauma incident reduction,[35] emotional freedom techniques,[36] and eye movement desensitization and reprocessing (EMDR)[37] are newer psychotherapeutic methodologies.

Francine Shapiro developed EMDR, which uses eye movements to process communication to different parts of the brain. Although initially a controversial psychotherapy method, research has supported it as a successful treatment modality for treating PTSD and anxiety disorders. The model purports that "all memory is associated, and that learning occurs through the creation of new associations" while "addressing those experiences which are dysfunctionally rather that adaptively stored."[38] EMDR "focuses not just on a person's troubled feelings, but on the thoughts, physical sensations, behaviors related to those feelings as well."[39] For victims of a single trauma, treatment length may be swift, whereas victims with multiple traumas or fewer support systems may require a lengthy treatment plan.

According to Shapiro, EMDR is responsible for the following:

It catalyzes learning and is used to help the client learn from negative experiences from the past, desensitize present triggers that are inappropriately distressing, and incorporate templates for appropriate future action that allow the client to excel individually and within her interpersonal system.[40]

The fundamental aim of treatment is "for the client to achieve the most profound and comprehensive effects possible, in the shortest period of time, while maintaining stability, within a balanced system."[41] EMDR has eight phases of treatment. Each phase has a specific goal or treatment modality that needs to be achieved before the next phase is begun.

In addition to cognitive-behavioral and adjunctive therapies, psychopharmacologic interventions assist significantly in alleviating symptoms and promoting normal functioning in victims who present with anxiety, PTSD, depression, or persistent obsessive thoughts (Table 8.2). The drug class for treatment of an anxiety disorder is dependent upon the type of anxiety. PTSD is classified as an anxiety disorder subtype and is treated with benzodiazepines, tricyclic antidepressants (TCAs), monoamine oxidase inhibitors (MAOIs), and SSRIs. TCAs and MAOIs are a second- and third-line use.[42] The treatment of choice appears to be the SSRIs as combination treatments for PTSD, but they are poorly documented and frequently used.[43] Depressive behavioral symptoms coupled with PTSD and obsessive thoughts may respond to TCAs as well as SSRIs. Obsessive thoughts may require the addition of atypical antipsychotics such as risperidone (Risperdal) or olanzapine (Zyprexa), whereas TCAs promote sleep.[44] Caution must be advised with the addition of benzodiazepines, because they have the potential to lose efficacy and create dependency.

Table 8.2
Psychopharmacological Treatment of Sexual Assault Victims

Disorder	Benzodiazepines: Xanax Valium Ativan	Non-Benzodiazepine Anxiolytic: BuSpar	SSRIs: Zoloft Paxil Prozac	TCAs: Tofranil Elavil Pamelor	MAOIs: Parnate Nardil Luvox
Generalized anxiety	X	X		X	
PTSD	X		X	X	X
Obsessive thoughts		X	X	X	
Depression			X	X	X

Note: SSRIs = selective serotonin reuptake inhibitors; TCAs = tricyclic antidepressants; MAOIs = monoamine oxidase inhibitors; PTSD = posttraumatic stress disorder.

Creating Healthy Relationships

April has been recognized as Sexual Assault Awareness Month. A positive approach to raising awareness and promoting prevention of sexual violence is to focus on creating healthy, respectful relationships. The CDC recommends emphasis on the following key concepts for developing healthy relationships.

Relationships are imperfect, and partners may have projected feelings of anger and frustration at times; this is normal. However, feelings of fear, lack of control, or humiliation are not a basis for a normal relationship. Partners should feel respected and loved while maintaining a sense of self. To encourage a healthy relationship, respect another person's decision to say no to sexual activity.

Communication is an essential element in a healthy relationship. Again, respect the other person's opinions, feelings, and values. Be comfortable about addressing and inquiring about sex. Take time to actively listen to the other person's viewpoints, and directly and clearly express your thoughts and feelings without confronting or belittling another person. Never pressure others into doing something that they have verbalized a desire not to do.

Family and friends are important keys to a healthy relationship and they are the source of many values, beliefs, and attitudes. They should also be a source of comfort and love. If this is not the case, speak up and address the issues of physical and emotional abuse. Conduct this confrontation in a realm of safety. It is important to let the abuser know of inappropriate sexual behavior.

Healthy relationships are built upon respect, trust, and honesty. If a partner does not desire to have sexual activity, honor that request. Violence is never acceptable under any circumstances. Violence does not always imply physical abuse; abuse may be emotional, sexual, or psychological.

Physical safety is the absence of verbal, sexual, emotional, and physical violence, suicidality, and self-destructive behavior. It encompasses the freedom from substance abuse and other addictions and the avoidance of unnecessary risks while maintaining good health practices. Physical safety includes shelter, food, clothing, health, nonviolent disciplinary practices, and the ability to perceive and avoid danger.

Safety does not only mean physical safety but also entails moral/ethical, social, and psychological safety. All of these areas must be addressed to create a truly safe environment. A morally and ethically safe environment is one that allows an unending ethical discourse and encourages commitment to human rights and life, respect, integrity, and courage.

Social safety is safety with others, such as in personal attachments and groups. Rape crisis centers and domestic violence programs provide social support and are usually community-based organizations. They traditionally offer 24-hour hotlines, short-term crisis counseling services, and accompaniment to hospital and court appointments. These organizations have a nonprofit status. Victim assistance programs provide economic support in terms of compensation services to survivors who report abuse to the police department, and they are usually funded through the state attorney general's office.

Community Support

The health care system offers acute care in assessment and treatment of injuries, initiation of preventive measures, provision of medical and emotional referrals, and collection of evidence. Medical personnel may be the first provider for the survivor and will begin the chain of events to promote the healing process and ensure a safe environment. Confidentiality is of primary consideration as is the establishment and safeguard of a caring health care environment. Other social supports are churches, religious groups, friends, and spouses. The encouragement of adaptive responses includes supportive empathy and expression of fears without fear of criticism.

Involvement of the multiple agencies (crisis and advocacy centers) and disciplines (emergency room departments, law enforcement, and judiciary) is imperative to the establishment of effective services. Regularly scheduled multidisciplinary meetings are necessary to ensure and maintain consistency, coordination, education, information, and engagement. Community support can be further optimized by developing or improving a community sexual assault response team network that includes community leaders as well as minority representation. Outreach development to neighboring schools would further strengthen the community's sexual mores.

Creating a Healthy Environment

Psychological safety is recognition of being able to be safe with oneself and the ability to protect oneself from self-destructive behaviors and to protect oneself by distancing from vulnerable positions. Sexual assault takes from the survivor a personal integrity and a clear and integrated sense of self. Attention and focus energies should be placed on self-knowledge, -efficacy, -esteem, -empowerment, -control, and -discipline.

To reduce the survivor's vulnerability, four types of safety elements should be addressed: physical safety (bodily safety), psychological safety (safe with oneself), social safety (safe with others), and ethical safety (safe with the world of values). Physical safety encompasses the following components: provision for basic needs; intolerance to physical, emotional, and sexual violence; absence of suicidal or self-destructive behavior; absence of substance abuse; safe sexual behavior and avoidance of risk-taking behaviors; good health practices; and ability to perceive or avoid danger. Psychological safety is the insurance of self-protection, -knowledge, -efficacy, -esteem, -empowerment, -control, and –discipline. Social safety includes a safe social network of both interpersonal and community attachments. To promote ethical safety, the survivor behaviors would include honesty, courage, integrity, respect, commitment to human rights, and commitment to life.

In summary, the development of healthy relationships is essential. Sexual assault victims may be at a higher risk of developing depression than the general population. The incidence of suicide increases in depressed individuals. "Studies estimate that 1/3 of women who are raped contemplate suicide, and 17 percent of rape victims actually attempt suicide."[45] The therapist should always remain cognizant of this fact and should assess for suicidal ideations by direct closed-end questioning.

TREATMENT CONSIDERATIONS AND STRATEGIES FOR BATTERED WOMEN

> Their pain is acute; their confusion becomes ours. What can be done for them and their children? These women clearly recognize that they are both hurt and hurters, victims and perpetrators. They also watched their siblings or mother or father hurt, and thus they are also observers. Whether they fill the role of victim, perpetrator, or observer depends on time and circumstance. For now, in this group, they are victims. The object of the first phase of treatment is to both recognize and realize how they were abused and neglected. They have to remember many painful events.[46]

In positing intervention methods and evaluating their potential positive outcomes, clinicians and advocates must take into consideration the healing journey of the survivor; specifically, the point in that journey at which the victim presents for treatment. An individual who is still in an abusive situation has a different set of needs than one who has escaped or fled the relationship. Therefore, it is vital to complete an extensive and thorough psychosocial and relationship history prior to developing a long-term treatment plan. Information gained through this process will help set the course of future efforts. The setting of the initial meeting between the professional and the victim is also important. Physicians who encounter the physical results of relationship violence will need an immediate intervention plan, whereas a counselor who meets with an individual in a shelter environment will certainly have different considerations.

A number of situations and personalities may present in the initial and subsequent stages of healing. Each has a separate set of considerations and possibilities.

The "Shopper," or a Victim Seeking the Power to Leave an Abusive Situation

Scenario: A woman accompanies a friend to a local crisis center appointment to provide support as the friend seeks shelter or support for her effort to free herself from an abusive relationship. As the counselor works with the friend, the companion appears to be taking more than a passing interest in the conversation and information provided.

Strategies: The development of a safety plan for both women is an essential component of this meeting. In the case of domestic terrorism, it is vital for the professional to lead the victim(s) through the steps for seeking disengagement and refuge from an abusive partner. Personal or physical safety is the number one consideration. Some victims may feel that an open confrontation with the abuser will be safe, especially if there is someone there to help defuse any potential immediate retaliation from the abuser who is faced with losing the base of his or her power. Many safety plans encourage the victim to make preparations well ahead of the planned leaving date. If possible, the victim should establish independent financial sources (such as a personal bank account) that will help her self-support after leaving the abuser. The victim should have extra sets of car and house keys and copies of insurance policies, marriage documents, birth certificates, retirement plans, income tax returns, and other important documents. The victim also needs to inform someone of her intention to leave; this person will serve as a contact point and confidante to help with the processing of feelings and fears. The door is always left open for the "shopper" to return to the crisis center to gather strength and further strategies for self-liberation.

Victim Needing Immediate/Emergency Intervention

Scenario: A woman is delivered to the local crisis center office as the result of law enforcement intervention in a domestic violence call. She is visibly shaken, with her emotions running the gamut from relief at being out of the situation to expressing a panicked concern for her abuser. Her physical injuries are not life-threatening, but bruises are beginning to show on various parts of her body, including finger marks around her neck. She has been forced to flee her home without any belongings due to the severity of the attack and volatility of her attacker. The authorities have taken her preliminary statement, but inform her (and the advocate) that they will want to ask more questions later. She is left in the interview room with little more than a tissue and the clothes on her back.

Strategies: At this point, the primary focus of the clinician is to help the client stabilize her emotions and relieve the effects of her ordeal. Adrenaline is still running in her system, making it essential that the clinician establish an atmosphere of safety and build rapport quickly. The attitude and actions of the clinician in establishing a therapeutic relationship are always an important part of the healing process, but they are most crucial at the beginning of the healing journey. The woman is still a victim at this juncture, and a major task for the professional is to model the ability to breathe, think, and connect. Providing ice for injuries (unless contraindicated by the need of medical documentation), a cool drink, and a relaxing environment are good initial steps. Again, the demeanor of the clinician is vital in providing a sense of safety and connection that will allow the victim to follow basic self-soothing instructions, such as breathing relaxation and purposeful muscle tension relief. The victim will respond best if the information-gathering process is done with empathy and compassion, with adequate explanation about the rationale for the questions asked and reassurance about her present safety from further physical or emotional harm. For this reason, persons who will have initial stage contact with victims should be chosen on the basis of their ability to respond with the care skills needed to enable the victim's recovery. The lack of these skills on the part of the professional can severely hinder, if not completely derail, the process. Persons called to this type of work must be high in empathy and boundary abilities.

Meeting the primary set of needs presented by a victim can pave the way for a better experience for both the interviewer and interviewee. Visually assess the client for clothing or comfort issues. A blanket or wrap to cover shivering shoulders can add to the client's sense of safety and can reduce the fear that can interfere with the disclosure process. Hunger, thirst, facilities and supplies for personal hygiene (unless evidence collection requirements force a postponement of doing so), and other considerations may provide the relief that will assist the beginning of healing. Move through the interview process at a speed comfortable to the victim. Let her know that she may answer questions in her own time and in her own way—even in her primary language if she would prefer (interpreters should be available if the clinic is located in a multicultural area). It is helpful for the initial contact person to speak in a calm, reassuring tone and to reinforce the elements of personal safety and the limits of confidentiality as they pertain to the ethics of the professional and the healing environment. It may be necessary to provide verbal reassurance to the victim repeatedly throughout the interview process to empower disclosure and to bridge silences stemming from fear or memory lapses due to the trauma experience. The goals of this initial session are to defuse the situation for the victim and then to provide a debriefing opportunity that will promote processing of information and de-escalating of emotions.

The need for safe shelter must be assessed, and the victim should be encouraged to consider her needs for security in any location she chooses after the interview session. Advocacy may be provided to the victim in subsequent meetings with authorities and other officials who need facts from the client. The provision of such a companion through the process of reporting, medical examinations, and prosecution of the abuser may make the difference between a rapid and healthy or complicated and prolonged recovery.

Unfortunately, it is possible that despite the best efforts of clinicians, advocates, law enforcement personnel, medical trauma specialists, crisis centers, and others, victims will choose to return to their abusers or move on to situations in their family of origin that will undo any progress made through initial healing efforts. Those involved in intervention work must be aware of the recidivism potential for victims given their lifelong patterns of accepting abusive behaviors and immature self-concepts that predispose them to victimization by persons who seek to fill their own power and control needs through the disempowerment of others.

Victim Moving to Survivor Status

Scenario: The same individual comes to the crisis center location several days or weeks following the abusive incident. The threat of immediate danger is past, and she presents as ready and willing to explore events through the more productive lenses of hindsight.

Strategies: The goals of this stage of intervention differ dramatically from the crisis stabilization focus of the initial meeting(s). The foci now shift to beginning the exploration of the abusive relationship for its past importance and future impact and beginning to empower the victim to engage in insight-gathering and truth-finding activities. It would be optimal to have contact with the victim over a period of time long enough to allow for full processing and integration of events and life lessons to set the stage for lasting growth or change, but the majority of victims will not choose to engage in counseling long enough to permanently impact their future choices. Many will return to their abusers, often leaving the counselor feeling frustrated and without the satisfaction of seeing their charge heal and move forward to productivity and healthier choices.

When the victim does make the effort to seek insight, the professional can lead her into a soul-searching exercise that helps her understand the predisposing factors for the relationship (i.e., why the victim chose the partner) and, if the experience is judged as unproductive or unpleasant (and therefore not desirable of repeating), how to form templates of judgment to avoid similar choices in the future. The counselor needs to obtain a more detailed client history, including family of origin information and impressions,[47] to enhance a platform for identifying the client's decision-making and problem-solving skills that led to the abusive involvement. This base of knowledge and understanding may hasten the healing process by allowing a cognitive restructuring process that has the potential to impact the individual's life planning strategies and outcomes. In the cognitive restructuring process, events are examined in terms of their outcomes and the automatic thought processes (cognitive distortions or filters) that serve as the lenses through which the client views these events. The ultimate goal of this restructuring is to change these lenses and thus change future choices and outcomes. The client is introduced to restructuring through a psychoeducational process wherein the professional explains the connection between events and actions and their outcomes or consequences. The process centers on three areas: emotions, physiological reactions, and behavioral choices. Behavioral choices are made as a result of the meanings the client attaches to the event by filtering the experience through automatic thoughts that reflect her life rule system. When the victim slows down this filtering process and demonstrates her mastery of challenging and changing automatic thoughts, she is better capable of making future choices that are unencumbered by unrealistic or irrational expectations.

This period of intensive work can provide an opportunity for the victim to learn self-regulation strategies for handling the many symptoms of their abusive past. Anxiety-reducing techniques such as systematic desensitization, relaxation breathing, progressive muscle relaxation, stress inoculation, and guided imagery can help change the client's internal state. Confronting her anxiety in a clinical setting can help the client with any posttraumatic stress symptom difficulty and, combined with cognitive restructuring efforts, can give her powerful tools for combating conditions that might lead to reentry into victimization and helplessness.

Provision of social supports is critical to the victim's recovery. Crisis centers, shelters, religious institutions, and even governmental agencies have been forerunners in engendering synergy between community service providers and individuals who need direction or resources to start a new life. This network of social support is another tool the victim can use to change her life prediction paradigms, allowing success and peace to take the place of hopelessness and failure.

Individual intervention is important at this point in the victim's journey, but the greatest and most rapid progress can often be seen in victims who engage in group processing of events and perceptions. Healing support groups provide a safe locale for the victim to try out new coping skills, such as active listening; assertive communication of thoughts, feelings, wants and needs; boundary recognition, communication, and consistent enforcement; and situational ethics. Practice with situational ethics helps the victim work on potential problem areas and set up templates of resolve that will keep them safe in the future.[48] The psychoeducational process continues in group settings; victims at differing stages of recovery offer help and hope to those just beginning their journeys. It is essential that the counselor who facilitates this group exhibit and enforce good boundary-setting and enforcement skills; the counselor will provide what is perhaps the first positive role model for victims to emulate as they chart their future course.

Survivor Moving to Victor Status

Scenario: After a prolonged period in one-on-one counseling and mentoring as well as in group processing, the victim feels more capable and competent to use her new skills outside of the safety of the counseling environment.

Strategies: As victims move toward survivor status, they will often express the desire to "pay forward" the privileges they have gained through the healing process. Many will seek places of leadership in group meetings, taking on the role of senior advisors to victims entering the process. Others will take time off from active participation in healing activities, but then will return and seek positions as volunteers or employees of agencies that provide services to victims. It is important that the crisis center or counseling program has a plan for keeping the healing victims involved as hotline responders, on-call advocates, policy board members, and more. It is also important for community resources to provide these opportunities to ensure that the survivors continue on a path that will result in them becoming integral and productive members of the local society. For all the power of counseling and advocacy training, there is no intervention more potent than that of the survivor giving hope to an individual who has none.

The victors now find themselves in the position of choosing to widen their circle of social support by joining a religious group or an educational organization that promotes scholarship opportunities for victims who seek to better their life circumstances through higher learning. The survivors internalize these external sources of support, and these victim-survivor-victors move even further forward and take full control of their destiny through self-motivation and an inherent belief in their ability not only to survive, but to thrive.

The healing journey does not end at this point. Growth continues through each day the fully functioning individual awakens and greets another opportunity to be free from oppression, fear, and shame.

Working to become free from abuse takes personal commitment and perseverance; it also offers tremendous liberation. As you go forward, acknowledge yourself and pay tribute to your strength, courage, and persistence. Build your nonabusive life with joy as well as dedication. Take care of yourself and those you love. Enjoy your safety, your peace, your happiness, your children, and your future. And remember to share and give of what you have learned to others.[49]

Chapter 9

Effects of Class and Culture on Intimate Partner Violence

Shelly L. Marmion
Donna Lee Faulkner

*What women don't understand is that there is a difference in cultures . . . .
[but] violence is there . . . It's in White homes, it's in Black homes, it's in
Hispanic homes, and it's in Asian homes. I mean, I know it's there. It's just
a matter, I think, of how you get brought up and whether you let yourself
believe that that's the way it's supposed to be. You can change things.*

—Unidentified Mexican American man[1]

OVERVIEW OF INTIMATE PARTNER VIOLENCE
AGAINST WOMEN OF COLOR

We are only too aware of the intimate partner violence that occurs
around us every day. One need only hear the names of Laci Peterson
or Lori Hacking—both women whose husbands were convicted of their
murders—and memories of extensive national media coverage immediately come to mind. But is there a woman of color who immediately
comes to mind from national press coverage because she was reported
missing and who was subsequently found to have been murdered by a
boyfriend or husband?

A huge part of the problem of intimate partner violence against
women of color is its invisibility. Although intimate partner violence
against women of color is just as physically, psychologically, and

emotionally harmful as it is for their white counterparts, it tends to be invisible. It is invisible in the sense that victims of intimate partner violence of non–Anglo American descent do not receive equivalent national media coverage. In fact, this lack of attention extends to most persons of color who have experienced violent crime. A sense of frustration regarding this issue was eloquently expressed by Dolores Childs in a petition created by the African American/Ethnic Community and Other Concerned Citizens and addressed to the *Today Show*, *Good Morning America*, and the national broadcast media during the search for the killer(s) of the little African American girl known at the time as Precious Doe.[2] "The African American/Ethnic people of the United States of America," the petition began, "are insulted and outraged at the broadcast media's lack of coverage for missing African American/Ethnic children." Thus far, 8,148 people have signed the petition.[3] Similarly, numerous Internet blogs have questioned the intense media exposure surrounding the disappearance and search for Natalee Holloway from her school trip to Aruba, while virtually ignoring the plight of many other girls who disappeared around the same time, such as Reyna Gabriella Alvarado-Carerra.[4]

The problem of invisibility in African American and other ethnic communities goes much deeper than a lack of national media coverage with regard to intimate partner violence. Invisibility also has occurred within the research arena, as attempts to document and investigate intimate partner violence within different ethnic and cultural communities began decades later than for "mainstream" Americans.

CULTURE AND ETHNICITY

Culture has been defined as the "beliefs, practices, values, norms, and behaviors that are shared by members of a group."[5] A society's culture often greatly influences the way its people perceive and interpret their world. Culture is generally passed down through and among generations. It might include teachings about history, food, traditions, and dress, for example. More important, culture also consists of attitudes, values, and beliefs, all of which influence behaviors. In the U.S. culture, the term *ethnicity* is used to refer to particular groups of non–Anglo Americans and their communities. So, for example, Asian Americans comprise a broad ethnic category that consists of people who have immigrated to the United States from many parts of Asia. Asian American families may have originally immigrated from one of at least 29 different countries such as China, the Philippines, Japan, Malaysia, India, Korea, Indonesia, Cambodia, and Vietnam.[6] Similarly, Hispanic Americans include people from numerous and diverse countries of origin including Mexico, Puerto Rico, Cuba, and many countries of

Central and South America. Even though each group within broader ethnic categories tends to share some cultural traditions, there will also be considerable differences between individuals or communities whose countries of origin are different.

In studies in which the prevalence of domestic violence within particular ethnic groups or subcultures in the United States has been examined, there is a tendency to blame the culture for the prevalence of battering, particularly if those rates are higher than the U.S. average. Anglo Americans often assume that minority cultures are more accepting of the abuse of women and that the influence of a minority group's culture is purely negative.[7] They fail to recognize that violence against women among members of the dominant Anglo American culture is similarly a reflection of the values and practices of "mainstream" culture.

All people exist within a cultural context, or combination of cultural contexts, but that context is less obvious to persons from the dominant or defining culture for a given society. It should be clear from the previous chapters of this book that many forms of violence against women are too common in virtually every American community and that American culture contains values, beliefs, and practices that support and maintain continued violence. Nevertheless, when violence occurs within immigrant communities or communities of color, it is often assumed that the behavior reflects the culture, rather than the individual, which serves to reinforce harmful cultural stereotypes.

On the other hand, there are cases in which batterers have used a cultural defense to justify brutal acts against their female partners.[8]

> Doug Lau Chen . . . a Chinese immigrant man in New York beat his wife to death with a hammer in 1987. Doug Lau Chen defended his actions by stating that in China, if a man believes his wife to be unfaithful, he has the right to kill her because she has brought shame upon him. Professor Pasternak from Hunter College [an anthropologist specializing in Chinese culture] provided expert testimony to verify that Chen's statement and actions under the circumstances were that of a "reasonable Chinese man."[9]

In this case, Mr. Chen's culture of origin was used as a defense against charges that his act constituted spousal murder. This defense was accepted, and Mr. Chen was found not guilty of murder.

GENDER INEQUALITIES

Patriarchy is a term used to describe a societal structure that is male centered and male identified and in which there is the prevalent belief that the man is the rightful head of the family. As such, men have power and authority over the women and children within the family unit, and this role passes directly from the father to the eldest son.[10] In patriarchal cultures worldwide, the social structure is one in which the most powerful roles in most sectors of society are held predominantly by men. Although not every man is powerful, male roles are organized around the concept of control. Such cultures are also male identified in that the personal attributes that are highly valued, such as strength and independence, are associated with men, whereas the attributes associated with women are less valued. Thus, a patriarchal culture is one in which gender inequality is maintained and promoted by the social structure. Research across cultures has consistently found that the lower the status of women within a culture, the greater the prevalence of rape and other forms of violence against women.[11] Thus, there appears to be a clear link between gender inequality and such violence. Within U.S. subcultures, however, such a link is indirect and tenuous, at best. Consider the following examples.

Those who have studied intimate partner violence within the Asian American community often point to the concept of patriarchy as being a possible contributor to intimate partner violence. Asian cultures are strongly patriarchal. The women from traditional Asian communities, for example, are often expected to observe the "three obediences."[12] These three obediences are obedience to their fathers before marriage, obedience to their husbands during marriage, and obedience to their sons during old age.[13] This family structure emphasizes the importance of the men and relegates the women in the family to a subordinate status. Another sociocultural distinction between many Asian cultures and the dominant U.S. culture is the emphasis on the family rather than the individual as the basic social unit and on self-worth as measured in terms of the success achieved by or for the entire family as a unit rather than by each family member.[14] Accomplishment and achievement in the Asian American family brings respect and honor, not to the individual but to the entire family, and misbehavior by any member brings shame or a loss of honor to the family. These norms create a climate in which the husband may feel entitled to forcefully correct any behavior perceived as inappropriate on the part of his wife or children to protect the family from the shame or dishonor such behavior would bring. Although Asian American cultures adhere to a patriarchal family structure and family-based code of honor, these factors alone do not explain the occurrence of intimate partner violence. After all, intimate partner violence does not occur in all homes where these traditional cultural values are held. When the prevalence of domestic violence has been measured in Asian American communities, reports of intimate partner violence tend to be lower than those for other racial categories.[15] These rates may reflect a tendency not to report domestic violence to the authorities. Under-reporting may be due to a greater acceptance of violence against women or an emphasis on preserving the family and "saving face." A fact sheet compiled by the Asian & Pacific Islander Institute on Domestic Violence reports that prevalence rates gathered in a large number of studies of specific Asian American groups are at least as high as those reported for the general population.[16]

Many African American families, on the other hand, are found to be considerably less male centered, perhaps as a result of the history of slavery. When people from the West African coast were brought to the United States and enslaved, both the male and female slaves were purchased to provide labor, and African slave women worked side-by-side with the male slaves.[17] Additionally, slaves were generally barred from forming family units, because it would interfere with the buying and selling of individual slaves. In present times, the African American woman is more likely than women in other cultural groups to work outside the home and is less likely to be married to the man who fathers her children, both of which would suggest a less patriarchal family structure. Despite the relative strength of the African American woman within both family and community, prevalence of reported intimate partner violence has consistently been measured as higher than for other ethnic groups. These higher rates probably reflect a number of factors, including environmental stressors and perhaps a greater willingness to report intimate violence.

Thus, the causes of any human behavior such as intimate partner violence are complex. Rather than looking to any one factor as the cause of violence, we should assume that a combination of factors contributes to the occurrence of intimate partner violence regardless of the community in which it occurs. We must consider other factors that contribute to the incidence of domestic violence.

VIOLENCE AND THE INTERSECTION OF OPPRESSIONS

The remains [Tamika Antonette Huston, African American woman] were found in a wooded area along Tyger River Road in . . . South Carolina. He [Christopher Hampton, African American male] told a reporter that he was ironing clothes before work and threw a hot iron at 24-year-old Tamika Huston and hit her in the head as they argued about money. . . . Huston and Hampton had dated for two or three months, he said. But another woman was bearing his child. Huston, he said, asked him for money but he refused, saying that he was saving money so he could take care of his baby. "She said, 'You care about the baby more than you care about me,'" Hampton said. "I just got mad—I just threw the iron," he said. "I didn't mean for it to hit her."[18]

A growing number of studies in the past two decades are giving voice to the battered women from a wide range of formerly excluded or ignored communities. Scholars have come increasingly to realize that although there are usually some commonalities in the experiences of domestic violence within different communities and across all cultural groups, there are also important differences that must be considered. These differences are often linked to the specific intersections of race, class, and culture that make up the context in which the battering occurs. For women who experience multiple oppressions such as racism, ethnocentrism, class privilege, or heterosexism, these forms of oppression will interact with or modify the oppression produced by gender inequality.[19] To provide effective interventions to such marginalized women, we must understand these interlocking forms of oppression and the unique struggles they produce in any specific case.[20]

The first report to consider the prevalence of intimate partner violence in a non–Anglo American community, National Family Violence Survey in 1986, looked at intimate partner violence experienced by both women and men in Anglo and African American families.[21] In their ground-breaking survey, the researchers reported that intimate partner violence against women in African American families was much more prevalent than in Anglo families. Surprised by the racial disparity in these numbers, researchers began to look more closely at the prevalence of intimate partner violence not only within the African American community but also within several other ethnic and cultural communities in the United States.

Studies conducted in subsequent decades vary across contexts, but they have a consistent finding that poor women of color are the most likely to be involved in dangerous relationships.[22] There is also increasing evidence that the most severe and lethal domestic violence occurs at higher rates among these low-income women of color.[23] The risk factors, however, are most likely not race or culture *per se* but are those factors related to living in poverty, often within the context of poor and more violent neighborhoods, high unemployment, and limited resources.

A recent report by the National Institute of Justice in 2004 describes research that merged data from a national survey and the U.S. Census to examine the context in which domestic violence occurs. Again, the study found that the rate of intimate violence against women in African American couples is almost twice that of Anglo couples. To find out why, the study considered levels of economic distress, community disadvantage, race, and ethnicity and concluded that African Americans are more likely than whites to suffer economic distress and to live in disadvantaged neighborhoods.

The researchers also found that the economic status of African Americans and Hispanics does not match the economic status of the neighborhoods in which they live. For example, 36 percent of the African American couples were economically disadvantaged, but twice that many (77 percent) lived in disadvantaged neighborhoods. The pattern for Hispanics was similar. The researchers found that the higher rates of intimate violence could be accounted for by the high levels of economic distress and the greater likelihood of living in disadvantaged neighborhoods. Disadvantaged neighborhoods are dangerous places to live, with higher rates of crime and all forms of violence. According to the study, women in such neighborhoods are more than twice as likely to be victims of intimate violence and are more likely to be victimized repeatedly and/or to be more severely injured by their domestic partners than women from more advantaged neighborhoods.

The study also found that economic problems or distresses such as job loss or the inability to make enough to support a family, and even chronic worry about finances, increase the risk of intimate violence. In fact, women whose male partners experienced two or more periods of unemployment over this five-year study were almost three times as likely to be victims of intimate violence than were women whose partners were in stable jobs.[24]

In contrast, the study found that in higher socioeconomic groups, rates of violence among African Americans and Anglo Americans were virtually identical. The authors conclude that it is poverty and the neighborhoods in which it is prevalent, rather than race or ethnicity, that predict higher intimate partner violence.[25] Many other studies have found that racial and ethnic differences in the rate of intimate partner violence largely disappear when socioeconomic factors are controlled.[26]

Additionally supporting the importance of economic determinants of intimate violence, studies consistently find that the majority of homeless women were once victims of domestic violence and that more than half of all women receiving public assistance were once victims of domestic violence.[27] Thus, it is very apparent that poverty and the circumstances surrounding it put women at much greater risk of being battered. The reason for higher rates of domestic violence among African Americans is at least partially explained by the high and extreme levels of poverty in African American communities.

Thus, domestic violence scholars struggle to find a balance between the roles of race, culture, and patriarchal social structure and emphasize that there are no simple explanations for the rates of intimate partner violence. We are urged to look instead at how patriarchy and gender inequalities operate differently in different cultures and within differing circumstances such as socioeconomic status, immigrant status, sexual orientation, and the context of racism.[28]

RACISM AND DISCRIMINATION

Undoubtedly, slavery and the culture of racism that it produced, and continues to produce in more subtle forms, have contributed to the occurrence of intimate partner violence. Even though both the African American man and woman in a family are often employed, the woman often bears the brunt of her partner's frustration with discrimination within the context of a predominately Anglo American, male-dominated culture. African American men are exposed to cultural messages and expectations that define the masculine role as that of provider and protector, while at the same time they often encounter numerous barriers in the form of subtle forms of racism and discrimination. When discrimination keeps many of these men unemployed or in low-paying jobs, minimizing the economic support they can bring to their families, the stress and the pressure they feel to prove their masculinity in other ways may contribute to the occurrence of intimate partner violence. One African American woman explained away her boyfriend's intermittent abuse by saying, "He gets abused by White people all day . . . he doesn't deserve trouble from me too . . . "[29]

Racism and discrimination also affect, to varying degrees, virtually all non-Anglo men and women. Discrimination manifests in any number of ways and continues to marginalize these groups, causing greater economic instability and resulting in less access to resources or interventions that are directed at reducing family violence. Recent immigrants and other marginalized groups are more likely to encounter problems with unemployment, lack of education, and unfamiliarity with English, and they may reside in very poor communities. These factors, along with the family's structure and beliefs, may contribute to the occurrence of intimate partner violence in these groups.[30]

PERCEPTIONS OF VIOLENCE

The prevalence of domestic violence within differing subcultures cannot be adequately measured or appropriately addressed without taking into account the fact that definitions of what is threatening or violent can differ. The meaning that a woman gives to her partner's act is shaped by her sociocultural background. For example, in a traditional Japanese household, overturning the dining table is an act of contempt that specifically questions the woman's legitimate role in the family. Dousing her with liquid implies that she is impure or contaminated. Therefore, Japanese women are likely to view these acts as being more severe than purely physical acts of aggression.[31]

Religious values can influence the interpretation of aggressive acts. Women of differing religious backgrounds and strong religious beliefs may have been taught that their husband is their superior and that it is his right as head of the family to control or "correct" her behavior.[32] Victims from tightly knit religious communities may find that their religious beliefs conflict with standard legal remedies for domestic violence. For example, victims or their family members may have religious beliefs that emphasize the sanctity of the family and prohibit or discourage divorce. Victims who live in insular religious communities may be afraid to reveal the family violence to service providers outside of their community. They may fear that if they seek outside assistance, members of their community will support the perpetrator, particularly if the religion emphasizes the rights of men to rule their families. In some cases, religious principles may require wives to obtain their husband's permission to divorce him, giving perpetrators an additional means of control.[33]

Thus, it is important that we understand a woman's cultural perspective concerning acts we perceive as harmful. The intersections of race, class, and culture can also affect the likelihood that a battered woman will seek safety or outside intervention. Cultural values and conditions can cause many women to keep silent concerning abuse. For example, a Vietnamese woman may have been taught that saving face and maintaining family unity are more important than her individual safety.[34] Women of color, especially African American women who have experienced racism, may fear that calling the police will subject their partners to further racist treatment within the criminal justice system, as well as confirm racist stereotypes of African Americans as violent.[35] Similarly, lesbians who are not open about their orientation may remain silent about partner abuse, because of the fear of how they might be treated by police or the fear of being "outed."[36] Latina women have often been socialized to have gender roles in which they are nurturing and submissive, in combination with the expectation that they should not disclose family issues to outsiders.[37]

ISSUES FOR IMMIGRANT WOMEN

Victoria, a 42-year-old Nicaraguan woman, experienced physical and sexual abuse from her husband Eduardo for six years. She had come to the U.S. eleven years earlier on a student visa, but began to work full-time when she was unable to continue her education. She eventually married Eduardo, a U.S. citizen originally from Nicaragua, who eventually became abusive. "He would come home at four or five o'clock in the morning when I was asleep and he didn't like it that I was sleeping; instead he wanted me up waiting for him. You see, he worked nights. So, he would drink, he would wake me up by hitting me and yelling at me to cook for him."[38]

A number of additional issues may complicate the experience of domestic violence among recent immigrant populations. Language barriers and social isolation may cause them to be unfamiliar with U.S. laws and customs and to be fearful of the authorities. An immigrant victim of domestic violence who does not speak English may not be able to communicate with the law enforcement officer who may believe an English-speaking perpetrator's claim that the victim initiated the violence or that nothing happened at all. Based solely on language barriers, a police officer may inappropriately arrest a victim, let a perpetrator go who should be arrested, or fail to provide a victim with information about her legal rights.[39]

In some cases, immigrants will have experienced major social upheaval prior to coming to the United States, including political oppression, war, or severe economic deprivation. In their home countries, they may have faced rape or torture for their political beliefs. They may have been forced into prostitution or state-sponsored sterilization programs or subjected to female genital mutilation. They may bear physical and psychological scars from this abuse and may still be fighting the effects of PTSD.[40]

For those women who enter the United States illegally, crossing the border can be a harrowing experience; women and children risk being robbed, raped, or detained. Once they are in the United States, they may experience discrimination, unemployment, isolation, and fear of being caught by the Immigration and Naturalization Services (INS). Immigrant women may also have difficulty obtaining employment in the United States, because they lack basic job or language skills. When they are able to find work, they often face low wages, sexual harassment, dangerous working conditions, or long hours because they work "under the table" and their immigration status prevents them from seeking the protection of U.S. laws. They may be under considerable pressure to work hard and send money to support their children and other family members in their home countries.[41]

Migrant farmworker women live a very transient lifestyle and often live in very isolated circumstances. They are paid extremely low wages, they work very long hours in hazardous conditions, and they are often forced to turn over their paychecks to their husbands. These pressures result in very difficult lives for immigrant women, particularly those who are undocumented. More vulnerable to abuse, and more likely to be trapped in the abusive relationship, battered migrant women are among the most marginalized victims of domestic violence in this country. A recent study found that 53 percent of almost 2,000 migrant women surveyed had experienced abuse in the last year.[42] Many immigrant women fear that reporting abuse will result in legal problems, loss of services, and even deportation. Lack of material resources and social support can be significant barriers, particularly for non-English-speaking women and those who have not previously worked outside of the home.[43]

The relationship between domestic violence rates and immigration status is important to acknowledge. Cases of battered immigrants can be further complicated by their abuser's use of immigration status as a tool of control. Research on domestic violence conducted among immigrants indicates that such women are extremely vulnerable to violence due to their immigration status. In one survey of immigrant women, 62 percent reported that they were subjected to weekly physical or emotional abuse. Forty percent of the women reported they experienced increased abuse or abuse for the first time after immigration to the United States. Twenty percent reported that their spouses used threats of deportation, of not filing immigration papers, or of withdrawing these papers as a power and control tactic in abusive relationships. One out of every four felt trapped in the abusive relationship because of fear related to their immigration status.[44]

Such an increase in the abuse experienced following immigration would suggest that the prevalence is not directly linked to the culture of origin as much as it is a reflection of the high levels of stress and psychological and structural disequilibrium that often accompanies the immigrant experience. For example, in home countries, extended families may exert collective pressure to prevent abuse of wives or to provide safety and support if it does occur. Migration to the United States often disrupts or breaks the links to extended families at the same time that racism, economic instability, and the pressure to fit into a new culture are experienced.

A major issue for many immigrants is the pressure to learn the customs, traditions, and values of mainstream U.S. society. Potentially, all forms of stress can increase the likelihood of violence being expressed within the family unit, and acculturation stress can create additional psychological difficulties. Men may feel powerless and out of control in an unfamiliar and racist cultural setting, and some may use domestic violence as a way to reestablish a sense of control and power.[45]

ADAPTING TO MAINSTREAM U.S. CULTURE

To gain success and economic stability within the majority culture, members of all minority populations often adjust their values and behaviors to better match those of the dominant race and culture. In doing so, they can be perceived by their families or communities as having rejected or abandoned the values of their ethnic communities. They may be accused of becoming "too white," or "too American." As one African American female journalist explains:

I run the gauntlet between two worlds, and I am cursed and blessed by both. I travel, observe and take part in both; I can also be used by both. I am a rope in a tug of war. If I am a token in my downtown office, so am I at my cousin's tea. I assuage white guilt. . . . I have a foot in each world, but I cannot fool myself about either. . . . Whites won't believe I remain culturally different; blacks won't believe I remain culturally the same.[46]

African Americans and members of many culturally diverse groups living within the Anglo culture of the United States may experience such two-fold discrimination. First, they may experience discrimination from outside their culture as they strive to become part of the predominately Anglo American, male-dominated middle class. Second, as they take on middle-class attitudes and behaviors, they may experience discrimination from members of their ethnic group who may view them as outsiders or traitors to their culture. These pressures may also cause them to question their identity or self-concept as they grapple to balance between cultures.

Additionally, family members from minority cultures can experience stress related to their differing rates of acculturation to the dominant culture. Oftentimes, older generations of immigrants or members of ethnic communities may retain many of the traditions and values of their original cultures, while the younger family members will adopt more quickly the values and behaviors of the U.S. culture because of their greater exposure to it through schools, television, and other cultural influences. Intergenerational conflict can result as individual family members adopt at differing rates the mainstream values of the new culture with respect to such issues as male/female relations, family structure, and the role of the individual in the family.[47]

In other cases, immigrant adult male family members may have greater exposure to the dominant U.S. culture because of employment, while their wives may remain more isolated at home. Differing rates of acculturation and the clash of values between "old" and "new" cultures, or non-Anglo and Anglo cultures, can be additional stressors that can increase family tensions. When combined with other factors, this can increase the risk for domestic violence.

A NEW FOCUS: THE SLOW MOVE TOWARD VISIBILITY

Domestic violence within different ethnic and cultural groups presents particular challenges to the efforts to eliminate such violence or to mediate its effects. To address some of these challenges, the VAWA reauthorization, signed into law on January 5, 2006, authorized the appropriations of funds to go to the U.S. Department of Justice and authorized various other grants for fiscal years 2006 through 2009, the funds of which have been specifically earmarked for the establishment of a new program for victims of intimate partner violence from ethnic communities.[48] One important implication of this law is its testament that the woman of color who suffers violence is no longer completely invisible.

Chapter 10

Global Violence against Women

Shelly L. Marmion

Why are women so often subjected to violence and abuse here in the United States and in many other cultures? Although there are many factors involved, research makes clear that one of the most important contributors to the frequency of such behaviors is a lack of equality between the genders. Whenever people are seen as belonging to one group or another, and one of those groups is routinely in a more powerful position within the culture, differences between groups are exaggerated and the more powerful group assumes an aura of superiority. Negative stereotypes and myths about the less valued group prevail, causing both groups to believe in the inferiority and dependence of the less powerful group.

Women who grow up in a system of inequality will often construct personalities, identities, and sexualities that defer to men, whereas men often grow up expecting deference from the women in their lives. Thus, gender inequality and other forms of discrimination create the conditions that allow for, or even encourage, the violence and exploitation of one group or gender by another.

Men as well as women can be the targets of violence and exploitation. In fact, men experience more forms of violence and more frequent violence than do women. The difference, though, is that men are most often assaulted by other men. As members of the more privileged gender, they are not abused or exploited because of their lack of status as a social group. Gendered violence, on the other hand, is an act against persons who are vulnerable because of their gender or sexuality. Gendered violence includes the forms of violence covered in the other chapters of this book, and also includes sexual harassment, pornography, prostitution, female infanticide, and female genital mutilation (FGM). This chapter examines a number of examples of gendered violence seen in various parts of the world.

FEMALE INFANTICIDE

As soon as the baby girl was born, my mother-in-law kicked it with her toe and said "Who wants this?" She wrapped it in a wet towel and left it on the floor. My husband's sister, weak after the delivery, just wept. It died within a few hours.[1]

Perhaps no other cultural behavior so obviously illustrates the devaluing of girls and women as the widespread practice of killing unwanted baby girls. Throughout recorded history, cultural, religious, economic, and social forces have served to devalue the lives of women, and this has led to the preference for male children. Some of the factors that appear to contribute to the common practice of killing girl babies include poverty or economic hardship; the view of girls as unproductive consumers who will leave home with marriage; the perceived need for military strength; marriage patterns that place heavy financial burdens on the bride's family, such as dowry; inheritance laws that favor sons; and religious and social attitudes that place great importance on sons. In India, for example, only sons are expected to support their parents in old age; daughters are married off and then belong to their husband's family. When parents die, only sons can perform religious rites considered necessary to benefit the soul. Although the practice of murdering baby girls is most associated with such countries as India and China, it occurs in many other cultures around the globe. In such cultures, it is considered a kindness to kill the girl as an infant rather than subject her to poverty and dependence or to hand her over to "strangers" to rear.[2]

Although the killing of infants is now against the law in almost every society, the practice of ridding the family of the economic burden represented by girl babies has not slowed; now the means by which it is accomplished have become more sophisticated so that it is less likely to be detected as murder.[3] In cultures where medical technology makes it possible, an alternative form of the practice is carried out. Ultrasound technology has made possible the identification of the sex of an unborn child, so that abortion can be used as a method of selecting the sex of the offspring.[4] The ratio of men to women in countries where the practice is most common is considerably skewed in favor of men. For example, in China where the state policy is for each family to have only one child, the strong preference for that child to be a boy results in the estimated deaths of more than half a million female babies each year.[5]

Although it might seem that such an imbalance might lead to an increase in women's value, the reverse is true. The relative scarcity of marriageable women has led to the kidnapping, trafficking, and forced marriage of tens of thousands of women.[6]

FEMALE GENITAL MUTILATION

More than 100 million women and girls each year undergo some form of genital mutilation. This is an extreme example of the widespread effort to control the sexuality of women by deadening their sex drives and ensuring their subjugation.[7] Most commonly seen in Africa and to a lesser extent in parts of Asia and the Middle East, FGM is frequently practiced in at least 28 countries.[8] Worldwide migration has led to the practice being introduced into the United States and other Western cultures.[9] FGM is practiced in many forms of varying severity, but it often includes the removal of the clitoris and surrounding tissues and the stitching together of the outer lips of the vagina, leaving only a small opening for urine and menstrual flow. It is often performed on young girls as a rite of passage, under brutal conditions. Generally, there is no anesthesia. It is performed by persons with no medical training, using unclean "surgical" instruments such as knives, razor blades, or broken glass. It leaves survivors vulnerable to lifelong medical complications, which may include frequent infections, infertility, and difficult childbirth.[10] As an adult, a woman who has undergone FGM often needs to be cut open to allow for sex with her husband and cut again to allow for the delivery of a baby. In some cultures, the woman will be stitched again following the delivery of the baby in order to be "tight" for her husband. Cutting and restitching of a woman's genitals with each birth can produce tough scar tissue.[11]

The custom is entrenched and is considered essential to a woman's identity—a sign of chastity, cleanliness, fertility, beauty, and docility. Girls who have not undergone FGM are viewed as being unsuitable for marriage, unclean, unchaste, and likely to engage in infidelity. An uncut woman is viewed as being so unclean that she is not allowed to handle food and water. Some cultures believe that if the procedure is not performed the clitoris of the girl will continue to grow to resemble the penis, thus destroying her femininity. Some believe that the clitoris is dangerous, and if it touches a man's penis he will die.

Girls who do not survive the procedure are often thought to be witches or bad girls and are blamed for their own deaths. So strong are the cultural beliefs surrounding these practices that parents feel they have no option to choose otherwise if they are to ensure the future of their daughters. Mothers who themselves have suffered FGM are instrumental in arranging the procedure for their daughters. Often the practice is carried out by an older woman of the village who is esteemed for her important social role.[12]

FGM is a clear example of an institutionalized form of violence against women that is tolerated by governments, encouraged by custom, and sanctioned by religion. Although not specific to any religion, tradition very often blurs any separation from religious doctrine. The influence of tradition is so strong that most often it is women themselves who enact the custom.

DOWRY DEATHS

> For nineteen-year-old Rinki, dreams of a happily married life was never to be. Barely a month after her marriage, she was allegedly tortured and then set ablaze by her in-laws for dowry. . . . Rinki was married to Anil on April 19. . . . However, soon after the marriage, Anil's father demanded a colour television instead of a black and white one and a motorcycle as well. When Rinki's mother failed to meet their demands, the teenage housewife was subjected to severe torture, allegedly by her husband and mother-in-law. On Saturday morning Rinki's mother was informed that Rinki was charred to death when a kerosene lamp accidentally fell on her and her clothes caught fire. . . . It appeared that the victim was first attacked as her teeth were found broken.[13]

Traditionally in India and similar cultures, marriages are arranged and the marriage market is a competitive one. Newspapers are filled with advertisements of young women whose families seek a "good" marriage as a means to advance up the social ladder and of men who declare their social prowess and eligibility. The price to be paid for a good marriage is in the form of a dowry. Although outlawed in India more than 40 years ago, the practice of dowry continues in which the family of a bride must bestow money and gifts to the man who will marry her. The size of the dowry depends on the family's social and economic standing, but the dowry can be financially crippling to the bride's family. Nevertheless, if the groom's family (with whom the bride lives) decides they want more dowry, they may harass, beat, and terrorize the bride into getting more money from her parents. Such demands for more dowry may go on for years; when the bride's family cannot comply, the terror all too often becomes deadly. Indian officials estimate that more than 6,000 young brides are killed in India each year over dowry.[14] Unofficial estimates place the number closer to 25,000 per year.[15] Harassment and even deaths related to dowry are common and generally ignored by the police, the courts, politicians, and the media. Failure to report the crime is also quite common, due to fear of retaliation and the expectation that the legal system will not intervene or will prosecute the bride's family.

The method of dousing the bride with flammable liquid and setting her on fire was so common that the Indian government was eventually forced to create a law so that a charge of murder could be made if the bride died by burning in the first seven years of marriage.[16] A groom whose bride dies in a "kitchen accident" is free to seek another bride who will bring another dowry. When evidence of foul play is too obvious to ignore, the groom's family often changes the explanation for the death to suicide. As with infanticide and FGM, women participate in this terrible practice, and women's prisons are crammed with women who have been charged with bringing about the injury or death of a sister-in-law or a daughter-in-law.[17]

HONOR KILLINGS

A 16-year-old mentally retarded girl who was raped in the Northwest Frontier province of Pakistan was turned over to her tribe's judicial council. Even though the crime was reported to the police and the perpetrator was arrested, the Pathan tribesmen decided that she had brought shame to her tribe and she was killed in front of a tribal gathering.[18]

Kajal Khidr was accused of adultery by her husband's family and held hostage by six family members in Iraqi Kurdistan. She was tortured and mutilated; family members cut off part of her nose and told her she would be killed after the birth of her child. After fleeing to Syria, two of her abusers were arrested, but released within 24 hours because authorities decided they had acted to safeguard the honor of the family. No charges were brought against them.[19]

A strong tradition exists in many cultures to kill a woman who "dishonors" her husband or father through even a suspicion of improper behavior, especially sexual behavior, so that the family honor can be restored. In Pakistan, for example, hundreds of girls and women are killed each year for a variety of reasons connected to perceptions of honor. The number of such killings is apparently on the rise as the perceptions of what behaviors put honor at risk steadily broaden. Marital infidelity, flirting, asking for a divorce, or failing to perform duties quickly and effectively have each been given as a reason for killing. A case was reported in which a husband murdered his wife after simply dreaming that she betrayed him. In Turkey, a girl's throat was slashed in the town square because a love ballad was dedicated to her on the radio.[20]

The only cure for these perceived sins is the woman's death, usually at the hands of her family. Perpetrators of these murders often are not prosecuted, or if prosecuted they receive light sentences and return to the community as heroes. Many people in the cultures involved, even urban and educated persons, share in these traditional conceptions of honor and approve of honor killings—including the mothers of those killed. Those who might oppose the practice are often silenced by the threat that their honor will be questioned.[21]

In the majority of cases, the murders are ignored or approved by the community. The women may be buried in unmarked graves and, in some cases, all records of their existence are destroyed. Women accused of destroying family honor are rarely given the opportunity to prove their innocence. Often the only form of protection available to these women is prison. In Jordan, a woman fearing her family's retaliation can check herself into prison, but she cannot check herself out. Only a male relative can release her.[22]

The United Nations Population Fund estimates that as many as 5,000 girls and women are killed each year for reasons of "honor."[23]

ACID ATTACKS

Dano, a teenage boy, had a crush on Bina's cousin, who did not return his affection. Asleep one night, Dano and his friends entered the girls' bedroom in order to throw acid in the face of Bina's cousin, but hit Bina instead. Sulfuric acid, used in car batteries and available in stores, dissolves iron. Imagine the effect on human flesh. Even after several surgeries, Bina's face bears the devastating effects of the acid attack. "With acid, they usually aim for the face. It symbolizes beauty. Taking away beauty takes away the woman's value," says the surgeon who has operated on Bina and others like her.[24]

In Bangladesh, where acid attacks have become increasingly common, it is assumed that a disfigured girl will not be able to marry, and she will often be rejected by her family. She is expected to live her life in a state of shame, give up school or work, keep her face covered, and remain dependent on others for her survival.[25]

Land and property disputes are a common reason for acid attacks. Refusals of marriage and dowry disputes account for others. The common root for this evil act, like the others described in this chapter, is a system in which women are viewed as property owned by a husband or father. In conflicts between men, these girls and women suffer attacks from one man who is attempting to weaken another through the destruction of his property. Acid attacks are most common among the poor who cannot protect their daughters. When someone is determined to carry out an attack, it can occur anywhere. It is nearly impossible for most families to pay for extensive reconstructive surgeries that could improve conditions for the victims. In fact, few hospitals are equipped to deal with such severe burn victims.[26]

SPOILS OF WAR

In the Bosnian ethnic conflict in the 1990s, Serb and Yugoslav armed forces "detained" Muslim and Croat women and girls, subjecting them to systematic rape and sexual enslavement. A 12-year-old girl, detained for 10 days in 1992, was taken 10 times to be raped; her mother was taken twice.[27]

Abduction, rape, and sexual slavery are also systematic and widespread in the conflict in Sierra Leone. Rape victims often suffer extreme brutality. In one case, a 14-year-old girl was stabbed in the vagina with a knife because she refused to have sex with the rebel soldier who abducted her. In another, a 16-year-old girl was so badly injured through rape, that after her escape she required a hysterectomy.[28]

Amnesty International reports that rape is routinely used as a weapon of war, and it has occurred in every armed conflict in modern times. Rape is used to intimidate people, to humiliate people, and to break community resistance and as a weapon of terror. It is used as a method of torture and as a system of reward for soldiers. It is also used to impregnate women of opposing ethnic groups as a technique of ethnic cleansing.[29]

Sexual violence in wartime is often perpetrated by armed forces or militia, but not all violence against women is linked to soldiers. Frequently civilians, sex traffickers, and even local security take advantage of the lack of law enforcement within combat zones, engaging in sexual violence for amusement, profit, or revenge.

Women and children who flee to refugee camps to escape war zones are often subjected to sexual abuse, both during transit and after their arrival. Women experience sexual violence from security forces, border guards, local civilians, smugglers, and other refugees. Camp guards and male refugees often seem to view unaccompanied women and girls as common sexual property to be used at will. In some countries, government-sponsored violence also exists in peacetime, with women being assaulted while in police custody or in prison and at the hands of any number of state officials. Correctional officers frequently coerce women into providing sex for "favors" such as food or to avoid a beating.

ABC News reported the widespread allegations of sexual exploitation and abuse of Congolese women, boys, and girls that have been made against the United Nations forces stationed in the Congo as peacekeepers. The range of abuse includes reported rapes of young girls by United Nations troops, an Internet pedophile ring run by a senior United Nations official, and hundreds of underage girls having babies fathered and abandoned by United Nations soldiers. Ravaged by decades of civil war, the impoverished country of Congo has relied on United Nations protection and humanitarian aid.[30] But who will protect the women and children from the "protectors"?

Sexual violence against women is rooted in a global culture of gender oppression that denies women equal rights with men and gives men rights over women's bodies. Because women have traditionally had a lower status in societies, they have often been excluded from definitions of human rights and the laws that uphold them. This makes them more vulnerable to sexual violence and creates barriers to seeking justice. Women who are victims of sexual violence often choose not to report the abuse for fear of being detested and shamed by communities that are quick to blame the victims. Violence against women is so deeply embedded in societies that it often fails to produce any public outrage.

In every war, the largest group of casualties is not armed soldiers but civilian women and children. Most of the world's refugees are women and children. Most of the world's poorest, those most likely to die of disease and starvation, are women and children. Gender inequity works to make these victims largely invisible, with the result that they are denied basic human rights protections intended to apply to all.

TRAFFICKING OF WOMEN AND CHILDREN

In Bangkok's Patpong district, famous for its sex clubs, a Thai man approached an Australian and offered him sex with two girls—a 12-year-old and her 6-year-old sister—who had been sold into prostitution by their relatives. The agent delivered the girls to the tourist's hotel room, where he abused and photographed them for months.[31]

The U.S. Department of Health and Human Services reports that human trafficking is a form of modern-day slavery, common in the United States and around the world. It is forced labor that uses techniques such as debt bondage, human smuggling, theft of passports, threats of imprisonment, and threats against family to maintain control over victims.

A form of human trafficking that targets young women and children is an international market for sex slaves, accounting for perhaps 90 percent of all trafficking. It is estimated that 4 million women and children worldwide are victims each year; they are forced into prostitution by kidnappers who profit by as much as $72 billion a year from this practice. In fact, trafficking of women for the purpose of forced prostitution now generates more profits than international trafficking of firearms or drugs.[32]

Third-world countries and countries experiencing economic instability, such as the former Soviet Bloc, provide the greatest number of
victims; these victims are lured by the promise of real jobs or are kid-
napped and forced to become sexual slaves. In the poorest of countries, families will sometimes sell their daughters or give them to
traffickers in the belief that they will be given regular employment.[33]
More economically advantaged countries, including the United States,
are frequent destinations where victims are sold into bondage. In
2000, the U.S. Central Intelligence Agency released a report stating
that as many as 50,000 women and children, some as young as nine
years old, are trafficked to the United States each year and held in sexual bondage.[34]

In Amsterdam, a preferred destination for sex tourism, 80 percent of
prostituted people are of foreign origin and probably 70 percent are
victims of trafficking. In Austria, 90 percent of prostitutes are from
other countries. These young women, who are frequently minors, can
be purchased outright in the markets in the Balkans for about $600 or
are required by pimps to have sex with 30 to 100 men per day.[35] The
International Labor Organization reports that prostitution in Thailand
has grown so much that it constitutes a major "commercial sector,"
employing more workers than the tourist industry. Male tourists and
business travelers from around the globe go to Thailand to indulge in
forbidden pleasures at bargain prices.[36] Organized pimping and the
running of brothels are generally controlled and supported by organized crime syndicates. In those countries where prostitution has been
made legal, the sex industry and sex trafficking have grown uncontrol-
lably and have increased such problems as child prostitution and HIV
exposure. Legalization of prostitution in these countries has not led to
improved conditions for sex workers as was hoped but has created
instead a gold mine for pimps and organized crime groups.[37] Sweden,
on the other hand, has changed its laws to prosecute the customers of
prostitution while decriminalizing the activities of prostitutes. Combined with government programs designed to help prostitutes leave
the profession and to educate police and the public, prostitution has
been dramatically reduced in just five years. In the capital of Stockholm, the number of women in street prostitution has been reduced by
two-thirds and the number of customers has been reduced by 80 percent. The Swedish government estimates that only about 200 to
400 women and girls have been trafficked into Sweden in recent years,
compared to 15,000 to 17,000 trafficked into neighboring Finland
where prostitution is still legal. Sweden's unique strategy treats prostitution as a form of violence. The prostitution policies were part of
the country's 1999 violence against women legislation. Government
literature states:

> In Sweden prostitution is regarded as an aspect of male violence against women and children. It is officially acknowledged as a form of exploitation of women and children and constitutes a significant social problem. . . . Gender equality will remain unattainable so long as men buy, sell and exploit women and children by prostituting them.[38]

To view prostitutes as victims of male coercion and violence, a government must first switch from seeing prostitutes from a male point of view. Most countries still see this issue from a primarily male point of view. (Witness the 2006 Academy Award for best song in a movie going to "It's Hard Out Here for a Pimp"!) Perhaps Sweden was able to take a different view, because the Swedish Parliament was composed of nearly 50 percent women when these laws were passed.[39]

The world and people in it need a radical shift in thinking, away from the male-centered customs and policies that have allowed violence against women to be a normal and expected part of almost every society. We must strive to create political systems in which women play an equal role, where the lives and experiences of women and children are given equal weight to those of men, where "women's issues" are issues of concern to all. Only when this country and others make it a priority to address issues of gender inequality that form the basis for so much violence against women will we begin to see significant reductions in the prevalence of these acts of indifference and hatred.

Chapter 11

To the Future

Shelly L. Marmion

In the preface to this book, we tried to contemplate a future in which women and children would not need to fear possible abduction, assault, and violence from intimate partners and others and where women would not be victimized because of being women.

In this final chapter, we will suggest how progress toward such a world might occur.

Cultural beliefs are transmitted from one generation to the next, and they greatly affect our perceptions of the world. Our beliefs about what the world and people in it are like, what is normal and abnormal, or even what can be done to influence the future are learned from our earliest moments from the culture into which we are born. These cultural influences on how we think tend to be invisible to us, because most of us are not sufficiently exposed to other ways of thinking or being, much as the fish in the sea cannot imagine a different reality.

Cultural ideas, norms, and expectations can greatly influence our choices and behaviors, but sometimes we fail to see the schism between what we *believe* to be our values and what our behaviors actually demonstrate. Few, if any, modern cultures have openly adopted the belief that women are less worthy than men and should be subjected to brutalities because of their sex. Although they differ in various small ways, virtually all cultures have avowed that women have equal (although perhaps different) value to men and that they should be treated with care and dignity. And yet, in each of these cultures, we find the prevalence of various forms of violence that are most often directed at women. In most cases, such treatment is denounced, laws are passed to define perpetrators as criminal, and we go about our lives as if the issue has been resolved. But one only has to look at the continued prevalence of these many forms of violence that specifically victimize women to understand that we have not done nearly enough and what we have done is simply not working. Most people do not want to see that a schism exists between what we believe as a culture and the multiple systems of oppression that are the reality within that culture. Such willful ignorance serves to keep in place the systems of oppression that allow for these kinds of violence.

The first step to changing the way things are is to identify those things that need to be changed and to identify those attitudes and behaviors that help to maintain the *status quo*. We also have to develop the belief that change is possible, that we can evolve as a culture, and that we can affect the direction in which change will occur. We must move beyond the myth that "it's always been this way and always will be."[1] We must understand that culture is a process and change is inevitable.

Once we have envisioned what could be, we must recognize the importance of each of us in reaching that goal. It is very easy to observe an immense problem and believe that our actions could never make a difference. Gandhi once said that nothing we do as individuals matters, but that it is vitally important that we do it anyway.[2] When each person strives toward a common goal, the critical mass of the effort is anything but insignificant. Whenever we choose a different path, we make it possible for others to see a new direction. The simplest way to influence others to make different and better choices is to make them yourself and to do so openly. Allan Johnson suggests the following behaviors for creating a world in which systems of oppression will fail to thrive:

1. Acknowledge the problem. Break the silence on which continued oppression depends. Once you become aware of the problem, hang on to that knowledge. It is easy to slip back into the bliss of willful ignorance, because life is simpler that way.

2. Pay attention. Be open to the idea that much of what we have been taught to believe is not necessarily true. Those beliefs are a product of the oppressive systems in which they are maintained.

3. Take small risks: do something. The more we attend to what is happening, the more we will see opportunities to do something about it. Stand up, volunteer, speak out, write letters, sign petitions, show up. Plant seeds of doubt about the desirability and inevitability of the way things are and, by example, plant the seeds of what might be. Choose, and model, alternative paths—creating tension in the system. As Gandhi put it, be the change we want to see happen.

4. Dare to make people feel uncomfortable, including ourselves. Small actions may seem like they do not amount to much, until we notice our own resistance to doing them. If that resistance is a measure of power, then the action itself has the power to be an influence. It may feel uncomfortable to challenge the assumptions of others, but discomfort is an unavoidable part of any meaningful process of education.

5. Actively promote change in how systems are organized around patriarchal values and male privilege:

   - Speak out for equality in every sphere;
   - Oppose the devaluing of women and the work that they do;
   - Support the well-being of mothers and children and defend women's rights to control their own lives;
   - Object to the dismantling of welfare and attempts to limit access to health services;
   - Speak out against violence and harassment against women wherever they occur, whether at home, at work, or on the street;
   - Support government and private services for women who are victimized by male violence;
   - Volunteer at the local rape crisis center or battered women's shelter;
   - Call for and support clear and effective sexual harassment policies in workplaces, unions, schools, professional associations, churches, and political parties, as well as in public spaces such as parks, sidewalks, and malls.

6. Pay attention to racism and other forms of oppression that draw from the same roots. Whatever we do that draws attention to those roots undermines all forms of oppression. Make contact; connect to other people who feel the same way.

7. Remember that you do not have to do it all. All we can do is what we can manage to do. Think small, humble, and doable rather than large, heroic, and impossible. Do not paralyze yourself with impossible expectations. Small acts can have great implications. If evil can be perpetuated when good people do nothing, then the choice is not between all or nothing but between nothing and something.[3]

GETTING STARTED

In the pages to follow, you will find our recommendations for needed changes in our current system. We have included suggestions for legislative responses to the issues of violence against women, as well as community and legal system responses. Suggestions to medical personnel, clergy, schools, and educators are also included. Additionally, in the appendices of this book, you will find very specific advice addressed to victims of violence and to the parents, family, and friends of victims or potential victims of violence against women.

NEEDED LEGISLATIVE REFORMS

- Legislation should compel changes in criminal justice systems that would ensure fair treatment of women and children and provide for their safety.
- Legislation should increase mechanisms to protect victims of IPV and their children so that victims can work and keep their jobs when IPV-related absences occur, because financial independence is crucial to nonvictimization. It is imperative that state and local governments design policies aimed at bolstering IPV victims' income and job support.
- Legislation should strengthen existing laws intended to protect women against sex- or victimization-related types of discrimination, and society must demand the enforcement of those laws.
- Legislators need to enact laws requiring employers to assist employees who are being threatened, stalked, or harassed at work by instituting preventive safety measures.
- Legislators should mandate the evaluation of welfare programs and job-training programs for IPV victims to be sure that these efforts succeed in teaching victims how to earn a living.
- Legislatures should mandate training for everyone in the legal system to be more responsive to victims and sensitive to cultural issues. Studies have found a great need for education of law enforcement officers and prosecutors to reduce the negative attitudes and misconceptions commonly held that cause them to treat domestic violence differently from violence occurring between strangers. Additionally, research consistently indicates that judges often minimize the criminal nature of acts of IPV. Some judges routinely dismiss the charge of noncompliance with restraining orders and rarely sanction even the most assaultive men in IPV cases. The result of the collective under-response to IPV is that only about one-fourth of batterers are arrested, about one-third of those arrested are prosecuted, and only 1 percent of those prosecuted receive jail time beyond the time served at arrest (often just a few hours).[4]
- In addition to receiving training, judges need to assume a community leadership role to reduce IPV.[5] To avoid bias, they should adopt protocols for granting and enforcing protective

orders and for sentencing IPV perpetrators with prior convictions. State bar associations should set guidelines for appropriate judicial behavior and establish a judicial body to discipline judges whose behavior in IPV cases is outrageous.

- Funding MUST be available to implement laws and statutes designed to address these issues. Laws without the resources to implement them are completely ineffective.

NEEDED LEGAL AND CRIMINAL JUSTICE SYSTEM REFORMS

- The principal problem pertaining to the criminal justice system in reducing IPV is the failure to implement the laws that already exist. Prevention of IPV requires vigorous action from police, prosecutors, judges, defense attorneys, jurors, and court advocates. Funding for vigorous action must be available. For example, half the victims of crime served by federal compensation programs are IPV victims, but they receive only 13 percent of compensation awards.[6]
- Better efforts to enforce critical statutes must be made. For example, the 1997 amendment to modify the Gun Control Act of 1968 that bans individuals who have been convicted of domestic assault from carrying weapons (including police officers) needs better enforcement, as does the Brady Bill, which is supposed to limit those who can legally purchase guns.
- Legal services and courts need to better address the IPV victim's privacy needs and security issues.
- Affordable legal services need to be more available.
- Fees to obtain an order of protection need to be eliminated.
- One group of IPV experts that has devised an integrated approach to batterer interventions and criminal justice strategies recommends that law enforcement officers comply with four major guidelines: (1) identify the primary aggressor, (2) execute a proarrest or mandatory arrest policy, (3) gather evidence at the scene for use in prosecutions, and (4) arrange for a temporary restraining or no-contact order.[7]
- The British criminal justice system has taken three paths in dealing with the problem of IPV: (1) victim choice, in which victims are encouraged to make a reasoned choice about whether arrest of the abuser will improve the situation; (2) proarrest policy, which implies that subsequent prosecution will be undertaken in such a way as to prevent retaliation against the victim by the perpetrator; and (3) victim empowerment strategies that attempt to understand the individual victim, to educate her about available services, and to find out what might work best for her.[8]

Specific recommendations to law enforcement for treatment of women who report rape, battery or sexual assault include the following:

- Every woman who reports rape or battering to the police should be kept informed of all the developments relating to her case. One officer, who has received specialist training, should be assigned for this purpose.
- Every woman should have the opportunity to be examined by a female doctor or sexual assault nurse examiner, who has received specialist training for this role. This should take place without delay and in facilities designed for such cases.
- Procedures for identifying perpetrators should not be intimidating for women who have been raped or sexually assaulted, and their identity should be protected if it was previously unknown to the accused, for example, by the use of one-way glass.
- Victims of rape or sexual assault should be informed when the suspect is bailed and about any conditions that involve or affect them.
- Women who have been battered, raped, or sexually assaulted must be given the opportunity to tell the police about any ongoing fears for their safety. The police and courts should take this information into account when bail is being considered and when deciding whether action should be taken to prevent further victimization or intimidation by the suspect or his associates.
- Victims of battery, rape, and sexual assault must be provided with any additional protection necessary to prevent further victimization or intimidation from the suspect or his associates.
- Rape, sexual assault, and battery cases should be fast-tracked and delays and adjournments kept to a minimum. Delays and adjournments in proceedings cause enormous distress and prolong the effects of the crime.
- Screens and closed-circuit television should be available and considered for all women complainants in sexual assault cases, when they give evidence in court. Cross-examination of rape and sexual assault complainants must be strictly regulated so as to minimize the trauma of giving evidence. It is unacceptable for any woman to be left feeling as if she has been "raped" again by lengthy, confusing, embarrassing, or intimidating questioning by counsel or defendants.
- The law and court procedures relating to rape and sexual assault must be reviewed with an eye to improving the experience of, and conferring greater dignity and respect to, women reporting rape, battery, and sexual assault. Clearing the court of

the public and the press during rape and sexual assault trials, as well as the conduct of cross-examination, should also be considered.

NEEDED COMMUNITY RESPONSES TO ADDRESS VIOLENCE AGAINST WOMEN

Victims who seek services all too often encounter significant obstacles. Harris and colleagues[9] list the following obstacles encountered by women in their study: cannot find service needed or service does not exist in that community; do not know which agency to contact; have difficulty contacting agencies because of language difference, literacy problem, or disabilities; cannot access agency because of exigencies, such as long waiting lists or service fees; and cannot receive help because agency lacks funding.

Battered women in one study listed the following needs in leaving their abusers: laws that impose sanctions on batterers; resources that allow independence, such as housing and money; education about abuse; more shelters; and provision of interim help during the decision-making phase.[10]

Community responses that are needed to help women include:

- Public awareness campaigns to dispel rape myths and to change beliefs about and acceptance of IPV. Campaigns designed to educate the public about relevant resources and services should also be carried out.
- The provision for more safe shelters. The greatest gap for services for IPV victims is inadequate shelter capacity, especially in nonurban settings.
- The provision of transitional housing and permanent affordable housing.
- To improve the efficiency of their responses to IPV, some jurisdictions have adopted a community collaboration approach that combines police action with social services. Social service agency staff members are trained about the resources available to IPV victims, the functions of various agencies, and their agencies' role in preventing IPV. They may provide an information packet that educates victims on available services and how to access them. Such programs have reported success in reducing victimization.[11]
- In more sizeable communities, local jurisdictions would be wise to establish specialized police units or courts to address IPV cases. This practice has been successful in increasing the rate of successful prosecution of cases.[12]

- Communities need to provide a more holistic approach or network of involved systems. Interagency collaborations are not easy to establish and maintain, often because of differing goals and standards of ethics, but they are important to victim outcomes. The health care community needs to be a part of this network.

As part of the holistic approach to prevention, detection, and treatment of intimate violence against women and children, we offer this list of recommendations.

RECOMMENDATIONS TO TEACHERS AND SCHOOLS

- Teach students about relationships and alert them to the dangers of interpersonal control;
- Present antidrug messages and alcohol misuse awareness programs;
- Provide guidance about avoiding date-rape drugs and the dangers of intoxication;
- Address sexist attitudes and peer-group support for aggression;
- Teach anger management, conflict resolution skills, and stress reduction skills; and
- Create partnerships with community agencies to provide after-school educational experiences on the above issues.

RECOMMENDATIONS TO UNIVERSITIES

- Offer more courses in family violence, interpersonal relationships, and sexual assault;
- Address women's fears about sexual assault, date rape, and associated actual risk;
- Offer rape prevention programs aimed at changing the behaviors of male students (some schools report success using all-male peer education programs); and
- Toughen rules for athletic eligibility (barring athletes found to have been involved in aggressive acts toward women).

RECOMMENDATIONS TO CLERGY

Studies show that clergy are the second most likely source of help (after police) contacted by victims of IPV. Therefore, their responses can be critical.

- Provide a safe outlet for women to confide their experiences of sexual violence or battering;

- Help women to name their experience of physical aggression by partners as "battery," and of sexual abuse in relationships as "rape";
- Hold men accountable for their violent acts, stop minimizing the damage caused, and stop blaming the victims;
- Do not counsel women to endure violence to maintain a marriage;
- Include the topic of IPV during premarital counseling; and
- Work to challenge the social conventions that perpetuate domestic violence and marital rape.

RECOMMENDATIONS TO THE MEDICAL PROFESSIONS

- Medical personnel need ongoing training to teach them how best to screen patients for abuse situations, how to document abuse, and how to intervene in such cases. These techniques should not be cumbersome or intrusive, and screeners need to be trained to display caring and nonjudgmental attitudes;
- Medical schools need to expand their curricula to incorporate training in these areas and in cultural competence;
- Medical personnel should be knowledgeable about the epidemiology of abuse of children, adolescents, and adults and about the current reporting requirements in their communities for all forms of abuse;
- Pediatricians and family care providers should screen adolescents for a history of sexual assault or relationship violence and potential sequelae and be prepared to offer psychological support or referral for counseling; and
- Medical personnel should be aware of the services in the community that provide management, examination, and counseling for patients who have been victimized.

There is only one key to eliminating sexual violence and violence against women—to view the prevalence of these behaviors as completely unacceptable, determine the factors that contribute to that prevalence, and make changes that will address these factors. We hope that in providing the information contained in this book, along with our list of recommendations, we can help others to focus on meaningful changes that must take place to make our world safe for women.

Appendix I

Safety Recommendations for Victims of Intimate Partner Violence

The following recommendations are from the American Bar Association Web site: http://www.abanet.org/domviol/victims.html.

1. Know what domestic violence is. When spouses, intimate partners, or dates use physical violence, threats, emotional abuse, harassment, or stalking to control the behavior of their partners, they are committing domestic violence. Most victims of domestic violence are women. Children who witness domestic violence are also victims; they suffer from behavioral and cognitive problems. Boys, especially, are more likely to be aggressive and engage in criminal behavior if they grow up in homes where domestic violence exists.

2. Develop a safety plan. If you, a relative, a friend, or a neighbor are experiencing domestic violence, think about ways to make yourself safer. Leave a spare set of keys, emergency money, important phone numbers, and documents like birth certificates, passports, bankbooks, and insurance papers in a safe place your batterer doesn't know about, for example, with a trusted friend or relative. Plan how to get out of your home quickly and safely, should a battering incident begin. Think about a safe place to go to once you leave your home. If you can, learn local crisis hotline numbers, so that you can call for advice or assistance.

3. Call 911. If you are being battered—or you know that a relative, friend, or neighbor is being battered—by a spouse or intimate partner, call the police right away for help, if you can get to a phone safely. Don't be afraid to ask for immediate help. Domestic violence is a crime, not a "private family matter."

4. Exercise your legal rights. You—or anyone else experiencing domestic violence—have the right to go to court and petition for an order of protection if you have been battered in one of the 50 states, Puerto Rico, or the District of Columbia. In most parts of the country, you can also ask for custody of your children and child support at the same time. You should try to get a lawyer to represent you and protect all of your rights under the law. Call your state or local coalition against domestic violence, a state or local crisis hotline, or the state or local bar association to learn more about where to find legal help.

5. Get help for your family so that the violence will stop. There are many services available to help families struggling with domestic violence. Look in the phone book for the number of your state or local domestic violence coalition or crisis hotline for help in locating the financial, housing, and counseling services needed to break free of domestic violence.

SAFETY WITH AN ABUSER

- Your abuser may have patterns to his abuse. Know how violent your abuser tends to get. Know any signs that show he's about to become violent. Know how dangerous a situation may be for you and your children.

- If it looks like violence may happen, try to leave if you can.

- Know things that your abuser can use as a weapon. He may use sharp or heavy objects, like a hammer or an ice pick, to hurt you.

- Know where guns, knives, and other weapons are kept. If you can, lock them up or make them as hard to get to as you can.

- Figure out "safe places" in your home—places where there aren't weapons. If it looks like your abuser is about to hurt you, try to get to a safe place. Stay out of the kitchen, garage, or workshop. Try to avoid rooms with tile or hardwood floors.

- Don't run to where the children are. Your abuser may hurt them too.

- If there's no way to escape violence, make yourself a small target. Dive into a corner and curl up into a ball. Protect your face and put your arms around each side of your head, wrapping your fingers together.

- If you can, always have a phone you can get to. Know the numbers to call for help. Know where the nearest pay phone is. Know your local battered women's shelter number. Don't be afraid to call the police or 911.

- If you need help in a public place, yell "FIRE." People respond more quickly to someone yelling fire than to any other cry for help.

- Let friends and neighbors you trust know what is going on. Make a plan with them for when you need help. Have a signal, like flashing the lights on and off or hanging something out the window, to tell them you need help.

- Teach your children how to get help. Tell them not to get involved if your abuser is hurting you. Plan a code word to let them know that they should get help or leave the house.

- Practice how to get out safely. Practice with your children.

- Plan for what you will do if your children tell your partner about your plan or if your partner finds out about your plan some other way.

- Make a habit of backing the car into the driveway and having a full tank of gas. Keep the driver's door unlocked and others locked—for a quick escape.

- Try not to wear scarves or long jewelry. Your abuser could use these things to strangle you.

- Create several reasons he'll believe for your departure from the house at different times of the day or night.

- Call a domestic violence hotline from time to time to talk about your options and to talk to someone who understands you.

- Tell your children that violence is never right, even when someone they love is being violent. Tell them that the violence isn't their fault or your fault. Tell them that when anyone is being violent, it is important to keep safe.

GETTING READY TO LEAVE

- Keep any evidence you can of physical abuse. Make sure to keep this evidence in a safe place that your abuser will not find. This might include:
  o Any pictures you have of bruises or other injuries. If you're taking pictures of your injuries, try to have these pictures dated;
  o Any household objects that your abuser tore or broke;
  o Any pictures that show your home is destroyed or messed up after violence happened;
  o Any records that you have from doctors or the police that document the abuse;

o A journal about the abuse. Write down how he abused you, any way that he threatened you, and when these things happened; and

o Anything else you think could help show that you've been abused.

- Know where you can go to get help. This Web site has listings of domestic violence organizations and legal resources in every state (http://www.abanet.org/domviol/victims.html). To find these listings, select your state from the drop-down menu at the top of this page. Then click on the Links and Resources link for your state. Also, the National Domestic Violence Hotline can connect you directly with someone in your area who can help you (1-800-799-SAFE [7233]).

- Tell someone you trust what is happening to you.

- If you are hurt, go to a doctor or an emergency room. Tell them what happened. Ask them to make a record of your visit and what happened. Get a copy.

- Plan with your children. Figure out a safe place for them to go. This might be a room with a lock or a friend's house where they can go for help. Make sure they know that their job is to stay safe, not to protect you.

- Contact your local domestic violence organization or battered women's shelter. They can tell you about laws and other resources available to you before you have to use them during a crisis.

- Try to set money aside. You can ask friends or family members to hold money for you.

GENERAL GUIDELINES FOR LEAVING AN ABUSIVE RELATIONSHIP

- Make a plan for how you are going to leave and where you're going to go. Make a plan for leaving if you have time to prepare. Make another plan for leaving if you have to leave in a hurry.

- A worker at a domestic violence organization can help you make a plan to leave as safely as you can. Also, "Leaving Abuse" (www.leavingabuse.com) can help you think of ways to leave safely.

- If you're going to leave secretly, plan ahead and cover your tracks. A domestic violence worker and "Leaving Abuse" (www.leavingabuse.com) can help you come up with a plan.

- You can ask the police to escort you out of the house as you're leaving. You can also ask them to be "on call" while you're leaving.
- Put aside as much emergency money as you can.
- Hide an extra set of car keys in a place you can get to easily.
- Get a bag together with:
  - spare car keys;
  - money;
  - phone numbers for friends, relatives, doctors, schools, taxi services, and your local domestic violence organization;
  - a change of clothing for you and your children;
  - medication that you or your children usually take;
  - copies of your children's birth certificates, social security cards, school records, and immunizations;
  - copies of legal documents for you and your abuser. This may include social security cards, passports, greencards, medical records, insurance information, birth certificates, marriage license, wills, and welfare identification information;
  - copies of financial documents for you and your abuser. This may include pay stubs, bank account information, and a list of credit cards you hold by yourself or together with your abuser;
  - the evidence you've been collecting to show that you've been abused; and
  - a few things you want to keep, like photographs, jewelry, or other personal items.

Hide this bag somewhere he will not find it. Try to keep it at a trusted friend or neighbor's house. Avoid using next-door neighbors, close family members, or mutual friends. Your abuser might be more likely to find it there.

If you're in an emergency and need to get out right away, don't worry about gathering these things. While they're helpful to have, getting out safely should come first.

As you are leaving:

- Grab the bag you hid, your driver's license, any checkbooks, and credit cards if you can. If there's time, take the originals of documents you might need, such as birth certificates, social security cards, legal documents, and financial documents.
- Create a false trail. Call motels, real estate agencies, and schools in a town at least six hours away from where you plan to go.

Ask them questions that will need to be answered by them calling you back. Give them your old phone number.

SAFETY WHEN GOING TO COURT

If you are going to court for a final protective order, your abuser may also be coming to court. Here are some ideas on keeping safe in court.

Getting to Court

- Plan on getting to court an hour or more before your hearing. That way, you may get to court before your abuser does. This can make it safer for you to get into the building.
- Try to get a domestic violence worker to go with you. It can really help with safety. Call the National Domestic Violence Hotline (1-800-799-SAFE [7233]) to find help near you.
- Bring a friend or family member with you.
- See if your police department or sheriff's department will take you to the courthouse. Ask them to meet you **away** from the courthouse. Ask the officer to walk you inside. Have the officer wait with you until the bailiff or courthouse security is around.
- Have a friend drive you. It's best to get someone whose car your abuser doesn't know. Ask your friend to drop you off at the courthouse entrance, instead of having you walk in from the parking lot.
- If you have to drive yourself, try to keep your abuser from recognizing your car. If you can, borrow or rent a car that your abuser doesn't know. If you drive your own car, cover it with a sheet once you've parked.

Inside the Courthouse

- Travel in a group with the people who came with you. Pick a person who will only pay attention to the surroundings and safety considerations.
- Find someone who knows the court well, such as the domestic violence worker or someone who works at the court. Ask them about safe places you can hide inside the court. Some safe places to hide might be witness rooms or where courthouse security is. Ask them where all the exits are, in case you have to leave in a hurry. In addition to the the main exit, there may be exits through the courtrooms, side exits, or exits through the judges' chambers (their offices).

- Let the bailiff or courthouse security know if your abuser sits next to you or tries to harass you. Ask the bailiff to keep your abuser away from you.

Leaving the Courthouse

- At the end of your hearing, ask the judge to "detain" your abuser, to hold him until you can leave.
- If the judge doesn't detain your abuser, think about letting your abuser leave first. Then wait a long time before leaving.
- Have a police officer or sheriff walk out with you.
- Have a friend pick you up at the exit.

LEAVING THE ABUSIVE RELATIONSHIP

If you are getting a restraining order and your abuser is leaving:

- Change your locks.
- Put dead bolt locks on your doors.
- If you can, replace any wood doors with steel or metal doors.
- If you have the money, think about installing a security system.
- Try to make sure that the outside of your house is well-lit. Think about getting a lighting system that lights up when a person is coming close to the house (motion sensitive lights).
- Keep bushes, trees, and other plants around your house well-trimmed. That way, you'll be able to see more of what is happening outside.
- Change your phone number. Tell the phone company to not list your new phone number.
- Call the telephone company to request caller ID. Ask that your phone be blocked so that if you call, neither your partner nor anyone else will be able to get your new, unlisted phone number.
- If you can, change the hours that you work. Take different routes to work. Avoid the route you took when you and your abuser were together.
- When you're taking the children to school, take different routes. Avoid the route you took when you were with your abuser.

- Tell anyone who takes care of your children the names of the individuals who are allowed to pick up your children. Explain your situation to them. Give them a copy of your restraining order.

- Take a different route to the grocery store, hardware store, restaurants, and any other place you go on a regular basis. Use different places if you can.

- Try not to travel alone. Stay in public and well-lit places as much as you can.

- Avoid walking or jogging alone.

- Keep a certified copy of your restraining order with you at all times.

- Let friends, neighbors, and employers know that you have a restraining order in effect.

- Give copies of your restraining order to your employers, neighbors, and schools. Also give them a picture of your abuser.

- Tell people you work with about the situation. See if a receptionist or someone else can screen your calls.

- Call law enforcement if your abuser violates the order.

- Carry a cell phone if you can, but don't count on it too much. Cell phones may not get good service in some places, and batteries do run out. Ask your local domestic violence organization if they give out cell phones. Have emergency numbers on speed dial.

- If you need help in a public place, yell "FIRE." People respond more quickly to someone yelling "fire" than to any other cry for help.

- Stay in touch with your local domestic violence organization for support.

- Get a full check-up with your doctor to see if you need medical treatment. Keep in mind that your abuser may not have been faithful. Consider getting tested for sexually transmitted diseases.

If you are leaving:

- Have an address that's different from where you're living. Think about renting a post office box or using a friend's address.

- Be aware that addresses are on restraining orders and police reports. Before filling out your new address on any forms, ask if there's any way to keep your address confidential.

- Tell the phone company to not list your new address and phone number.
- Call the telephone company to request caller ID. Ask that your phone be blocked to keep other people from getting your new, unlisted phone number.
- Be careful about giving out your new address and phone number.
- Change your work hours if you can.
- If you have children, let their school know what is going on.
- Consider changing your children's schools.
- Reschedule appointments you made before leaving that your abuser may know about.
- Take a different route to the grocery store, hardware store, restaurants, and any other place you go on a regular basis. Use different places if you can.
- Consider telling your new neighbors about the situation. Make a plan with them for when you need help. Have a signal, like flashing the lights on and off or hanging something out the window, to tell them you need help.
- Talk to people you trust about the violence.
- Put dead bolt locks on your doors.
- If you can, replace any wood doors with steel or metal doors.
- If you have the money, think about installing a security system.
- Try to make sure that the outside of your house is well-lit. Think about getting a lighting system that lights up when a person is coming close to the house (motion sensitive lights).
- Keep bushes, trees, and other plants around your house well-trimmed. That way, you'll be able to see more of what is happening outside.
- Tell people you work with about the situation. See if a receptionist or someone else can screen your calls.
- Tell anyone who takes care of your children the names of the individuals who are allowed to pick up your children. Explain your situation to them. Give them a copy of your restraining order if you have one.
- Carry a cell phone if you can, but don't count on it too much. Cell phones may not get good service in some places, and batteries do run out. Ask your local domestic violence organization

if they give out cell phones. Have emergency numbers on speed dial.

- If you need help in a public place, yell "FIRE." People respond more quickly to someone yelling "fire" than to any other cry for help.
- Stay in touch with your local domestic violence organization for support.
- Get a full check-up with your doctor to see if you need medical treatment. Keep in mind that your abuser may not have been faithful. Consider getting tested for sexually transmitted diseases.

SAFETY IN RURAL AREAS

If you live in a rural area or a small town, there are some additional things to keep in mind when you're making a safety plan.

It may take police or sheriff a long time to get to you.

- If you call the police, get to a safe place to wait for the police. You may want to go to a friend or neighbor's house or a public place you think is safe.
- If you decide to leave your abuser, think about leaving your area, at least for a little while. Think about it even if you get a protective order.

A lot of times, there aren't any buses, taxis, or other types of public transportation and your abuser may keep you from using the car.

- Make a plan with a friend you trust to give you a ride when you need one.
- See if your local sheriff's office or police department can help you.
- See if any local churches, synagogues, or spiritual groups can help you.
- Talk with a domestic violence worker. She or he can help you make a plan to get a ride when you need one.

Your abuser may have weapons.

- Be aware of things that your abuser can use as a weapon. He may use sharp or heavy objects, like a hammer or an ice pick, to hurt you.

- Know where guns, knives, and other weapons are kept. If you can, lock them up or make them as hard to get to as you can.
- Figure out "safe places" in your home—places where there aren't weapons. If it looks like your abuser is about to hurt you, try to get to a safe place. Stay out of the kitchen, garage, or workshop. Try to avoid rooms with tile or hardwood floors.

There may be many isolated areas in your community. These isolated areas can be dangerous for you.

- Try to stay away from isolated areas when you can.
- Travel in a "pack." If you can, have someone in charge of paying attention to safety and what's going on around you.
- Consider leaving the area, at least for a little while. Consider it even if you get a protective order.
- Carry a cell phone if you can, but don't count on it too much. Cell phones may not get good service in some places, and batteries do run out. Ask your local domestic violence organization if they give out cell phones. Have emergency numbers on speed dial.

Safe places, like a friend's house or a shelter, may be far away.

- If you can use a car, try to keep a full tank of gas.
- In winter, keep clothing for cold weather (like a hat, scarf, and jacket) in an accessible place. If you can, keep them in your car.
- Be aware of where neighbors live along the road in case you need to pull over.

In your area, people may know where the domestic violence shelter is; the shelter location may not be confidential.

- Be aware that your abuser and other people may know where the shelter is.
- Think about going to a shelter outside of where you live, even if it's only for a little while.
- If you go to the shelter, cover your car with a sheet. This can help keep your abuser and other people from seeing your car in the parking lot.

Appendix 2

Teen Dating Violence

The following recommendations are from the WomensLaw.org Web site: http://www.womenslaw.org/teens.htm.

Dating violence (or relationship abuse) is a pattern of overcontrolling behavior that someone uses against a girlfriend or boyfriend. Dating violence can take many forms, including mental/emotional abuse, physical abuse, and sexual abuse. So, you may experience dating violence even if you are not being physically abused. It can occur in both casual dating situations and serious, long-term relationships.

How Is Teen Dating Violence Different from Adult Domestic Violence?

There are several things that make teenage dating violence different from adult domestic violence. Usually, when a teen is abused, he or she becomes isolated from his or her peers because of the controlling behavior of the abusive partner.

The isolation teens face in abusive dating situations often makes it hard to:

- Develop new and mature relationships with peers of both sexes;
- Feel emotionally independent;
- Develop personal values and beliefs; and
- Stay focused on school and get good grades.

Am I Being Abused?

Many people don't recognize that they are in an abusive relationship. They don't realize how they have gradually changed because of the abuse. Answer the questions below. If you answer yes to two or more of them, you are probably in an abusive relationship or your relationship is likely to become abusive. Abuse isn't just hitting.

It's yelling; threatening; name-calling; saying things like "I'll kill myself if you leave me"; obsessive phone calling; and extreme possessiveness.

Are you going out with someone who:

- is jealous and possessive, won't let you have friends, checks up on you, won't accept breaking up?
- tries to control you by being bossy, giving orders, making all the decisions, not taking your opinions seriously?
- puts you down in front of friends, tells you that you would be nothing without him or her?
- scares you?
- makes you worry about his or her reactions to things you say or do?
- threatens you?
- uses or owns guns or other weapons?
- is violent?
- has a history of fighting, loses temper quickly, brags about mistreating others?
- grabs, pushes, shoves, or hits you?
- pressures you for sex or is forceful or scary about sex?
- gets too serious about the relationship too fast?
- abuses alcohol or other drugs and pressures you to take them?
- has a history of failed relationships and blames the other person for all the problems?
- makes your family and friends uneasy and concerned for your safety?
- makes you feel like you need to apologize to yourself or others for your partner's behavior when he or she treats you badly?

The following recommendations are from the Boulder Colorado Police Department Web site: http://www3.ci.boulder.co.us/police/prevention/teen-dating.htm.

If you want out:

- Tell your parents, a friend, a counselor, a clergyman, or someone else whom you trust and who can help. The more isolated you are from friends and family, the more control the abuser has over you;
- Alert the school counselor or security officer;
- Keep a daily log of the abuse;

- Do not meet your partner alone. Don't let him or her in your home or car when you are alone;
- Avoid being alone at school, your job, or on the way to and from places;
- Tell someone where you are going and when you plan to be back;
- Plan and rehearse what you would do if your partner became abusive.

Being a Friend to a Victim of Abuse

Most teens talk to other teens about their problems. If a friend tells you he or she is being victimized, here are some suggestions on how you can help.

- If you notice a friend is in an abusive relationship, don't ignore signs of abuse. Talk to your friend.
- Express your concerns. Tell your friend you're worried. Support, don't judge.
- Point out your friend's strengths—many people in abusive relationships are no longer capable of seeing their own abilities and gifts.
- Encourage your friend to confide in a trusted adult. Talk to a trusted adult if you believe the situation is getting worse. Offer to go with your friend for help.
- Never put yourself in a dangerous situation with the victim's partner. Don't be a mediator.
- Call the police if you witness an assault. Tell an adult, a school principal, parent, guidance counselor.

What You Can Do

- Start a peer education program on teen dating violence.
- Ask your school library to purchase books about living without violence and the cycle of domestic violence.
- Create bulletin boards in the school cafeteria or classroom to raise awareness.
- Perform a play about teen dating violence.

ADDITIONAL TEEN DATING VIOLENCE INFORMATION

There are many great resources available on-line that provide information on teen dating violence. Listed below are some sites that are invaluable resources to teen dealing with relationship violence:

- **Love Is Not Abuse**
  www.loveisnotabuse.com
- **Break the Cycle**
  www.breakthecycle.org
  310-286-3366
  888-988-TEEN
  help@break-the-cycle.org
- **Teen Outreach Program**
  www.teenrelationships.org/
  Teen hotline: 650-259-8136
  Hotline hours: Monday–Wednesday, 5–7 P.M. Pacific Time
- **U Have the Right**
  www.uhavetheright.net
- **West Virginia Department of Health & Human Resources**
  www.wvdhhr.org/bph/trust/index.htm
- **Safe Youth**
  www.safeyouth.org/scripts/index.asp
- **The Quiet Storm Project**
  www.thequietstormproject.com/tqsp.html
- **Love Doesn't Have to Hurt**
  www.apa.org/pi/pii/teen
- **KidsHealth**
  www.kidshealth.org/teen/your_mind/relationships/abuse.html
- **SeeItAndStopIt.Org**
  www.seeitandstopit.org
- **Cool Nurse**
  www.coolnurse.com/teen_dating_violence.htm

Appendix 3

What Parents, Teachers, and Other Caregivers Should Know about Child Sexual Abuse

The following recommendations are from the Queensland government Web site: http://www.communities.qld.gov.au/projectaxis/booklet_carers. html.

- About half the children who are sexually abused suffer in silence. They never tell another person.
- Most of the time, the offender is known by both the child and the child's parents.
- Most child sex offending occurs within or close to the child's home.
- One in five child sexual abuse offenders found their victims in the organizations in which they worked or volunteered.

Talk to Them to Protect Them

- Anyone who cares for children must help educate and protect them from sexual abuse.
- For the sake of our children, it's a topic that must be permanently removed from the taboo list. It must be discussed as openly in our society as road safety and stranger danger.
- Children need to know it's OK to talk to parents and caregivers when anything of a sexual nature worries them. This helps children feel more confident about raising the subject with adults they can trust.
- Children have the right to expect adults will protect them.

Ways You Can Protect Your Child

- Be suspicious if an adult wants to spend time alone with your child.

- Be wary of people who are overly affectionate or generous with gifts to your child.

- Be careful about the company your children keep. Watch children's behavior for signs of stress; their reactions to certain individuals may be telling you something.

- Teach children that parts of their bodies covered by underwear are private.

- Encourage children to tell someone they trust if anyone tries to touch their private parts.

- Teach children never to keep secrets that make them feel uncomfortable or bad.

- Check who is supervising your children when they are away from home.

- Listen to your children and trust what they say, even if it shocks you. Children rarely make up stories about sexual abuse.

Telltale Signs of Sexual Abuse

Children will often say things, do things, or exhibit physical signs that are clues to sexual abuse.

Watch for the following:

- Children displaying greater sexual knowledge than normally expected for their age;

- Unexpected redness, soreness, or injury around the penis, vagina, mouth, or anus;

- Children playing sex games with much younger children and being more preoccupied with sex talk and sex games than other children;

- Excessive masturbation or masturbation in public after kindergarten age;

- Children always drawing the sexual parts of bodies; and

- Children being afraid or upset when people talk about their bodies or sex.

If any of these signs are present, the children may need parents or other adults to keep them safe from further harm.

What Parents and Caregivers Can Do

- Try to teach children about being safe in a way that does not frighten them.
- Teach your child your home address and telephone number as early as possible.
- Speak to children who are under school age about personal safety, in simple language and repeat the same rules often. Play "what if" games to reinforce the message.
- Teach children of primary school age basic family safety rules and how to apply them in potentially dangerous situations.
- Assist adolescents to think independently and to develop the skills of decision making and assertiveness.
- Teach adolescents to assess potentially risky situations and to act in a preventive manner, for example, not walking alone in deserted places or keeping some money aside for emergency calls or transport.

Appendix 4

Legal and Advocacy Resources

Abusive Men Exploring New Directions (AMEND)
Provides counseling to men who have been the abusers in intimate partner violence, supports their partners and children, and provides education services to the community.
2727 Bryant Street, Suite 350
Denver, CO 80211
http://www.amendinc.org

Asian & Pacific Islander Institute on Domestic Violence
Serves as a clearinghouse for information, resources, research, and other services about intimate partner violence against women specifically from the Asian and Pacific Islander communities.
450 Sutter Street, Suite 600
San Francisco, CA 94108
http://www.apiahf.org/apidvinstitute

Asian Task Force Against Domestic Violence
Maintains a 24-hour confidential hotline that serves women from 15 different ethnic groups in 12 Asian languages for women in the Boston area.
P.O. Box 120108
Boston, MA 02112
http://www.atask.org

Battered Women's Justice Project—Civil Division
Works with advocates and victim service providers to educate communities about domestic violence and ensure targeted, appropriate responses to cases of domestic violence. BWJP functions through a partnership of three organizations: the Domestic Abuse Intervention Project, which addresses the criminal justice system's response to

domestic violence; the Pennsylvania Coalition Against Domestic Violence, which addresses civil court access and legal representation issues of battered women; and the National Clearinghouse for the Defense of Battered Women, which addresses issues raised when battered women are accused of committing crimes, including killing an abusive partner.

Commission on Domestic Violence—American Bar Association

The Commission on Domestic Violence Web site provides American Bar Association policies, training materials, legal briefs, and sample legal forms relevant to domestic violence issues and proceedings. The site also includes information about upcoming events and training opportunities and links to other resources and organizations.
740 15th Street NW, Ninth Floor
Washington, DC 20005-1022
Phone: 202-662-1737
www.abanet.org/domviol

Criminal Justice Information Services Division—National Crime Information Center, Federal Bureau of Investigation

Serves as the FBI's central repository for criminal justice information services. Programs include the National Crime Information Center, Uniform Crime Reporting, the Integrated Automated Fingerprint Identification System, and the National Incident-Based Reporting System.
1000 Custer Hollow Road
Clarksburg, WV 26306
Phone: 304-625-2000
www.fbi.gov/hq/cjisd/cjis.htm

FaithTrust Institute

Provides information about date and marital rape and provides education through speakers, publications, and consultation. International in scope, working with communities including Asian and Pacific Islander, Latino/a, Buddhist, Jewish, Muslim, African American, Indigenous, Protestant, and Roman Catholic.
2400 North 45th Street #10
Seattle, WA 98103
http://www.faithtrustinstitute.org

Institute on Domestic Violence in the African American Community

Provides numerous educational resources about intimate partner violence in the African American community to its victims, seeking to educate practitioners.

University of Minnesota, School of Social Work
290 Peters Hall
1404 Gortner Avenue
St. Paul, MN 55108-6142
http://www.dvinstitute.org

Islamic Society of North America
Devoted to issues that affect the male and female of Middle Eastern descent, including several resources for the Islamic women suffering from intimate partner violence.
P.O. Box 38
Plainfield, IN 46168
http://www.isna.net

Muslim Women's League
Addresses the religious, legal, and civil rights concerns of the woman of Middle Eastern descent who may be experiencing intimate partner violence in the United States.
3010 Wilshire Blvd., Suite 519
Los Angeles, CA 90010
http://www.mwlusa.org

The National Alliance for Hispanic Health
Provides general health information for both Hispanic men and women and includes a brief overview of intimate partner violence.
1501 Sixteenth Street NW
Washington, DC 20036
Hotline: 1-866-SU-FAMILIA or 1-866-783-2645
http://www.hispanichealth.org

National Center for Victims of Crime
Mission is to help victims of crime and their families rebuild their lives. NCVC works with local, state, and federal agencies to enact legislation and provide resources, training, and technical assistance. The NCVC Web site provides relevant statistics, links to publications, and referrals to participating attorneys.
2000 M Street NW, Suite 480
Washington, DC 20036
Phone: 202-467-8700 or 1-800-FYI-CALL
http://www.ncvc.org

National Center on Full Faith and Credit
Promotes interjurisdictional enforcement of civil and criminal protection orders. The project provides ongoing assistance and training on full faith

and credit, federal firearms prohibitions, and federal domestic violence and stalking crimes to law enforcement officers, prosecutors, judges, court administrators and other court personnel, private attorneys, victim advocates, and others who work with victims of domestic violence and stalking.
1601 Connecticut Avenue NW, Suite 701
Washington, DC 20009
Phone: 1-800-256-5883, ext. 2

National Immigration Project of the National Lawyers Guild

Provides important overviews and interpretations of immigration provisions included in the Violence Against Women and Department of Justice Reauthorization Act of 2005 for noncitizens of the United States who are women and also the victims of intimate partner abuse.
14 Beacon Street, Suite 602
Boston, MA 02108
http://www.nationalimmigrationproject.org

National Latino Alliance for the Elimination of Domestic Violence (Alianza)

Goals include raising community awareness of intimate partner violence and options for the victim within the Latino community, helping to formulate policies to help prevent and end intimate partner violence in Latino communities, and fostering competent research and training to help Latino/a practitioners.
P.O. Box 672
Triborough Station
New York, NY 10035
http://www.dvalianza.org

The National Organization for Men Against Sexism (NOMAS)

Holds conferences and has chapters to educate and provide counseling to men who have been the abusers and has programs that stress non-violence, the assumption of personal responsibility, and ways to deal with emotions and anger, relationships, and parenting.
P.O. Box 455
Louisville, CO 80027-0455
http://www.nomas.org

National Tribal Justice Resource Center

A comprehensive Web site dedicated to tribal justice systems for Native American and Alaska Native tribal courts. Includes information for female victims of intimate partner violence.

4410 Arapahoe Avenue, Suite 135
Boulder, CO 80303
http://www.tribalresourcecenter.org

Pennsylvania Coalition Against Domestic Violence
6400 Flank Drive, Suite 1300
Harrisburg, PA 17112
Phone: 1-800-903-0111, ext. 2
www.pcadv.org/projects.html

Resource Center on Domestic Violence: Child Protection and Custody
National Council of Juvenile and Family Court Judges
Provides professionals involved with domestic violence and child protection and custody issues with access to information and assistance.
P. O. Box 8970
Reno, NV 89507
Phone: 1-800-527-3223
http://www.dvlawsearch.com/res_center

Standing Committee on the Delivery of Legal Services—American Bar Association
Focuses on improving the delivery of legal services to the public, specifically people of moderate income.
541 North Fairbanks Court
Chicago, IL 60611
Phone: 312-988-5761
http://www.abanet.org/legalservices/delivery/home.html

Violence Against Women in American Indian/Native American & Alaska Native Communities
Provides educational and legal information for female victims of intimate partner violence from American Indian/Native American and Alaska Native communities.
6400 Flank Drive, Suite 1300
Harrisburg, PA 17112-2778
http://www.vawnet.org

Women's Law Project (Insurance Discrimination)
Works to advance the legal and economic status of women and their families through litigation, advocacy, public education, and direct

services including a telephone counseling and referral service. Project staff are experts in insurance discrimination.
125 South Ninth Street, Suite 300
Philadelphia, PA 19107

Young Women's Christian Association (YWCA)
Local branches of this organization may offer such services as infant care, food banks, children's programs, and abuse counseling. It is recommended that you contact the local chapter of the YWCA in your area.
1015 18th Street NW, Suite 1100
Washington, DC 20036
http://www.ywca.org

ADDITIONAL RELEVANT ORGANIZATIONS AND WEB SITES

2005 National Crime Victims' Rights Week Resource Guide
http://www.ojp.usdoj.gov/ovc/ncvrw/2005/pg4c.html#d

Acquaintance Rape of College Students (Department of Justice, 2002)
This guide describes the problem of acquaintance rape of college students, addressing its scope, causes, and contributing factors; methods for analyzing it on a particular campus; tested responses; and measures for assessing response effectiveness. http://www.cops.usdoj.gov/mime/open.pdf?Item=269

American Bar Association Commission on Domestic Violence http://www.abanet.org/domviol/home.html

American Indian & Alaska Native Affairs (Office of Justice Programs, U. S. Department of Justice)
Addresses the many concerns of male and female Native American and Alaskan Natives, including a good deal of legal information for female victims of intimate partner violence from these tribes.
http://www.ojp.usdoj.gov/americannative

American Psychological Association, Presidential Task Force on Violence and the Family
http://www.apa.org/pi/pii/issues/homepage.html

Antistalking Web Site
http://www.antistalking.com/

Asian Task Force Against Domestic Violence
http://www.atask.org/

Battered Women's Justice Project
Resource for legal issues involving domestic violence, and information on finding an attorney. http://www.bwjp.org/

By the Numbers (Illinois Coalition against Sexual Assault, 2001)
Facts and statistics on sexual violence
http://www.icasa.org/uploads/adult_victimss.pdf

Information on nonstranger sexual assault
http://www.icasa.org/uploads/acquaintance_rape-final.pdf

Physical and emotional effects of sexual violence
http://www.icasa.org/uploads/Health_information.pdf

Center for Women Policy Studies
Contains information on policies that affect women, covering not only violence, but also health, education, foreign policy, and information on trafficking.
http://www.centerwomenpolicy.org/

Clearinghouse on Abuse and Neglect of the Elderly (CANE) at the University of Delaware
http://db.rdms.udel.edu:8080/CANE/index.jsp

Communities Against Violence Network (CAVNET)
A searchable, authoritative source of information about violence against women, children, persons with disabilities, gays and lesbians, and others.
http://www.cavnet2.org/

Costs of Intimate Partner Violence Against Women in the United States (report from the Centers for Disease Control and Prevention, National Center for Injury Prevention and Control, March 2003)
http://www.cdc.gov/ncipc/pub-res/ipv_cost/00_preface.htm

Division of Violence Prevention (Centers for Disease Control and Prevention) http://www.cdc.gov/ncipc/dvp/dvp.htm

Family Violence Prevention Fund
Works to prevent violence within the home, and in the community, to help those whose lives are devastated by violence.
http://endabuse.org/

Guidelines for Preventing Workplace Violence for Health Care and Social Service Workers (U.S. Department of Labor, Occupational Safety and Health Administration, 1998, revised 2003)

An extensive document with screening materials, references, and more.
http://www.osha-slc.gov/Publications/osha3148.pdf

Guidelines for the Evaluation of Sexual Abuse of Children (subject review from the American Academy of Pediatrics, January 1999)

http://aappolicy.aappublications.org/cgi/content/full/pediatrics;103/1/186

Indicators of School Crime and Safety: 2003 (Bureau of Justice Statistics, U.S. Department of Justice)

http://www.ojp.usdoj.gov/bjs/abstract/iscs03.htm

International Society for Research on Aggression

http://www.israsociety.com/

Jewish Women International

Striving to break the cycle of violence through education, advocacy, and action locally, nationally, and around the world.
http://www.jewishwomen.org/

Management of Imminent Violence

Clinical practice guidelines for mental health services, UK.
http://www.psychiatry.ox.ac.uk/cebmh/guidelines/violence/violence_full.html

Men Can Stop Rape (formerly the Men's Rape Prevention Project)
http://www.mencanstoprape.org/

Minnesota Center Against Violence and Abuse

One of the largest and best organized meta-sites for resources and Web links on all aspects of violence.
http://www.mincava.umn.edu/

Nation to Nation: Promoting the Safety of Native Women (Chapter 14 of *Toolkit to End Violence Against Women* from the National Advisory Council on Violence Against Women and the Violence Against Women Office)

http://toolkit.ncjrs.org/default.htm

National Center for Missing and Exploited Children

Resources available include an extensive document on sexually victimized children and their recovery.
http://www.missingkids.com/

National Center for PTSD PILOTS Database

An electronic index to the worldwide literature on posttraumatic stress disorder (PTSD) and other mental health consequences of exposure to traumatic events.
http://www.ncptsd.va.gov/publications/pilots/index.html

National Center for Victims of Crime

http://www.ncvc.org/ncvc/Main.aspx

National Center on Domestic and Sexual Violence

Trains professionals who work with victims and perpetrators of domestic violence, including law enforcement, health care professionals, counselors, and advocates.
http://www.ncdsv.org/

National Center on Elder Abuse

http://www.elderabusecenter.org/

National Clearinghouse on Family Violence in Canada

http://www.phac-aspc.gc.ca/ncfv-cnivf/familyviolence/bilingual.htm

National Coalition Against Domestic Violence

http://www.ncadv.org/

National Domestic Violence Hotline, 1-800-799-SAFE (7233)

http://www.ndvh.org/

National Network to End Domestic Violence

Contains a full summary of the Violence Against Women Act as well as legal information on specific cases involving domestic violence.
http://www.nnedv.org/

National Organization for Women

Comprehensive site containing updated news and information on issues affecting women. There are also links for advocacy and a store.
http://www.now.org/index.html

National Resource Center on Domestic Violence

Contains information on domestic violence including a collection of searchable electronic resources.

http://www.nrcdv.org/

National Sexual Violence Resource Center

Comprehensive collection and distribution center for information, statistics, and resources related to sexual violence.

http://www.nsvrc.org

National Women's Health Information Center

Provides free, reliable health information for women everywhere.

http://www.4woman.gov/faq/sexualassault.htm

Nonfamily Abducted Children: National estimates and characteristics (on-line report from the U.S. Department of Justice)

http://www.ncjrs.org/pdffiles1/ojjdp/196467.pdf

Nursing Network on Violence Against Women International

http://www.nnvawi.org/

Office of Violence Against Women of the U.S. Department of Justice

http://www.ojp.usdoj.gov/vawo/

Partnerships Against Violence Network

"Virtual library" of information about violence and youth-at-risk, representing data from seven different federal agencies.

http://www.pavnet.org/

Prevalence, Incidence, and Consequences of Violence against Women: Findings from the National Violence Against Women Survey (National Institute of Justice, 1998)

This report summarizes the results of a national survey on men's and women's experiences with violence, including the prevalence of rape and physical assault among women of different racial and ethnic backgrounds, the rate of injury among rape and physical assault victims, and injured victims' use of medical services.

http://www.ncjrs.org/pdffiles/172837.pdf

Psychological Abuse

Contains information on psychological abuse including definitions, prevalence, and information for victims.

http://psychabuse.info/

Rape, Abuse & Incest National Network (RAINN)
Nation's largest anti–sexual assault organization. Statistics, counseling resources, prevention tips, and more.
http://www.rainn.org/

Rape and Sexual Assault: Reporting to Police and Medical Attention, 1992–2000 (Bureau of Justice Statistics, 2002)
This report presents information on the consequences of rape and sexual assault for female victims.
http://www.ojp.usdoj.gov/bjs/pub/pdf/rsarp00.pdf

Rape Myths & Facts (Colorado Coalition against Sexual Assault, 2000)
Addresses 13 common myths about sexual assault. http://www.ccasa.org/documents/Rape_Myths_&_Facts.pdf

Sexual Assault and Rape Crisis Resource List (Feminist Majority Foundation; National and State Resources)
http://www.feminist.org/911/resources.html

Sexual Assault Support Services (Duke University)
http://wc.studentaffairs.duke.edu

Sexual Victimization of College Women (National Institute of Justice, 2000)
Reports prevalence of sexual assault using a sample of 4,446 randomly selected women who attended a two- or four-year college during the fall of 1996. http://www.ojp.usdoj.gov/bjs/abstract/svcw.htm

StopFamilyViolence.org
A comprehensive resource on domestic violence with information on the Violence Against Women Act as well as updated news and legal decisions affecting women.
http://www.stopfamilyviolence.org/

United Nations Fourth World Conference on Women: Platform for Action: Violence Against Women
http://www.un.org/womenwatch/daw/beijing/platform/violence.htm

U.S. Department of Health and Human Services
Includes information on domestic violence, elder abuse, and stalking. It also includes updated news, information on detecting abuse, and a checklist for leaving an abuser.
http://www.4woman.gov/violence/index.cfm

U.S. Department of Justice's Victims of Crime
http://www.usdoj.gov/crimevictims.htm

Victim Information and Notification Everyday (VINE)
Allows crime victims across the country to obtain timely and reliable information about criminal cases and the custody status of offenders 24 hours a day, over the telephone, through the Internet, or by E-mail. 1-866-277-7477.
http://www.appriss.com/VINE.html

Violence Against Women
Provides law, criminal justice, advocacy, and social service professionals with updated information on interventions.
http://www.vaw.umn.edu

Violence Against Women Act of 1994 (U.S. Department of Justice)
http://www.ojp.usdoj.gov/vawo/laws/vawa/vawa.htm

Violence as a Public Health Problem
Position statement from the American Association of Colleges of Nursing.
http://www.aacn.nche.edu/Publications/positions/violence.htm

Violence Prevention (American Medical Association)
http://www.ama-assn.org/ama/pub/category/3242.html

VioLit: Violence Literature database (Center for the Study and Prevention of Violence at the University of Colorado at Boulder)
http://ibs.colorado.edu/cspv/infohouse/violit/

Womenslaw.org
Resource for legal information, includes state-by-state information and resources. There is also a mirror site in Spanish.
http://www.womenslaw.org/

World Health Report on Violence and Health
The goals of the 2002 report are to raise awareness about the problem of violence globally and to highlight the crucial role that public health has to play in addressing its causes and consequences.
http://www.who.int/violence_injury_prevention/violence/world_report/wrvh1/en/ and http://www.who.int/violence_injury_prevention/violence/world_report/factsheets/en/index.html

STATE CRISIS LINES (24-HOUR FREE CALLS)

Alabama
Crisis Services of N. Alabama, Inc.
256-716-1000

Alaska
Central Peninsula Counseling Services
907-283-7511

Arizona
EMPACT-Suicide Prevention Center
480-784-1500 or 866-205-5229

Arkansas
NW Arkansas Crisis Intervention Center
888-274-7472 or 479-756-2337 (local)

California
Suicide Prevention Center
Didi Hirsch Community Mental Health Center
877-727-4747

Colorado
Jefferson Center for Mental Health
800-201-5264 or 303-432-5049 (TDD)

Connecticut
River Valley Services
860-344-2100
Wheeler Clinic, Inc.
860-747-3434 or 860-524-1182

Delaware
CONTACT Delaware, Inc.
800-262-9700 or 302-761-9100 (local)

District of Columbia
Access Helpline
888-793-4357

Florida
Switchboard of Miami, Inc.
305-358-4357

Georgia
Emergency Mental Health Services
404-730-1600

Hawaii
Crisis Line
800-877-7999

Idaho
Idaho Suicide Prevention Hotline
800-564-2120
Region VII Mental Health 24-hour emergency
208-528-5700

Illinois
Mental Health Association of Illinois Valley
888-799-7373 or 309-673-7373

Indiana
Community Health Center
877-849-1248
Crisis Center—Rape Line
800-519-0469

Iowa
Foundation 2 Crisis Line
319-362-2174
Crisis Line: Service of the American Red Cross
800-244-7431 or 515-244-1000

Kansas
Headquarters Counseling Center
785-841-2345

Kentucky
River Valley Behavioral Health
800-433-7291

Life Skills Hotline
800-223-8913

Louisiana
Baton Rouge Crisis Intervention Center, Inc.
225-924-3900

Maryland
Grassroots Crisis Intervention Center, Inc.
410-531-6677

Maine
Ingraham
888-568-1112
Crisis Response Service
888-568-1112

Massachusetts
The Samaritans on Cape Cod and the Islands, Inc.
800-893-9900 or 508-548-8900

Michigan
Third Level Crisis Center
800-442-7315
University of Michigan Health System
734-996-4747

Minnesota
Crisis Line & Referral Service
800-462-5525
Listening Ear Crisis Center
800-854-9001

Mississippi
CONTACT Crisis Line
601-713-4357 or 866-322-9832 (Spanish)

Missouri
St. Louis Life Crisis Services
314-647-4357

St. Louis Behavioral Health Response
314-469-6644 or 800-811-4760

Montana
Crisis Line—Voices of Hope
888-587-0199

Nebraska
Girls & Boys Town National Hotline
800-448-3000

New Hampshire
Riverbend Community Mental Health Services
800-852-3323
The Samaritans of the Monadnock Region
603-357-5505

New Jersey
Center for Family Services
800-648-0132
Contact We Care, Inc.
908-490-1900

New Mexico
Crisis Response of Santa Fe
888-920-6333 or 505-820-6333 (local)
The Dutchess County Department of Mental Hygiene
877-485-9700 or 845-486-2866 (TTY)

North Carolina
Riverstone Counseling and Personal Development
252-537-2909 or 800-742-2572

North Dakota
Mental Health Association HELP-LINE
800-472-2911
West Central Human Service Center
888-328-2112 or 800-366-6888 (TTY)

Ohio
Portage Path Community Mental Health Center
330-434-9144 or 330-434-1706 (TTY)

Crisis Intervention Center of Stark County
800-956-6630

Oklahoma
Contact Telephone Hotline
405-848-2273

Oregon
NW Human Services Inc., Crisis & Information Hotline
800-560-5535 or 503-581-5535 (TTY)

Pennsylvania
Montgomery County Emergency Service, Inc.
800-452-4189 or 610-279-6100
Adams/Hanover Counsel Service
800-673-2426

Rhode Island
The Samaritans of Rhode Island
800-365-4044

South Carolina
Aiken County Help Line, Inc.
803-648-9900
United Way 2-1-1
866-744-7778

South Dakota
Help! Line Center
605-339-4357

Tennessee
Centerstone Community Health Centers, Inc.
800-681-7444

Texas
Suicide and Crisis Center
214-828-1000
Crisis Intervention of Houston, Inc.
713-468-5463

Utah
Valley Mental Health Crisis Service
801-261-1442

Vermont
Clara Martin Center
800-639-6360

Virginia
New River Community Services—ACCESS Services
888-717-3333
ACTS Helpline
703-368-4141

Washington
North Islands Mental Health
800-584-3578
Crisis Clinic of the Peninsulas
800-843-4793 or 360-479-3033

West Virginia
Contact Huntington Inc.
304-523-3448

Wisconsin
Walworth Co. Department of Human Services
800-365-1587

Wyoming
Victims of Violence Center
307-347-4991

Notes

Preface

1. Yaroslava Krestovskaya, "Condolezza Rice's ant-Russian stance based on sexual problems,"*Pravda, RU*, January 11 2006, Online News Publication.

Chapter 1

1. Shannan M. Catalano, *Criminal Victimization, 2004*, special report prepared for the U.S. Department of Justice, Office of Justice Programs (Washington, DC: Government Printing Office, 2005), 10.

2. Marcia Clark and Teresa Carpenter, *Without a Doubt* (New York: Viking Penguin, 1997).

3. Margaret Carlson, "Preventable Murders," *Time*, October 16, 1995.

4. Howard Chua-Eoan and Elizabeth Gleick, "Making the Case: A Behind-the-Scenes Look at the Missteps, Triumphs, Animosities and Egos of the Trial of the Century," *Time*, October 16, 1995.

5. Carlson.

6. Ibid.

7. Patricia Edmonds, "Messages Mixed on Domestic Violence," *USA Today*, October 18, 1996, http://usatoday.com/news/index/nns091.htm (accessed September 20, 2005).

8. The Associated Press, "Key Dates in the O.J. Simpson Case," *USA Today*, February 4, 1997, http://www.usatoday.com/news/index/nns171.htm (accessed January 9, 2006).

9. "Key Dates in the Peterson Trial," *CNN.com*, December 13, 2004, http://www.cnn.com/2004/LAW/11/12/peterson.timeline/index.html (accessed January 9, 2006).

10. Amanda Bower and Laura A. Locke, "Murder in the Family," *Time*, April 28, 2003.

11. "Peterson Sentenced to Death for Wife's Slaying," *CNN.com*, March 16, 2005, http://www.cnn.com/2005/LAW/03/16/peterson.case/index.html (accessed January 9, 2006).

12. "Peterson Guilty of Murder," *CNN.com*, November 13, 2004, http://www.cnn.com/2004/LAW/11/12/peterson.verdict/index.html (accessed September 4, 2005).

13. Jane Roh, Adam Housley, and The Associated Press, "Mark Hacking Pleads Guilty to Murder," *FOXNews.com*, April 15, 2005, http://www.foxnews.com/story/0,2933,153607,00.html (accessed January 9, 2006).

14. "Missing Woman's In-laws: Son Lied About Medical School," *CNN.com*, July 21, 2004, http://www.cnn.com/2004/US/West/07/21/missing.-jogger/index.html (accessed January 9, 2006).

15. Roh, Housley, and The Associated Press.

16. "Remains of Missing Utah Woman Found in Landfill," *CNN.com*, October 1, 2004, http://www.cnn.com/2004/LAW/10/01/hacking.case/index.html (accessed January 8, 2006).

17. Ruth Teichroeb, "Why Rein in the Police? 5-year-old David Brame Jr. Knows: Crystal Brame's Family Seeks Reforms That Will Help Others Embroiled in Domestic Violence," *Seattle Post-Intelligencer*, July 25, 2003, http://seattlepi.nwsource.com/printer2/index.asp?ploc=t&refer=http://seattlepi.nwsource.com/local/132287_dvbrame25.html (accessed January 9, 2006).

18. Teichroeb.

19. Lewis Kamb et al., "Tacoma Police Chief Shoots Wife, Kills Himself," *Seattle Post-Intelligencer*, April 26, 2003, http://seattlepi.nwsource.com/printer2/index.asp?ploc=t&refer=http://seattlepi.nwsource.com/local/119458_chief26ww.html (accessed January 8, 2006).

20. Kamb et al.

21. "Peterson Guilty of Murder," *CNN.com*, December 14, 2004, http://www.cnn.com/2004/LAW/11/12/peterson.verdict/index.html (accessed January 9, 2006).

22. Rusty Dornin, "Peterson Guilty of Murder," *CNN.com*, December 14, 2004, http://www.cnn.com/2004/LAW/11/12/peterson.verdict/index.html (accessed September 4, 2005).

23. V. Frye, "Examining Homicide's Contribution to Pregnancy-Associated Deaths," *The Journal of the American Medical Association* 285, no. 11 (2001): 1510–11.

24. Dornin.

25. Rochelle Steinhaus, "Carruth Playing for His Life," *COURTTV.com*, October 31, 2000, http://www.courttv.com/trials/carruth/background.html (accessed January 9, 2006).

26. Dawn Bradley Berry, *The Domestic Violence Sourcebook* (Los Angeles: Lowell House, 1998).

27. District of Columbia Coalition Against Domestic Violence, "Domestic Violence Statistics," August 1995, http://www.dccadv.org// (accessed November 7, 2005).

28. U.S. Department of Justice, Bureau of Justice Statistics Crime Data Brief, *Intimate Partner Violence, 1993–2001*, February 2003, http://endabuse.org/resources/facts/DomesticViolence.pdf (accessed January 9, 2006).

29. Family Violence Prevention Fund, "Domestic Violence Is A Serious, Widespread Social Problem In America: The Facts," http://endabuse.org/resources/facts/DomesticViolence.pdf (accessed May 13, 2006).

30. Berry.

31. Catalano.

32. National Center on Domestic and Sexual Violence, "Sexual Assault Statistics," http://www.ncdsv.org/images/SexualAssaultStatistics.pdf (accessed September 10, 2005).

33. U.S. Department of Justice, *Intimate Partner Violence*.

34. D. G. Kirkpatrick, C. Edmunds, and A. Seymour, *Rape in America: A Report to the Nation* (Charleston, SC: National Victim Center & the Crime Victims Research and Treatment Center, 1992).

35. Berry, 3.

36. "Psychological Abuse: Prevalence and Consequences," *Psychabuse.info*, 2005, http://psychabuse.info// (accessed January 10, 2006).

37. L. Heise, M. Ellsberg, and M. Gottemoeller, "Ending Violence Against Women, Population Reports," *Issues in World Health* series L, no. 11 (December 1999), http://www.infoforhealth.org/pr/l11edsum.shtml

38. Berry.

39. Centers for Disease Control and Prevention, *Costs of Intimate Partner Violence Against Women in the United States* (Atlanta, GA: Centers for Disease Control and Prevention, 2003).

40. Berry.

41. Murray A. Straus, J. Richard Gelles, and Christine Smith, *Physical Violence in American Families: Risk Factors and Adaptations to Violence in 8,145 Families* (New Brunswick, NJ: Transaction Publishers, 1990).

42. American Psychological Association Presidential Task Force on Violence and the Family, *Violence and the Family* (Washington, DC: American Psychological Association, 1996), 11.

43. Jody Raphael and Richard M. Tolman, *Trapped by Poverty, Trapped by Abuse: New Evidence Documenting the Relationship Between Domestic Violence and Welfare* (Ann Arbor, MI: University of Michigan, 1997).

44. Berry.

45. Michael S. Kimmel, *The Gendered Society* (New York: Oxford University Press, 2004).

46. Ibid.

Chapter 2

1. L. E. A. Walker, *The Battered Woman Syndrome*, 2nd ed. (New York: Springer, 2000).

2. Mary Ann Dutton, "The Dynamics of Domestic Violence: Understanding the Response from Battered Women," *Florida Bar Journal* 68, no. 9 (1994).

3. Nancyann N. Cervantes and Marsali Hansen, "Spouse/Partner Maltreatment: Issues, Intervention and Research," in *Violence and Sexual Abuse at Home*, ed. R. Geffner, S. Sorenson, and P. Lundberg-Love (Binghamton, NY: Haworth Maltreatment & Trauma Press, 1997).

4. B. Birns, "Battered Wives: Causes, Effects, and Social Change," in *Readings in the Psychology of Women: Dimensions of the Female Experience*, ed. C. Forden, A. E. Hunter, and B. Birns (Boston: Allyn & Bacon, 1999).

5. Margaret W. Matlin, *The Psychology of Women*, 5th ed. (Belmont, CA: Wadsworth/Thomson, 2004).

6. K. D. O'Leary and R. D. Maiuro, eds., *Psychological Abuse in Violent Domestic Relations* (New York: Springer, 2001).

7. L. L. Alexander, J. H. LaRosa, and H. Bader, *New Dimensions in Women's Health*, 2nd ed. (Boston: Jones & Bartlett, 2001).

8. J. Hamlin, "List of Rape Myths," University of Minnesota, Duluth, www.d.umn.edu/cla/faculty/jhamlin/3925/myths.html (accessed March 11, 2006).

9. Diana Scully, *Understanding Sexual Violence: A Study of Convicted Rapists* (New York: HarperCollins, 1990).

10. A. Bandura, *Social Learning Theory* (New York: General Learning Press, 1977).

11. J. C. Campbell, "Nursing Assessment for Risk of Homicide with Battered Women," *Advances in Nursing Science* 8 (1986).

12. M. D. Pagelow, "Adult Victims of Domestic Violence: Battered Women," *Journal of Interpersonal Violence* 7 (1992): 87–120.

13. Matthew R. Durose et al., *Family Violence Statistics*, NCJ Publication No. 207846 (Washington, DC: U.S. Department of Justice, 2005), 52.

14. Walker.

15. F. S. Christopher and S. A. Lloyd, "Physical and Sexual Aggression in Relationships," in *Close Relationships*, ed. C. Hendrick and S. S. Hendrick (Thousand Oaks, CA: Sage, 2000).

16. Allan Johnson, "On the Prevalence of Rape in the United States," *Signs* 6, no. 1 (1980).

17. Naomi Neft and Ann D. Levine, *Where Women Stand: An International Report on the Status of Women in 140 Countries* (New York: Random House, 1997).

18. Alexander, LaRosa, and Bader.

19. Ola Barnett, Cindy L. Miller-Perrin, and Robin D. Perrin, *Family Violence Across the Lifespan: An Introduction*, 2nd ed. (Thousand Oaks, CA: Sage, 2002).

20. C. Warshaw, "Women and Violence," in *Psychological Aspects of Women's Health Care*, 2nd ed., ed. N. L. Stotland and D. E. Stewart (Washington, DC: American Psychiatric Press, 2001).

Chapter 3

1. *Merriam-Webster's Collegiate Dictionary Eleventh Edition* (Springfield, MA: Merriam-Webster, Inc., 2005).

2. Marti Tamm Loring, *Emotional Abuse* (San Francisco: Jossey-Bass, 1994).

3. Kay-Laurel Fischer and Michael McGrane, *Journey Beyond Abuse: A Step-by-Step Guide to Facilitating Women's Domestic Abuse Groups* (St. Paul, MN: Wilder Publishing, 1997).

4. Mary Ellen Copeland and Maxine Harris, *Healing the Trauma of Abuse: A Women's Workbook* (Oakland, CA: New Harbinger Publications, 2000).

5. Loring.

6. Ibid.

7. Mildred D. Pagelow, *Family Violence* (New York: Praeger Publishers, 1984).

8. In order to protect the confidentiality of the interviewee by the author, and mutually agreed upon by both parties, the name of the interviewee was withheld.

9. C. Brené Brown, *Women and Shame: Reaching Out, Speaking Truths and Building Connection* (Austin, TX: 3C Press, 2004).

10. Fischer and McGrane.

11. Copeland and Harris.

12. Erik H. Erikson, *Childhood and Society* (New York: Norton, 1950).

13. John Bowlby, *Attachment and Loss: Vol. 1: Attachment* (New York: Basic Books, 1969/1982).

14. Albert Bandura, *Social Learning Theory* (New York: General Learning Press, 1977).

15. In order to protect the confidentiality of the interviewee by the author, and mutually agreed upon by both parties, the name of the interviewee was withheld.

16. In order to protect the confidentiality of the interviewee by the author, and mutually agreed upon by both parties, the name of the interviewee was withheld.

Chapter 4

1. In order to protect the confidentiality of the interviewee by the author, and mutually agreed upon by both parties, the name of the interviewee was withheld.

2. K. J. Wilson, *When Violence Begins at Home: A Comprehensive Guide to Understanding and Ending Domestic Violence* (Alameda, CA: Hunter House, 1997), 8–13.

3. Ibid., 25–28.

4. Lenore Walker, *The Battered Woman* (New York: Harper & Row, 1979).

5. Ola Barnett, Cindy L. Miller-Perrin, and Robin Perrin, "Intimate Partner Violence in Adult Relationships," in *Family Violence Across the Lifespan: An Introduction* (Thousand Oaks, CA: Sage, 2005).

6. Murray Straus and Richard Gelles, "Societal Change and Change in Family Violence from 1975 to 1985 as Revealed by Two National Surveys," *Journal of Marriage and the Family* 48 (1986): 465–79.

7. Murray Straus, Richard Gelles, and Suzanne Steinmetz, *Behind Closed Doors: Violence in the American Family* (Garden City, NY: Doubleday, 1980).

8. Patricia Tjaden and Nancy Thoennes, *Prevalence, Incidence, and Consequences of Violence Against Women: Findings from the National Violence Against Women Survey*, NCJ Publication No. 172837 (Washington, DC: U.S. Department of Justice, 2000).

9. C. K. Zlotnick et al., "Partner Physical Victimization in a National Sample of American Families," *Journal of Interpersonal Violence* 13 (1998): 156–66.

10. Callie Marie Rennison and Sarah Welchans, *Intimate Partner Violence*, NCJ Publication No. 178247 (Washington, DC: U.S. Department of Justice, 2000).

11. R. Bachman and L. E. Saltzman, *Violence Against Women: Estimates from a Redesigned Survey*, NCJ Publication No. 154348 (Rockville, MD: U.S. Department of Justice, 1995).

12. P. Tjaden and N. Thoennes, *Extent, Nature and Consequences of Intimate Partner Violence: Findings from the National Violence Against Women Survey*, NCJ Publication No. 181867 (Washington, DC: U.S. Department of Justice, 2000).

13. J. E. Stets and M. A. Straus, "The Marriage License as a Hitting License: A Comparison of Assaults in Dating, Cohabitating, and Married Couples," in *Violence in Dating Relationships: Emerging Social Issues*, ed. M. A. Pirog-Good and J. E. Stets (New York: Praeger, 1989).

14. S. C. Turell, "A Descriptive Analysis of Same Sex Relationship Violence for a Diverse Sample," *Journal of Family Violence* 15 (2000): 281–94.

15. D. A. Brownridge and S. S. Halli, "Double Jeopardy? Violence Against Women in Canada," *Violence and Victims* 17 (2002): 455–71.

16. In order to protect the confidentiality of the interviewee by the author, and mutually agreed upon by both parties, the name of the interviewee was withheld.

17. V. A. Moss et al., "The Experience of Terminating an Abusive Relationship from an Anglo and African American Perspective: A Qualitative Descriptive Study," *Issues in Mental Health Nursing* 18 (1997): 433–54.

18. M. Hyden, "The World of the Fearful: Battered Women's Narratives of Leaving Abusive Husbands," *Feminism and Psychology* 9 (1999): 449–69.

19. Joan Zorza, "Battering," in *Violence Against Women*, ed. J. Zorza (Kingston, NJ: Civic Research Institute, 2002).

20. G. C. L. Davey, "Classical Conditioning and the Acquisition of Human Fears and Phobias: A Review and Synthesis of the Literature," *Advances in Behaviour Research and Therapy* 14 (1992): 29–66.

21. M. T. Rogan, "Fear Conditioning Induces Associative Long-Term Potentiation in the Amygdala," *Nature* 390 (1997): 604–7.

22. Barnett et al.

23. K. Hoefeller, *Social, Psychological, and Situational Factors in Wife Abuse* (Palo Alto, CA: R&E Research Associates, 1982).

24. W. A. Stacey and A. Shupe, *The Family Secret* (Boston: Beacon, 1983).

25. C. A. Byrne et al., "The Socioeconomic Impact of Interpersonal Violence on Women," *Journal of Consulting and Clinical Psychology* 67 (1999): 362–66.

26. A. M. Moe and M. P. Bell, "Abject Economics: The Effects of Battering and Violence on Women's Work and Employability," *Violence Against Women* 10 (2004): 29–55.

27. Zorza, 3.

28. Ibid.

29. In order to protect the confidentiality of the interviewee by the author, and mutually agreed upon by both parties, the name of the interviewee was withheld.

30. C. R. Brewin, B. Andrews, and S. Rose, "Fear, Helplessness, and Horror in Posttraumatic Stress Disorder: Investigating DSM-V Criterion A2 in Victims of Violent Crime," *Journal of Traumatic Stress* 68 (2000): 748–66.

31. *Psychology, An Introduction*, 2nd ed. (Glenview, IL: Scott, Foresman, 1989), 193.

32. C. M. Clements and D. K. Sawheny, "Coping with Domestic Violence: Control Attributions, Dysphoria, and Hopelessness," *Journal of Traumatic Stress* 13 (2000): 221–40.

33. J. C. Campbell et al., "Voices of Strength and Resistance: A Contextual and Longitudinal Analysis of Women's Responses to Battering," *Journal of Interpersonal Violence* 14 (1998): 21–40.

34. E. W. Gondolf, *Battered Women as Survivors: An Alternative to Treating Learned Helplessness* (Lexington, MA: Lexington, 1998).

35. Barnett et al., 288.

36. K. J. Ferraro, "The Words Change, but the Melody Lingers," *Violence Against Women* 9 (2003): 110–29.

37. Barnett et al., 290.

38. L. A. Goodman et al., "The Intimate Partner Violence Strategies Index," *Violence Against Women* 14 (2003): 163–86.

39. Clements and Sawheny, 211–40.

40. C. F. Lerner and L. T. Kennedy, "Stay-Leave Decision Making in Battered Women: Trauma, Coping and Self-Efficacy," *Cognitive Therapy and Research* 24 (2000): 215–32.

41. A. Towns and P. Adams, "If I Really Loved Him Enough, He Would Be Okay," *Violence Against Women* 6 (2000): 558–85.

42. P. S. Fry and L. A. Barker, "Female Survivors of Violence and Abuse: Their Regrets of Action and Inaction in Coping," *Journal of Interpersonal Violence* 16 (2001): 320–42.

43. B. Andrews and C. R. Brewin, "Attributions of Blame for Marital Violence. A Study of Antecedents and Consequences," *Journal of Marriage and the Family* 52 (1990): 757–67.

44. M. A. Strauss and C. Smith, "Family Patterns of Primary Prevention of Family Violence," in *Physical Violence in American Families: Risk Factors and Adaptations to Violence in 8,145 Families*, ed. Murray A. Strauss, J. Richard Gelles, and Christine Smith (New Brunswick, NJ: Transaction Publishers, 1990), 507–26.

45. J. M. Golding, "Intimate Partner Violence as a Risk Factor for Mental Disorders: A Meta-Analysis," *Journal of Family Violence* 14 (1999): 99–132.

46. Zorza, 4–5.

47. E. B. Carlson and C. J. Dahlenberg, "A Conceptual Framework for the Impact of Traumatic Experiences," *Trauma, Violence & Abuse* 1 (2000): 4–28.

48. American Psychiatric Press, *Diagnostic and Statistical Manual of Mental Disorders*, 4th ed. (Washington, DC: American Psychiatric Press, 1994).

49. P. G. Mertin and P. B. Mohr, "A Follow-Up Study of Posttraumatic Stress Disorder, Anxiety and Depression in Australian Victims of Domestic Violence," *Violence and Victims* 16 (2001): 645–53.

50. S. J. Woods and M. A. Isenberg, "Adaptation as a Mediator of Intimate Abuse and Traumatic Stress in Battered Women," *Nursing Science Quarterly* 14 (2001): 213–21.

51. C. Laffaye, C. Kennedy, and M. Stein, "Posttraumatic Stress Disorder and Health-Related Quality of Life in Female Victims of Intimate Partner Violence," *Violence and Victims* 18 (2003): 227–38.

52. Dee L. R. Graham, Edna Rawlings, and Nelly Rimini, "Survivors of Terror: Battered Women, Hostages, and the Stockholm Syndrome," in *Feminist Perspectives on Wife Abuse*, ed. Kersti Yllo and Michele Bograd (Beverly Hills, CA: Sage Publishers, 1988), 217–34.

53. National Center for Injury Prevention and Control, *Costs of Intimate Partner Violence Against Women in the United States* (Atlanta, GA: Centers for Disease Control and Prevention, 2003).

54. Y. C. Ulrich et al., "Medical Care Patterns in Women with Diagnosed Domestic Violence," *American Journal of Preventive Medicine* 24 (2003): 9–15.

55. Barnett et al., 262.

56. Ibid.

57. Barnett et al., 262–263.

Chapter 5

1. In order to protect the confidentiality of the interviewee by the author, and mutually agreed upon by both parties, the name of the interviewee was withheld.

2. Erna Olafson, "Child Sexual Abuse," in *Sexualized Violence Against Women and Children: A Psychology and Law Perspective*, ed. B. J. Cling (New York: Guilford, 2004), 151–87.

3. Richard A. Roth, *Child Sexual Abuse: Incest, Assault, and Sexual Exploitation* (Washington, DC: U.S. Department of Health and Human Services, 1978).

4. Ola W. Barnett, Cindy Miller-Perrin, and Robin Perrin, "Child Sexual Abuse," in *Family Violence Across the Lifespan* (Thousand Oaks, CA: Sage, 2005), 87–125.

5. Olafson, 151.

6. Barnett et al., "Child Sexual Abuse," 89.

7. Diana Russell, "The Prevalence of Incestuous Abuse in Contemporary America," in *The Secret Trauma: Incest in the Lives of Girls and Women* (New York: Basic Books, 1986), 59–74.

8. Stephanie D. Peters, Gail E. Wyatt, and David Finkelhor, "Prevalence," in *A Sourcebook on Child Sexual Abuse*, ed. David Finkelhor (Beverly Hills: Sage, 1986).

9. Lucy Berliner and Diana Elliott, "Sexual Abuse of Children," in *The APSAC Handbook on Child Maltreatment*, 2nd ed., ed. J. E. B. Myers et al. (Thousand Oaks, CA: Sage, 2002), 55–78.

10. Barnett et al., "Child Sexual Abuse," 90.

11. Russell, "The Prevalence of Incentuous Abuse," 59.

12. Barnett et al., "Child Sexual Abuse," 90.

13. Peters et al., 18.

14. Barnett et al., "Child Sexual Abuse," 94.

15. Berliner and Elliott, 56.

16. Barnett et al., "Child Sexual Abuse," 91.

17. Russell, "The Prevalence of Incestuous Abuse," 60–61.

18. Berliner and Elliott, 57.

19. Barbara Everett and Ruth Gallop, "The Research Story," in *The Link Between Childhood Trauma and Mental Illness: Effective Interventions for Mental Health Professionals* (Thousand Oaks, CA: Sage, 2001), 37–56.

20. David Finkelhor and Larry Baron, "High-Risk Children," in *A Sourcebook on Child Sexual Abuse*, ed. David Finkelhor (Beverly Hills: Sage, 1986).

21. Barnett et al., "Child Sexual Abuse," 94–95.

22. David Finkelhor and I. A. Lewis, "An Epidemiological Approach to the Study of Child Molestation," *Annals of the New York Academy of Sciences* 528 (1988), 64–66.

23. Barnett et al., "Child Sexual Abuse," 94–95.

24. Finkelhor and Baron, 72–79.

25. Barnett et al., "Child Sexual Abuse," 95.

26. Berliner and Elliott, 57.

27. Barnett et al., "Child Sexual Abuse," 95.

28. Diana Russell, "Who Are the Perpetrators?" in *The Secret Trauma: Incest in the Lives of Girls and Women* (New York: Basic Books, 1986).

29. Barnett et al., "Child Sexual Abuse," 95.

30. Finkelhor and Lewis.

31. John Briere and M. Runtz, "The Trauma Symptoms Checklist (TSC-33): Early Data on a New Scale," *Journal of Interpersonal Violence* 4 (1989), 151–63.

32. Barnett et al., "Child Sexual Abuse," 95–96.

33. Berliner and Elliott.

34. Barnett et al., "Child Sexual Abuse," 96–98.

35. Ibid., 96–99.

36. Berliner and Elliott.

37. Barnett et al., "Child Sexual Abuse," 99.

38. In order to protect the confidentiality of the interviewee by the author, and mutually agreed upon by both parties, the name of the interviewee was withheld.

39. Berliner and Elliott, 59.

40. Diana Russell, "Trauma Through the Eyes of the Victims," in *The Secret Trauma: Incest in the Lives of Girls and Women* (New York: Basic Books, 1986).

41. Barnett et al., "Child Sexual Abuse," 103–5.

42. Berliner and Elliott, 59–60.

43. Barnett et al., "Child Sexual Abuse," 105.

44. Berliner and Elliott, 60–61.

45. Barnett et al, "Child Sexual Abuse," 104.

46. Berliner and Elliott, 61.

47. Barnett et al., "Child Sexual Abuse," 104.

48. Berliner and Elliott, 61–64.

49. Barbara Everett and Ruth Gallop, "Recognizing the Signs and Symptoms," in *The Link Between Childhood Trauma and Mental Illness: Effective Interventions for Mental Health Professionals* (Thousand Oaks, CA: Sage, 2001), 57–79.

50. Berliner and Elliott, 64.

51. Everett and Gallop, "Recognizing the Signs and Symptoms," 67.

52. National Security Institute, "Child Sexual Abuse," http://nsi.org/Tips/sexabuse.htm (accessed March 11, 2006).

53. In order to protect the confidentiality of the interviewee by the author, and mutually agreed upon by both parties, the name of the interviewee was withheld.

54. Mary P. Koss and Mary R. Harvey, "The Crime of Rape," in *The Rape Victim: Clinical and Community Interventions*, 2nd ed. (Newbury Park, CA: Sage Library of Social Research, 1991), 1–41.

55. Safehome, "What Is Sexual Assault?" http://www.safehome-ks.org/abuse/edu/sassault.htm (accessed November 17, 2005).

56. Koss and Harvey, "The Crime of Rape," 5.

57. L. B. Bienen, "Rape III-National Developments in Rape Reform Legislation," *Women's Rights Law Reporter* (1981): 171–213.

58. Koss and Harvey, "The Crime of Rape," 2–3.

59. Mary Koss et al., "Uniting All Women: Fear of Rape," in *No Safe Haven: Male Violence Against Women at Home, at Work, and in the Community* (Washington, DC: American Psychological Association, 1994).

60. Ibid.

61. Koss and Harvey, "The Crime of Rape," 5–8.

62. Koss et al., "Uniting All Women," 160–63.

63. Ola Barnett, Cindy Miller-Perrin, and Robin Perrin, "Dating Violence, Stalking, and Sexual Assault," in *Family Violence Across the Lifespan* (Thousand Oaks, CA: Sage, 2005), 222–50.

64. Koss and Harvey, "The Crime of Rape," 11–15.

65. Robin Warshaw, *I Never Called It Rape: The Ms. Report on Recognizing, Fighting, and Surviving Date and Acquaintance Rape* (New York: Harper & Row, 1988).

66. Koss et al., "Uniting All Women," 164.

67. Mary P. Koss, C. A. Gidycz, and N. Wisniewski, "The Scope of Rape: Incidence and Prevalence of Sexual Aggression and Victimization in a National Sample of Higher Education Students," *Journal of Consulting and Clinical Psychology* 55 (1987): 162–70.

68. D. E. H. Russell, "The Prevalence and Incidence of Forcible Rape and Attempted Rape of Females," *Victimology: An International Journal* 7 (1982): 81–93.

69. Koss and Harvey, "The Crime of Rape," 24–27.

70. Martha Burt, "Rape Myths," in *Confronting Rape and Sexual Assault*, ed. Mary E. Odem and Jody Clay-Warner (Wilmington, DE: Scholarly Resources, Inc., 1998).

71. Warshaw, 3–49.

72. Karen Bachar and Mary P. Koss, "From Prevalence to Prevention: Closing the Gap Between What We Know About Rape and What We Do," in *Sourcebook on Violence Against Women*, ed. Claire M. Renzetti, Jeffrey L. Edleson, and Raquel Kennedy Bergen (Thousand Oaks, CA: Sage, 2001), 117–42.

73. Warshaw, 49–52.

74. Warshaw, 51.

75. Ibid.

76. Joanne Belknap, "The Sexual Victimization of Unmarried Women by Nonrelative Acquaintances," in *Violence in Dating Relationships: Emerging Social Issues*, ed. Maureen A. Pirog-Good and Jan E. Stets (New York: Praeger, 1989).

77. Warshaw, 50–64.

78. Koss and Harvey, "The Crime of Rape," 29–41.

79. Warshaw, 92.

80. Koss and Harvey, "The Crime of Rape," 39–40.

81. Barnett et al., "Dating Violence, Stalking, and Sexual Assault," 235.

82. Jerrold S. Meyer and Linda F. Quenzer, "'Date Rape' Drugs," in *Psychopharmacology: Drugs, the Brain and Behavior* (Sunderland, MA: Sinauer Associates Inc., 2005), 371.

83. Joan Zorza, "Rape and Sexual Assault," in *Violence Against Women*, ed. J. Zorza (Kingston, NJ: Civic Research Institute, 2002).

84. In order to protect the confidentiality of the interviewee by the author, and mutually agreed upon by both parties, the name of the interviewee was withheld.

85. Koss et al., "The Scope of Rape."

86. Warshaw, 65–66.

87. Mary P. Koss and Mary R. Harvey, "The Trauma of Rape," in *The Rape Victim: Clinical and Community Interventions*, 2nd ed. (Newbury Park, CA: Sage Library of Social Research, 1991).

88. Alan W. McEvoy and Jeff B. Brookings, "Responding to Long Term Consequences," in *If She is Raped: A Guidebook for Husbands, Fathers, and Male Friends*, 2nd ed. (Holmes Beach: Learning, 1991).

89. Koss and Harvey, "The Trauma of Rape," 61–79.

90. McEvoy and Brookings, 20.

91. Warshaw, 68–73.

92. McEvoy and Brookings, 20.

93. Warshaw, 69–75.

94. Koss and Harvey, "The Crime of Rape," 64.

95. Warshaw, 78.

96. Koss and Harvey, "The Crime of Rape," 61–80.

97. Warshaw, 70.

98. Koss and Harvey, "The Crime of Rape," 66–67.

99. David B. Sugarman and Gerald T. Hotaling, "Dating Violence: Prevalence, Context, and Risk Markers," in *Violence in Dating Relationships: Emerging Social Issues*, ed. Maureen A. Pirog-Good and Jan E. Stets (New York: Praeger, 1989).

100. Office of Victims of Crime, *Strengthening Antistalking Statutes*, NCJ Publication No. 189192 (Washington, DC: U.S. Department of Justice, 2002).

101. Barnett et al., "Dating Violence, Stalking, and Sexual Assault," 224–27.

102. Patricia Mahoney, Linda M. Williams, and Carolyn M. West, "Violence Against Women by Intimate Relationship Partners," in *Sourcebook on Violence Against Women*, ed. Claire Renzetti, Jeffrey L. Edleson, and Raquel Kennedy Bergen (Thousand Oaks, CA: Sage, 2001), 143–78.

103. Barnett et al., "Dating Violence, Stalking, and Sexual Assault," 232–49.

Chapter 6

1. In order to protect the confidentiality of the interviewee by the author, and mutually agreed upon by both parties, the name of the interviewee was withheld.

2. Barbara Everett and Ruth Gallop, "The Research Story," in *The Link Between Childhood Trauma and Mental Illness* (Thousand Oaks, CA: Sage, 2001).

3. David Finkelhor, "The International Epidemiology of Child Sexual Abuse," *Child Abuse & Neglect*, 18 (1994): 409–17.

4. Everett and Gallop, 40.

5. Ibid., 41.

6. Ibid., 42.

7. Paula Lundberg-Love, "Adult Survivors of Incest," in *Treatment of Family Violence: A Sourcebook*, ed. Robert Ammerman and Michel Hersen (New York: John Wiley & Sons, 1990).

8. Paula Lundberg-Love, "The Resilience of the Human Psyche: Recognition and Treatment of the Adult Survivor of Incest," in *The Psychology of Sexual Victimization: A Handbook*, ed. Michele Paludi (Westport, CT: Greenwood Publishing, 1999).

9. In order to protect the confidentiality of the interviewee by the author, and mutually agreed upon by both parties, the name of the interviewee was withheld.

10. Lundberg-Love, "The Resilience of the Human Psyche," 5–6.

11. Kathleen Kendall-Tackett, "Emotional Pathways—Depression and Post-traumatic Stress Disorder," in *Treating The Lifetime Health Effects of Childhood Victimization* (Kingston, NJ: Civic Research Institute, 2003).

12. Ibid., 7.

13. Ibid., 8.

14. Ibid.

15. In order to protect the confidentiality of the interviewee by the author, and mutually agreed upon by both parties, the name of the interviewee was withheld.

16. Lundberg-Love, "The Resilience of the Human Psyche," 6.

17. American Psychiatric Association, *Diagnostic and Statistical Manual of Mental Disorders*, 4th ed. (Washington, DC: American Psychiatric Association, 1994).

18. Lundberg-Love, "The Resilience of the Human Psyche," 6–7.

19. Judith Herman, *Trauma and Recovery* (New York: Basic Books, 1992).

20. Everett and Gallop, 58–59.

21. Kendall-Tackett, 10–11.

22. Paula Lundberg-Love, "Personality Mapping: Differentiation to Assimilation, Fission to Fusion" (speech, Southwest Conference on Dissociative Disorders and Sexual Abuse, Tyler, TX, October 1993).

23. Bennett Braun, "Multiple Personality Disorder: An Overview," *The American Journal of Occupational Therapy* 44 (1990): 872.

24. American Psychiatric Association, 478–90.

25. Bennett Braun, "The BASK (Behavior, Affect, Sensation, Knowledge) Model of Dissociation," *Dissociation* 1 (1998): 4–23.

26. J. Brickman, "Female Lives, Feminist Deaths: The Relationship of the Montreal Massacre to Dissociation, Incest, and Violence Against Women," *Canadian Psychology* 33 (1992): 128–49.

27. Frank Putnam, *Diagnosis and Treatment of Multiple Personality Disorder* (New York: Guilford, 1989).

28. Paula Lundberg-Love, "Current Treatment Strategies for Dissociative Identity Disorder in Adult Sexual Abuse Survivors," in *Violence and Sexual Abuse at Home: Current Issues in Spousal Battering and Child Maltreatment*, ed. Robert Geffner, Susan Sorenson, and Paula Lundberg-Love (Binghamton, NY: Haworth Maltreatment & Trauma Press, 1997).

29. Lundberg-Love, "Current Treatment Strategies," 315.

30. In order to protect the confidentiality of the interviewee by the author, and mutually agreed upon by both parties, the name of the interviewee was withheld.

31. S. C. Wilsnack et al., "Childhood Sexual Abuse and Women's Substance Abuse," *Journal of Studies of Alcohol* 58 (1997): 264–71.

32. Kathleen Kendall-Tackett, "Behavioral Pathways," in *Treating Lifetime Health Effects of Childhood Victimization* (Kingston, NJ: Civic Research Institute, 2003).

33. John Briere and Marsha Runtz, "Post Sexual Abuse Trauma: Data and Implications for Clinical Practice," *Journal of Interpersonal Violence* 2 (1987): 367–79.

34. J. L. Jasinski, L. M. Williams, and J. Siegel, "Childhood Physical and Sexual Abuse as Risk Factors for Heavy Drinking Among African-American Women: A Prospective Study," *Child Abuse and Neglect* 24 (2000): 1061–71.

35. Kendall-Tackett, "Behavioral Pathways," 5.

36. In order to protect the confidentiality of the interviewee by the author, and mutually agreed upon by both parties, the name of the interviewee was withheld.

37. F. E. Springs and W. N. Friederich, "Health Risk Behaviors and Medical Sequelae of Childhood Sexual Abuse," *Mayo Clinic Proceedings* 67 (1992): 527–32.

38. V. J. Felitti, "Long-Term Medical Consequences of Incest, Rape and Molestation," *Southern Medical Journal* 84 (1991): 328–31.

39. T. K. King, M. M. Clark, and V. Pera, "History of Sexual Abuse and Obesity Treatment Outcome," *Addictive Behaviors* 21 (1996): 283–90.

40. National Institute of Mental Health, *Brief Notes on the Mental Health of Children and Adolescents* (Washington, DC: National Institute of Mental Health, 2000).

41. Kendall-Tackett, "Behavioral Pathways," 9.

42. D. C. Jimerson et al., "Decreased Serotonin Function in Bulimia Nervosa," *Archives of General Psychiatry* 54 (1997): 529–34.

43. E. Stice, "The Neglect of Obesity," *Monitor on Psychology* 33 (2002): 33.

44. T. DeAngelis, "Promising Treatments for Anorexia and Bulimia," *Monitor on Psychology* 33 (2002): 38–41.

45. K. Heffernan, "Bulimia Nervosa," in *Behavioral Medicine & Women: A Comprehensive Handbook*, ed. E. A. Blechman and K. D. Brownell (New York: Guilford Press, 1998).

46. In order to protect the confidentiality of the interviewee by the author, and mutually agreed upon by both parties, the name of the interviewee was withheld.

47. Barbara Everett and Ruth Gallop, "The Healing and Recovery Process," in *The Link Between Childhood Trauma and Mental Illness* (Thousand Oaks, CA: Sage, 2001).

48. Ibid., 144–48.

49. Ibid., 148–59.

50. Lundberg-Love, "The Resilience of the Human Psyche," 22–25.

51. John Briere, "Exploring the Solution: Abuse-Focused Psychotherapy," in *Child Abuse Trauma: Theory and Treatment of the Lasting Effects* (Newbury Park, CA: Sage, 1992).

Chapter 7

1. Roberta L. Valente et al., "The Violence Against Women Act of 1994," in *Sourcebook on Violence Against Women*, ed. Claire M. Renzetti, Jeffrey L. Edleson, and Raquel Kennedy Bergen (Thousand Oaks, CA: Sage, 2001), 286–87.

2. K. J. Wilson, "Living Underground," in *When Violence Begins at Home* (Alameda, CA: Hunter House, 1997).

3. Lenore E. A. Walker, *Abused Women and Survivor Therapy* (Washington, DC: American Psychological Association, 1994), 255, 257, 265.

4. Del Martin, *Battered Wives* (Volcano, CA: Volcano Press, 1976), 17.

5. Donna Ferrato, *Living with the Enemy* (New York: Aperture Foundation, 1991), 34.

6. S. Deller Ross et al., *The Rights of Women: The Basic ACLU Guide to Women's Rights* (Carbondale, IL: Southern Illinois University Press, 1993), 155.

7. Ola Barnett, Cindy L. Miller-Perrin, and Robin Perrin, *Family Violence Across the Lifespan*, 2nd ed. (Thousand Oaks, CA: Sage, 2005), 301.

8. Martin, 101.

9. Valente et al., 282.

10. Ibid., 287–88.

11. Texas Council on Family Violence, Public Policy Department, *Do No Harm: Protective Orders in Texas*, comp. Jodie Reaver, Nancy Flores, and Lori-Ann Lima (Austin, TX: 2003), 2, 6. Available on CD-ROM.

12. Ibid., 3–5.

13. Office of the Law Revision Council, U.S. House of Representatives, 18 U.S. Code § 922. (Washington, DC: U.S. Government Printing Office, 2000).

14. Texas Council on Family Violence, Public Policy Department, *To Protect and Serve: Law Enforcement's Response to Family Violence*, comp. Debbie McDaniel Carter (Austin, TX: 2003), 145. Available on CD-ROM.

15. Valente et al., 291–93.

16. Merriam-Webster, Inc., "serious bodily injury," in *Merriam-Webster's Dictionary of Law*, 1996 ed., http://dictionary.lp.findlaw.com.

17. Gerald Hill and Kathleen Hill, "assault, aggravated assault," in *The People's Law Dictionary*, 2005, http://dictionary.law.com/. See also Texas Council on Family Violence, *To Protect and Serve*, 145.

18. Callie Marie Rennison and Sarah Welchans, *Intimate Partner Violence*, NCJ Publication No. 178247 (Washington, DC: U.S. Department of Justice, 2000), 2.

19. Gerald Hill and Kathleen Hill, "first degree murder, second degree murder, manslaughter, homicide, injury," in *The People's Law Dictionary*, 2005, http://dictionary.law.com/. See also Texas Council on Family Violence, *To Protect and Serve*, 145.

20. Marilyn French, *The War Against Women* (New York: Ballantine Books, 1992), 191.

21. Kathleen Maguire and Ann L. Pastore, eds., *Sourcebook of Criminal Justice Statistics*, 30th ed. (Washington, DC: U.S. Department of Justice, 2002), http://www.albany.edu/sourcebook.

22. Susan Brownmiller, *Against Our Will* (New York: Simon & Schuster, 1975), 15.

23. B. J. Cling, "Rape and Rape Trauma Syndrome," in *Sexualized Violence against Women and Children: A Psychology and Law Perspective*, ed. B. J. Cling (New York: Guilford Press, 2004), 13–35.

24. Gerald Hill and Kathleen Hill, "rape," in *The People's Law Dictionary*, 2005, http://dictionary.law.com/.

25. Barnett et al., 12.

26. Walker, 25, 255, 257.

27. Laura Russo, *Date Rape: A Hidden Crime* (Canberra, Australia: Australian Institute of Criminology, 2000), 3. http://www.aic.gov.au/publications/tandi/ti157.pdf.

28. Diana E. H. Russell, *Rape in Marriage* (New York: Macmillan Press, 1990), 17.

29. Barnett et al., 34.

30. Ibid., 12.

31. Ibid., 307.

32. *1998 State Law Chart* (Berkeley, CA: National Clearinghouse on Marital and Date Rape), http://members.aol.com/ncmdr/state_law_chart.html.

33. Raquel Kennedy Bergen, *Marital Rape* (Harrisburg, PA: National Resource Center on Domestic Violence 1999), 2, http://vawnet.org/Domestic-Violence/Research/VAWnetDocs/AR_mrape.php.

34. Ibid., 1, 4.

35. Barnett et al., 254.

36. John E. B. Myers, *Legal Issues in Child Abuse and Neglect Practice*, 2nd ed. (Thousand Oaks, CA: Sage, 1998), 1–2.

37. Andrea J. Sedlak and Diane D. Broadhurst, *Executive Summary of the Third National Incidence Study of Child Abuse and Neglect* (Washington, DC: U.S. Department of Health and Human Services, Administration on Children, Youth and Families, 1996), http://nccanch.acf.hhs.gov/pubs/statsinfo/nis3.cfm.

38. U.S. Department of Health and Human Services, Administration on Children, Youth and Families, *National Child Abuse and Neglect Data System (NCANDS) Summary of Key Findings from Calendar Year* 2000, as cited in Barnett et al., *Family Violence Across the Lifespan*, 3.

39. M. A. Strauss and R. J. Gelles, "Societal Change and Change in Family Violence from 1975 to 1985 as Revealed by Two National Surveys," *Journal of Marriage and the Family* 48 (1986): 465–79; and M. A. Strauss et al., "Identification of Child Maltreatment with the Parent-Child Conflict Tactics Scales: Development and Psychometric Data for a National Sample of American Parents," *Child Abuse & Neglect* 22 (1998): 249–70, as cited in Barnett et al., 60.

40. Erna Olafson, "Child Sexual Abuse," in *Sexualized Violence against Women and Children: A Psychology and Law Perspective*, ed. B. J. Cling (New York: Guilford Press, 2004), 155.

41. Ibid., 170. See also Barnett et al., *Family Violence Across the Lifespan*, 90.

42. Olafson, 169.

43. Myers, 30–34.

44. Kathleen C. Faller, *Understanding Child Sexual Maltreatment* (Newbury Park, CA: Sage, 1990), 72–73.

45. Peter G. Jaffe, David A. Wolfe, and Susan K. Wilson, *Children of Battered Women* (Newbury Park, CA: Sage, 1990), 28–29.

46. K. J. Wilson, *When Violence Begins at Home* (Alameda, CA: Hunter House, 1997), 17.

47. Gerald Hill and Kathleen Hill, "kidnapping," in *The People's Law Dictionary*, 2005, http://dictionary.law.com/.

48. Merriam-Webster, Inc., "stalking," in *Merriam-Webster's Dictionary of Law*, 1996 ed., http://dictionary.lp.findlaw.com.

49. Wilson, 81.

50. Valente et al., 293.

51. Matthew R. Durose et al., *Family Violence Statistics*, NCJ Publication No. 207846 (Washington, DC: U.S. Department of Justice, 2005), 52.

52. Texas Council on Family Violence, *To Protect and Serve*, 145. Also see: Gerald Hill and Kathleen Hill, "harassment," in *The People's Law Dictionary*, 2005, http://dictionary.law.com/.

53. Valente et al., 283.

54. Ibid., 299.

55. Ibid., 286.

56. Ibid., 283–93. See also Durose et al., 51.

57. Durose et al., 21, 35.

58. Valente et al., 294. See also Durose et al., 51.

59. U.S. Department of Justice, Office on Violence Against Women, *The Violence Against Women Act of 2000* (Washington, DC: DOJ, 2001), http://www.ojp.usdoj.gov/vawo/laws/vawa_summary2.htm.

60. Wilson, 90.

61. Barnett et al., 273.

62. Callie Marie Rennison and Sarah Welchans, *Intimate Partner Violence*, NCJ Publication No. 178247 (Washington, DC: U.S. Department of Justice, Bureau of Justice Statistics, 2000).

63. Barnett et al., 274–76.

64. Ibid., 276.

65. Rennison and Welchans, 3–5.

66. Barnett et al., 277–78.

67. Kathryn B. Hagans and Joyce Case, *When Your Child Has Been Molested: A Parent's Guide to Healing and Recovery* (Lexington, MA: Lexington Books, 1988), 49.

68. R. A. Berk, S. Fenstermaker, and P. J. Newton, "An Empirical Analysis of Police Responses to Incidents of Wife Battery," in *Coping with Family Violence*, ed. G. T. Hotaling et al. (Newbury Park, CA: Sage, 1988).

69. Barnett et al., 274–75.

70. Ibid., 274–78.

71. Ibid., 276–78.

72. D. Epstein, "In Search of Effective Intervention in Domestic Violence Cases: Rethinking the Roles of Prosecutors, Judges, and the Court System," *Yale Journal of Law & Feminism* 11 (1999): 25.

73. Diana E. H. Russell, *Rape in Marriage* (New York: Macmillan Press, 1990), 18.

74. Wilson, 86.

75. Ola Barnett, Cindy L. Miller-Perrin, and Robin D. Perrin, "Intimate Partner Violence: Abusive Partners," in *Family Violence Across the Lifespan* (Thousand Oaks, CA: Sage, 2005).

76. J. L. Edleson, "Controversy and Change in Batterer's Programs," in *Future Interventions with Battered Women and Their Families*, ed. J. L. Edleson and Z. C. Eisikovits (Thousand Oaks, CA: Sage, 1996), 156.

77. D. G. Saunders, "Interventions for Men Who Batter: Do We Know What Works?" *Insession Psychotherapy* 2/3 (1996): 81–94.

78. Wilson, 86.

79. Wilson, 224.

80. Debbie M. Carter, "The Legal System: A Brief Overview," in *The Legal Advocate's Guide: A Training Manual for Domestic Violence Advocates* (Austin, TX: Texas Council on Family Violence, 2003). Available on CD-ROM.

81. Myers, 63.

82. National Association of Crime Victim Compensation Boards, "National Victim Advocates Brief U.S. Congress," http://www.nacvcb.org (accessed April 1, 2005).

83. Wilson, 76–77.

84. Daniel G. Saunders, *Child Custody and Visitation Decisions in Domestic Violence Cases: Legal Trends, Research Findings, and Recommendations* (National Resource Center on Domestic Violence [VAWnet], 1998), 1–2. http://www.vawnet.org/DomesticViolence/Research/VAWnetDocs/AR_custody.pdf.

85. National Council of Juvenile and Family Court Judges, *Model Code on Domestic and Family Violence* (Reno, NV: NCJFCJ, 1993), 33.

86. Saunders, (1998), 4–5.

Chapter 8

1. P. Tjaden and N. Thoennes, *Full Report of the Prevalence, Incidence, and Consequences of Violence Against Women Survey* (Washington, DC: National Institute of Justice, 2000).

2. D. G. Kilpatrick, C. Edmunds, and A. Seymour, *Rape in America: A Report to the Nation* (Charleston, SC: National Victim Center and the Crime Victims Research and Treatment Center, Medical University of South Carolina, 1992).

3. B. S. Fisher, F. T. Cullen, and M. G. Turner, *The Sexual Victimization of College Women* (Washington, DC: National Institute of Justice, Department of Justice, 2000).

4. Centers for Disease Control and Prevention, "Youth Risk Behavior Surveillance-United States," *Morbidity and Mortality Weekly Report* 53, no. SS02 (2003): 1–96.

5. Centers for Disease Control and Prevention, *Developing Healthy Relationships: Talking Points*, http://www.cdc.gov/ncipc/dvp/Healthy%20Relationship%20Messages%20Final.pdf (accessed June 30, 2005).

6. Mary Koss and Mary Harvey, *The Rape Victim: Clinical and Community Interventions*, 2nd ed. (Newbury Park, CA: Sage Library of Social Research, 1991).

7. Mary Koss and L. Heslet, "Somatic Consequences," *Archives of Family Medicine* 1 (1992): 53–59.

8. J. C. Campbell and K. Soeken. "Women's Responses to Battering Over Time," *Journal of Interpersonal of STD and AIDS* 14 (1990): 21–41.

9. A. Patel et al., "Under-Use of Emergency Contraception for Victims of Sexual Assault," *International Journal of Fertility and Women's Medicine* 49, no. 6 (Nov-Dec 2004): 269–73.

10. S. M. Murphy, "Rape, Sexually Transmitted Diseases, and Human Immunodeficiency Virus Infection," *International Journal of STD and AIDS* no. 1 (1990): 1–79.

11. V. J. Felitti, R. F. Anda, and D. Nordenberg, "The Relationship of Adult Health Status to Childhood Abuse and Household Dysfunction," *American Journal of Preventive Medicine* 14 no. 4 (May 1998): 245–58.

12. Koss and Harvey.

13. B. Everett and R. Gallop, *Effective Interventions for Mental Health Professionals* (Thousand Oaks, CA: Sage, 2001).

14. National Center for Post-traumatic Stress Disorder, "Fact Sheets," http://www.ncptsd.va.gov/facts/treatment/fs_treatment.html (accessed March 11, 2006).

15. Ibid.

16. Ibid.

17. Ibid.

18. A. W. Burgess, "Crisis and Counseling Requests of Rape Victims," *Journal of Nursing Research* 23 (1974): 196–202.

19. A. W. Burgess and L. L. Holstrom, "Rape Trauma Syndrome," *American Journal of Psychiatry* 131 (1974): 981–86.

20. A. W. Burgess and L. L. Holstrom, "The Rape Victim in the ER," *American Journal of Nursing* 73, no. 10 (1974): 1740.

21. A. W. Burgess and L. L. Holstrom, "Coping Behavior of the Rape Victim," *American Journal of Psychiatry* 133 (1976): 413–18.

22. A. W. Burgess and L. L. Holstrom, "Rape: Sexual Disruption and Recovery," *American Journal of Orthopsychiatry* 49 (1979): 648–57.

23. W. G. Doerner and S. P. Lab, *Victimology*, 2nd ed. (Cincinnati, OH: Anderson Publishing Company, 1998).

24. B. Forman, "Psychotherapy with Rape Victims," *Psychotherapy: Theory, Research, and Practice* 17 (1980): 304–11.

25. S. Roth and L. Lebowitz, "The Experience of Sexual Trauma," *Journal of Traumatic Stress* 1, no. 1 (1988): 79–107.

26. S. Sutherland and D. J. Scherl, "Patterns of Response Among Victims of Rape," *American Journal of Orthopsychiatry* 28 (1970): 527–29.

27. M. Symounds, "Victims of Violence: Psychological Effects and Aftereffects," *American Journal of Orthopsychiatry* 35 (1975): 19–26.

28. Koss and Harvey.

29. Symounds.

30. S. K. Burge, "Post Traumatic Stress Disorder in Victims of Rape," *Journal of Traumatic Stress* 1, no. 2 (1988): 193–209.

31. Forman.

32. Koss and Harvey.

33. L. S. Brown and Maria P. P. Root, *Diversity and Complexity in Feminist Therapy* (Binghamton, NY: Harrington Park Press, 1990).

34. J. Worell and P. Remer, *Feminist Perspectives in Therapy: Empowering Diverse Women*, 2nd ed. (Hoboken, NJ: John Wiley and Sons, 2002).

35. G. D. French and C. J. Harris, *Traumatic Incidence Reduction* (New York: CRC Press, 1999).

36. P. Mountrose and J. Mountrose, *Getting Thru to Your Emotions with EF* (Sacramento, CA: Holistic Communications, 2000).

37. F. Shapiro, *Eye Movement Desensitization and Reprocessing: Basic Principles, Protocols, and Procedures*, 2nd ed. (New York: Guilford Press, 2001).

38. F. Shapiro and L. Maxfield, "EMDR and Information Processing in Psychotherapy Treatment" in *Healing Trauma: Attachment, Mind, Body, and Brain*, ed. M. F. Soloman and D. J. Siegel (New York: WW Norton and Company, 2003).

39. F. Shapiro and M. Forrest, *The Breakthrough Therapy for Overcoming Anxiety, Stress, and Trauma* (New York: Harper Collins, 1997).

40. Shapiro.

41. Shapiro and Maxfield.

42. S. M. Stahl, *Essential Psychopharmacology: Neuroscientific Basis and Practical Applications* (New York: Cambridge University Press, 2000).

43. Ibid.

44. K. R. Delaney et al., *Psychiatric-Mental Health Nursing* (Philadelphia: Lippincott, Williams and Wilkins, 2006).

45. National Center for Post-traumatic Stress Disorder.

46. Philip G. Ney and Ana Peters, *Ending the Cycle of Abuse* (New York: Bruner/Mazel, 1995).

47. Kay-Laurel Fischer and F. Michael McGrane, *Journey Beyond Abuse: A Step-by-Step Guide to Facilitating Domestic Abuse Groups* (St. Paul, MN: Wilder Publishing Center, 1997).

48. Mary Ellen Copeland and Maxine Harris, *Healing the Trauma of Abuse: A Woman's Workbook* (Oakland, CA: New Harbinger Publications, 2000).

49. Andrea Lisette and Richard Kraus, *Free Yourself from an Abusive Relationship* (Alameda, CA: Hunter House, 2000).

Chapter 9

1. Susan B. Sorenson, "Violence Against Women: Examining Ethnic Differences and Commonalities," *Evaluation Review* 20 (1996): 123–45.

2. See petition at http://www.petitiononline.com. Precious Doe has since been identified as Erica Michelle Marie Green who was allegedly killed by her stepfather. Dolores Childs, *Precious Doe/Rilya Wilson*, http://www.petitiononline.com/ (accessed March 11, 2006).

3. As of January 10, 2006. See petition at http://www.petitiononline.com.

4. See, for example, http://kuro5hin.org/story/2005/7/3/491/18474 (accessed March 11, 2006).

5. Aarati Kasturirangan, Sandhya Krishnan, and Stephanie Riger, "The Impact of Culture and Minority Status on Women's Experience of Domestic Violence," *Trauma, Violence, & Abuse* 5, no. 4 (October 2004): 319.

6. Mo Yee Lee and Phyllis F. M. Law, "Perception of Sexual Violence Against Women in Asian American Communities," *Journal of Ethnic & Cultural Diversity in Social Work* 10, no. 2 (2001): 9.

7. S. D. Dasgupta and S. Warrier, "In the Footsteps of 'Arundhati': Asian Indian Women's Experience of Domestic Violence in the United States," *Violence Against Women* 2 (1996): 238–59.

8. H. Maguigan, "Cultural Evidence and Male Violence: Are Feminist and Multiculturalist Reformers on a Collision Course in Criminal Courts?" *New York University Law Review* 70 (1995): 36–99.

9. Doris Williams Campbell, Beckie Masaki, and Sara Torres, "Water on Rock: Changing Domestic Violence Perceptions in the African American, Asian American, and Latino Communities," in *Ending Domestic Violence: Changing Public Perceptions/Halting the Epidemic*, ed. Ethel Klein et al. (Thousand Oaks, CA: Sage, 1997), 78.

10. Carla K. Bradshaw, "Asian and Asian American Women: Historical and Political Considerations in Psychotherapy," in *Women of Color: Integrating Ethnic and Gender Identities in Psychotherapy*, ed. Lillian Comas-Díaz and Beverly Greene (New York: The Guilford Press, 1994), 82.

11. Peggy Reeves Sanday, *Female Power and Male Dominance* (New York: Cambridge University Press, 1981).

12. Bradshaw, 82.

13. Ibid.

14. Mo-Yee Lee, "Understanding Chinese Battered Women in North America: A Review of the Literature and Practical Implications," in *Violence: Diverse Populations and Communities*, ed. Diane de Anda and Rosina M. Becerra (Binghamton, NY: The Haworth Press, 2000), 220.

15. John Durose et al., *Family Violence Statistics: Including Statistics on Strangers and Acquaintances*, NCJ Publication No. 207846 (Washington, DC: U.S. Department of Justice, Bureau of Justice Statistics, 2005).

16. Asian & Pacific Islander Institute on Domestic Violence, "Fact Sheet: Domestic Violence In Asian Communities," July 2005, http://www.apiahf.org/apidvinstitute/PDF/Fact_Sheet.pdf (accessed March 11, 2006).

17. Beverly Greene, "African American Women," in *Women of Color: Integrating Ethnic and Gender Identities in Psychotherapy*, ed. Lillian Comas-Diaz and Beverly Greene (New York: The Guilford Press, 1994), 11.

18. *America's Most Wanted*, "Tamika Antonette Huston," 2005, http://www.amw.com/ (accessed January 8, 2006).

19. Natalie J. Sokoloff and Ida Dupont, "Domestic Violence at the Intersections of Race, Class, and Gender," *Violence Against Women* 11, no. 1 (January 2005): 38–64.

20. M. Anderson and P. H. Collins, *Race, Class and Gender: An Anthology* (Belmont, CA: Wadsworth, 2001).

21. Robert L. Hampton and Richard J. Gelles, "Violence Toward Black Women in a Nationally Representative Sample of Black Families," *Journal of Comparative Family Studies* 25, no. 1 (1994): 105–19.

22. B. Richie, "A Black Feminist Reflection on the Antiviolence Movement," *Signs* 25 (2000): 1133–37.

23. C. West, "Black Women and Intimate Partner Violence: New Directions for Research," *Journal of Interpersonal Violence* 19 (2004): 1487–93.

24. M. L. Benson and G. L. Fox, *When Violence Hits Home: How Economics and Neighborhood Play a Role*, DOJ Publication No. 193434 (Washington, DC: U.S. National Institute of Justice, Office of Justice Programs, 2004).

25. Ibid.

26. C. Rennison and M. Planty, "Non-Lethal Intimate Partner Violence: Examining Race, Gender and Income Patterns," *Violence and Victims* 18, no. 4 (2003): 433–43.

27. A. Browne and S. Bassuk, "Intimate Violence in the Lives of Homeless and Poor Housed Women: Prevalence and Patterns in an Ethnically Diverse Sample," *American Journal of Orthopsychiatry* 67 (1997): 261–78.

28. Sokoloff and Dupont.

29. Beverly Greene, "African American Women," in *Women of Color: Integrating Ethnic and Gender Identities in Psychotherapy*, ed. Lillian Comas-Diaz and Beverly Greene (New York: The Guilford Press, 1994), 15.

30. Jana L. Jasinski, Glenda Kaufman Kantor, and Etiony Aldarondo, "Sociocultural Status and Incidence of Marital Violence in Hispanic Families," *Violence and Victims* 9, no. 3 (1994): 209.

31. M. Yoshihama, "Domestic Violence Against Women of Japanese Descent in Los Angeles: Two Methods of Estimating Prevalence," *Violence Against Women* 5 (1999): 869–97.

32. N. Nason Clark, "When Terror Strikes at Home: The Interface Between Religion and Domestic Violence," *Journal for the Scientific Study of Religion* 43, no. 3 (2004): 303–10.

33. Beverly Horsburgh, "Lifting the Veil of Secrecy: Domestic Violence in the Jewish Community," *Harvard Women's Law Journal* 18 (1995): 171–85.

34. H. N. Bui and M. Morash, "Domestic Violence in the Vietnamese Immigrant Community: An Exploratory Study," *Violence Against Women* 5 (1999): 769–95.

35. Richie.

36. J. Ristock, *No More Secrets: Violence in Lesbian Relationships* (New York: Routledge, 2002).

37. E. Gondolf, "Appreciating Diversity Among Battered Women," in *Assessing Woman Battering in Mental Health Services*, ed. E. W. Gondolf (Thousand Oaks, CA: Sage, 1998).

38. Gloria Gonzalez, "Barriers and Consequences for Battered Immigrant Latinas," http://www-mcnair.berkeley.edu/96journal/gloriagonzalez.html (accessed March 11, 2006).

39. L. E. Orloff and R. Little, *Somewhere to Turn: Making Domestic Violence Services Accessible to Battered Immigrant Women. A "How to" Manual for Battered Women's Advocates and Service Providers* (Washington, DC: Ayuda, Inc., 1999).

40. Ibid.

41. Ibid.

42. Migrant Clinicians Network, "Domestic Violence in the Farmworker Population," 2002, http://www.migrantclinician.org/_resources/DVClinical-Supplement2002.pdf (accessed March 11, 2006).

43. K. Senturia et al., "Cultural Issues Affecting Domestic Violence Service Utilization in Ethnic and Hard to Reach Populations," *Seattle and King County Public Health*, November 1, 2000, www.metrokc.gov/health/dv// (accessed March 11, 2006).

44. Leslye Orloff and Nomi Dave, "Identifying Barriers: Survey of Immigrant Women and Domestic Violence in the D.C. Metropolitan Area," *Poverty and Race* 6 no. 4 (July–August 1997): 9–10.

45. E. K. Thomas, "Domestic Violence in the African American and Asian American Mental Health Service Provision for Women of Color," *A Journal of Human Behavior* 37 (2000): 32–43.

46. Jeanne Spurlock, "The World of Work," in *Black Families in Crisis: The Middle Class*, ed. Alice F. Coner-Edwards and Jeanne Spurlock (New York: Brunner/Mazel, 1988), 11.

47. Sorenson, "Violence Against Women."

48. *Violence Against Women and Department of Justice Reauthorization Act of 2005*, Public Law 109-162, 109th Cong., 1st sess. (January 4, 2005), 2–4.

Chapter 10

1. Gita Aravamudan, "Chilling Deaths," *The Week*, January 1999.

2. R. Muthulakshmi, *Female Infanticide, Its Causes and Solutions* (New Delhi: Discovery Publishing House, 1997).

3. Mala Sen, *Death by Fire: Sati, Dowry Death and Female Infanticide in Modern India* (London: Weidenfeld & Nicholson, 2001).

4. Radhika Balakrishnan, "The Social Context of Sex Selection and the Politics of Abortion in India," in *Power and Decision: The Social Control of Reproduction* (Cambridge, MA: Harvard School of Public Health, 1994).

•

5. T. H. Hull, "Recent Trends in Sex Ratios at Birth in China," *Population and Development Review* 16 (1990).

6. Johnathan Manthorpe, "China Battles Slave Trading in Women: Female Infanticide Fuels a Brisk Trade in Wives," *The Vancouver Sun*, January 11, 1999.

7. A. Rahman and N. Toubia, eds., *Female Genital Mutilation: A Guide to Laws and Policies Worldwide* (London: Zed Press, 2000).

8. K. M. Abusharaf, "Unmasking Tradition," *The Sciences* 38, no. 2 (1998).

9. A. E. White, "Female Genital Mutilation in America: The Federal Dilemma," *Texas Journal of Women & the Law* 10, no. 2 (2001).

10. Amnesty International, "AI Index," http://www.amnestyinternational. org/ (Female Genital Mutilation Report [accession number 77/006/1997]) (accessed December 15, 2005).

11. Ibid.

12. Ibid.

13. Amanda Hitchcock, "Rising Number of Dowry Deaths in India," *World Socialist Web Site*, July 4, 2001, http://www.wsws.org/articles/2001/jul2001/ind-j04.shtml (accessed March 11, 2006).

14. Ibid.

15. Himendra Thakur, "Are Our Sisters and Daughters for Sale?" *India Together*, June 1999, http://www.indiatogether.org/wehost/nodowri/stats.htm (accessed March 11, 2006).

16. Hitchcock.

17. "Dowry Battles Pack Indian Jail With Broken Women," *Independent Online*, September 29, 2000, http://www.iol.co.za/ (accessed January 3, 2006).

18. Hillary Mayell, "Thousands of Women Killed for Family 'Honor,'" *National Geographic*, February 12, 2002, http://www.nationalgeographic.com/news/2002/02/0212_020212_honorkilling.html (accessed March 11, 2006).

19. Amnesty International, "AI Index."

20. Mayell.

21. J. Goodwin, *Price of Honor: Muslim Women Lift the Veil of Silence on the Islamic World* (Boston: Little, Brown, 1994).

22. Mayell.

23. United Nations Population Fund, December 11–17, 2004, http://www.unfpa.org/news/coverage/2004/december11-17-2004.htm. (accessed January 2, 2006).

24. Liz Welch, "Uppity Women: Bina Akhter," *Ms. Magazine*, June 1999, http://www.geocities.com/HotSprings/Bath/5900/uppitywo.htm (accessed March 11, 2006).

25. Ibid.

26. Shadnaz Khan, "Acid Attacks—Heinous Crimes Against Women," *Human Rights SOLIDARITY* 15, no. 3–4 (May–July 2005).

27. Amnesty International, "Violence Against Women In Armed Conflict: A Fact Sheet," http://www.amnestyusa.org/stopviolence/factsheets/armed-conflict.pdf (accessed March 11, 2006).

28. Amnesty International, "Rape as a Tool of War: A Fact Sheet," http://www.amnestyusa.org/stopviolence/factsheets/rapeinwartime.pdf (accessed March 11, 2006).

29. Amnesty International, "A Fact Sheet on Sexual Violence: A Human Rights Violation," http://www.amnestyusa.org/women/violence/sexualviolence.html (accessed March 11, 2006).

30. Brian Ross, David Scott, and Rhonda Schwartz, "U.N. Sex Crimes in Congo," *ABC News*, February 11, 2005, http://abcnews.go.com/2020/ (accessed January 2, 2006).

31. Betty Rogers, "Bitter Harvest," *Ms. Magazine*, October 1999, http://www.msmagazine.com/oct99/bitterharvest.asp (accessed March 11, 2006).

32. U.S. Department of Health and Human Services, "Human Trafficking Fact Sheet," http://www.acf.hhs.gov/trafficking/about/fact_human.html (accessed March 11, 2006).

33. Richard Poulin, "Globalization and the Sex Trade: Trafficking and the Commodification of Women and Children," *Sisyphe: Un Regard Feministe Sur Le Monde*, February 12, 2004, http://sisyphe.org/article.php3?id_article=965 (accessed January 4, 2006).

34. Amy O'Neill Richard, "International Trafficking in Women to The United States: A Contemporary Manifestation of Slavery and Organized Crime," Center for the Study of Intelligence, November, 1999, http://www.cia.gov/cis/monograph/women/trafficking.pdf (accessed January 4, 2006).

35. Ibid. Poulin 2005.

36. Ibid. Poulin, 2005.

37. "The Need for a Public Debate on Prostitution and Its Social Consequences," *Sisyphe: Un Regard Feministe Sur Le Monde,* 2005, http://sisyphe.org/article.php3?id_article=1635/ (accessed January 4, 2006).

38. Ibid. De Santis.

39. Ibid. De Santis.

Chapter 11

1. Allan G. Johnson, *The Gender Knot: Unraveling Our Patriarchal Legacy* (Philadelphia: Temple University Press, 1997).

2. Ibid., 236.

3. Ibid., 232–53.

4. M. L. Coulter et al., "Police-Reporting Behavior and Victim-Police Interactions as Described by Women in a Domestic Violence Shelter," *Journal of Interpersonal Violence* 14 (1999): 1290–98.

5. A. E. Fenton, "Mirrored Silence: Reflections on Judicial Complicity in Private Violence," *Oregon Law Review* 78 (1999): 995–1060.

6. F. S. Danis, "Domestic Violence and Crime Victim Compensation," *Violence Against Women* 9 (2003): 374–90.

7. K. M. Healey, C. Smith, and C. O'Sullivan, *Batterer Intervention: Program Approaches and Criminal Justice Strategies*, DOJ Publication No. 168638 (Washington, DC: U.S. Department of Justice, 1998).

8. C. Hoyle and A. Sanders, "Police Response to Domestic Violence: From Victim Choice to Victim Empowerment," *British Journal of Criminology* 40 (2000): 14–36.

9. R. Harris et al., "Searching For Help and Information: Abused Women Speak Out," *Library & Information Science Research* 23 (2001): 123–41.

10. L. M. Short et al., "Survivors' Identification of Protective Factors and Early Warning Signs for Intimate Partner Violence," *Violence Against Women* 6 (2000): 272–85.

11. C. D. Uchida et al., *Evaluating a Multi-Disciplinary Response to Domestic Violence: The DVERT Program in Colorado Springs*, DOJ Publication No. 190230 (Washington, DC: U.S. Department of Justice, 2001).

12. E. S. Buzawa, G. T. Hotaling, and A. Klein, "The Response to Domestic Violence in a Model Court: Some Initial Findings and Implications," *Behavioral Sciences and the Law* 16 (1998): 185–206.

Index

About the Editors and Contributors

CAROL ANN BROADDUS is a Senior Lecturer and Clinical Instructor at the University of Texas at Tyler (UTT), where she teaches undergraduate nursing courses in mental health and health of the older adult. She has presented nationally in the realm of care of the sexual assault survivor and of the suicidal patient. In 2004, she received the most distinguished graduate student Award of Excellence in Nursing from UTT College of Nursing. She is completing her second year of doctoral studies at the University of Texas Health Science Center in Houston School of Nursing with an emphasis on nursing education and vulnerable populations.

BOBBIE K. BURKS, M.A., is a Licensed Professional Counselor on staff as a Counseling Associate at Green Acres Baptist Church in Tyler, Texas. She also maintains a private practice in the community. Her undergraduate and graduate degrees were obtained through study at UTT, where she has also served as an adjunct faculty member. The focus of her practice work is in women's issues, particularly in the area of empowerment after abusive relationships and/or life histories, a result of her study emphasis and licensure internship at the East Texas Crisis Center.

DONNA LEE FAULKNER earned a B.A. in English from UTT. Currently, she is pursuing a master of science degree in clinical psychology with an emphasis in neuropsychology. Additionally, Ms. Faulkner has been a research assistant for Dr. Shelly Marmion. Her research interests involve posttraumatic stress disorder. Upon graduation, Ms. Faulkner hopes to work with victims of trauma and individuals suffering from mood disorders.

CAROL A. GROTHUES, Ph.D., is a Licensed Psychologist in private practice in Longview, Texas. She obtained her doctorate in clinical psychology at the University of Southern Mississippi, received postdoctoral training at the University of Mississippi Medical Center, and later earned a postgraduate degree in clinical pharmacology. She was an Assistant Professor of Psychology at UTT for seven years, where she was recognized for her outstanding teaching of graduate and undergraduate courses. While at UTT, she was responsible for establishing a psychology clinic and neuropsychology laboratory. She has conducted a number of studies in the area of psychological symptomatology related to surviving child sexual abuse and other topics. She is currently engaged in a full-time private practice and is active in the Texas Psychological Association.

MELINDA S. HERMANNS, M.S.N., R.N., B.C., is a Senior Lecturer of Nursing at UTT, where she teaches undergraduate courses in mental health and community health and has an on-line course for the R.N. students. She is board certified as a psychiatric mental health nurse through the American Nurses Credentialing Center. She has presented nationally and has published several articles. In November 2004 she received the Outstanding Faculty Award from Texas Xi Alpha Chi National Honor Society. She is completing her second year of doctorate studies at the University of Texas Health Science Center in Houston and is a partner scholar.

PAULA K. LUNDBERG-LOVE is a Professor of Psychology at UTT and was the Ben R. Fisch Endowed Professor in Humanitarian Affairs for 2001–2004. Her undergraduate degree in chemistry was obtained from Xavier University in Cincinnati, Ohio, and her doctorate in physiological psychology with an emphasis in psychopharmacology was awarded by the University of Cincinnati. After a three-year postdoctoral fellowship in nutrition and behavior in the Department of Preventive Medicine at Washington University School of Medicine in St. Louis, she assumed her academic position at UTT, where she teaches classes in psychopharmacology, behavioral neuroscience, physiological psychology, sexual victimization, and family violence. Subsequent to her academic appointment, Dr. Lundberg-Love pursued postgraduate training and is a licensed professional counselor. She is a member of Tyler Counseling and Assessment Center, where she provides therapeutic services for victims of sexual assault, child sexual abuse, and domestic violence. She has conducted a long-term research study on women who were victims of childhood incestuous abuse, constructed a therapeutic program for their recovery, and documented its effectiveness upon their recovery. She is the author of nearly 100 publications and presentations and is co-editor of *Violence and Sexual Abuse at Home: Current Issues in Spousal Battering and Child Maltreatment.* As a result of her training in psychopharmacology and child maltreatment, her expertise has been sought as a consultant on various death penalty appellate cases in the state of Texas.

SHELLY L. MARMION, Ph.D., is an Associate Professor of Psychology at UTT. After earning a doctorate in experimental psychology from Texas Tech University, she taught for several years at Mississippi State University, where she helped to develop both the Gerontology Council and the women's studies program. While teaching, she held joint research appointments as a senior researcher at the MSU Social Science Research Center and then later with the MSU Rehabilitation, Research and Training Center for the Blind and Visually Impaired. Currently at UTT, she has taught a variety of graduate and undergraduate courses in such areas as cognition, statistics, experimental design, gender, client diversity, and gerontology and for which she has received a number of teaching awards. She has also served as a statistics and design consultant for several government agencies and nonprofit organizations and is the author of many presentations, book chapters, and journal publications on a variety of topics. Her current research is in the area of cognition and emotion.

BRITTNEY NICHOLS earned her B.F.A. in musical theatre from Emerson College and is currently pursuing her master's degree in clinical psychology at UTT. She is a volunteer/advocate for the East Texas Crisis Center where she was awarded a HOPE award for her work in 2005.

CAMILLE N. WARD is a recent graduate of UTT, where she earned a master of science in clinical psychology. She is a Behavior Specialist at the Compass Center, an alternative education program serving children grades kindergarten through 12 in the Jacksonville Independent School District in Jacksonville, Texas.

D. KAREN WILKERSON holds a B.S. in advertising from the University of Texas at Austin and an M.S. in psychology from UTT. Originally employed in advertising account management and creative services for regional and national clients, Ms. Wilkerson chose to leave the business world to train for a career in social service. Upon completion of her graduate degree, she worked directly with victims of domestic violence, sexual assault, and other crimes at the East Texas Crisis Center for several years. Still a resident of East Texas, she currently devotes much of her time to political activism.